Cooking with the

kitchen

Witch

About the Author

Patricia "Trish" Telesco (Western New York) is a passionate wordsmith and fusion cook with thirty years of experience. She is the author of more than fifty metaphysical titles, including *A Kitchen Witch's Cookbook*. Endeavoring to make life a ritual, and even an act of worship, is always in her mind. Visit her at Facebook.com /Trish.Telesco.

To Write to the Author

If you wish to contact the author or would like more information about this book, please write to the author in care of Llewellyn Worldwide Ltd. and we will forward your request. Both the author and the publisher appreciate hearing from you and learning of your enjoyment of this book and how it has helped you. Llewellyn Worldwide Ltd. cannot guarantee that every letter written to the author can be answered, but all will be forwarded. Please write to:

Patricia Telesco
℅ Llewellyn Worldwide
2143 Wooddale Drive
Woodbury, MN 55125-2989
Please enclose a self-addressed stamped envelope for reply,
or $1.00 to cover costs. If outside the U.S.A., enclose
an international postal reply coupon.

Many of Llewellyn's authors have websites with additional information and resources.

For more information, please visit our website at http://www.llewellyn.com.

Cooking with the
kitchen

Magical Recipes from the Hearth

Patricia Telesco
Foreword by Lilith Dorsey

LLEWELLYN
WOODBURY, MINNESOTA

First Edition
First Printing, 2024

Book design by Samantha Peterson
Cover design by Kevin R. Brown
Editing by Stephanie Finne

Llewellyn Publication is a registered trademark of Llewellyn Worldwide Ltd.

Library of Congress Cataloging-in-Publication Data (Pending)
ISBN: 978-0-7387-7630-9

Llewellyn Worldwide Ltd. does not participate in, endorse, or have any authority or responsibility concerning private business transactions between our authors and the public.

All mail addressed to the author is forwarded, but the publisher cannot, unless specifically instructed by the author, give out an address or phone number.

Any internet references contained in this work are current at publication time, but the publisher cannot guarantee that a specific location will continue to be maintained. Please refer to the publisher's website for links to authors' websites and other sources.

Llewellyn Publications
A Division of Llewellyn Worldwide Ltd.
2143 Wooddale Drive
Woodbury, MN 55125-2989
www.llewellyn.com

Printed in the United States of America

Other Books by Patricia Telesco

A Kitchen Witch's Cookbook (2002)

Disclaimer

Acknowledgments

Over the years, many people have blessed me with wisdom and insights that gleaned into my writing. A list would take a hefty book unto itself, so know y'all are not forgotten.

Specifically, I owe gratitude to Elysia, for giving me the opportunity to write for Llewellyn again. Throughout the process of acquisitions, her ideas were invaluable. Speaking of Llewellyn, thanks to the entire team there that did such an amazing job. Every part is more beautiful than I could have imagined.

Lilith, I appreciate you taking time out of your schedule to write the foreword more than you know. You are one busy lady!

Of course, there's family in the mix, all of whom have their favorite ways of cooking—three boys and their partners (whew) and two sisters! If my mom and dad were alive, they would love to see all the passionate activity in our kitchens. I suspect they're watching afar from somewhere that has a stove and grill.

Last, but hardly least, are my readers. The kind words you've said again and again gave me the courage to write again. It is such a blessing. I appreciate you.

contents

foreword

When it comes to Kitchen Witchery, Patricia Telesco's work is the gold standard. In her new book, *Cooking with the Kitchen Witch: Magical Recipes from the Hearth,* she explains how "food changes life, and life changes food." There is some serious truth in those words. When Telesco's first cookbook, *A Kitchen Witch's Cookbook,* appeared decades ago, it was truly revolutionary. There was nothing available of its kind. The work detailed magickal recipes for almost every occasion and showed how the act of creating nourishment for yourself and those you care about was a transformative blessing in every way. Over the years I have opened her books numerous times for recipes and inspiration, and I still do.

If I look back, I've always been a Kitchen Witch. Some of my earliest memories are dragging a chair over to the counter and helping my nana cook. It was always magick to me to watch her combine simple ingredients, such as milk, butter, flour, and sugar, and produce a delicious cake. Food always meant family for us. On holidays, we would have elaborate four- or five-course meals and sit around the table for hours, laughing and enjoying ourselves. Now that I'm older, I have never lost sight of the importance of food. Every ritual or ceremony with my spiritual family is also a feast. Herbs and other powerful foods are included to bring protection, joy, success, and other delightful intentions to the table, quite literally. We eat and we honor the Divine.

Telesco examines food from a social, cultural, and most importantly magickal context. For food impacts each and every one of these areas. Water is life, but food is also life. Humans can't survive without it. We feed ourselves multiple times a day, but few think of the nourishing possibility it contains. When I was a much younger Witch, people didn't focus much attention on Kitchen Witchery. In fact, Trish Telesco was the first person to ever discuss it with me, and the first person I ever saw write about this delicious topic. However, make no mistake, this is not the same work first published decades ago—everything is new and innovative. In this book, everything is included, such as the advice to stir your coffee clockwise for positivity, which when you think about it may be simple but is also sublime. No detail or opportunity is overlooked.

Despite the fact that cooking is a necessary skill, the number of people who only have a basic understanding of it astonishes me. Years ago when my daughter was young, I was a leader for her scout troop. One week I decided to help the girls with their outdoor cooking badge to proudly display on their sash. The scouts were required to cook outside using three different ways to create heat. We ended up using propane, campfire, and a solar oven. I was a little nervous. Before we started, I decided to ask the eight-year-olds how many of them were able to use the stove or the oven at home. Other than my own child, the answer was not a one. Most of them weren't even allowed to use the microwave. I was quite amazed. We got through the session, and hopefully everyone had a great experience and still loves cooking today.

Cooking with the Kitchen Witch: Magical Recipes from the Hearth contains helpful sidebars and advice for Witches of all culinary skill levels. Seriously, this book holds something for everyone. I really enjoyed the sections utilizing magic and metaphysics as they relate to herbs and spices. These are, in most instances, simple and readily available ingredients that can be a welcome addition to a variety of dishes. These sacred botanicals are one of my favorite ways to brings blessings to my food. Attention is also given to something often forgotten when talking about this topic: kitchen design and maintenance. In many ways this is about crafting space for working ritual. Each meal you make and each pot you stir is an opportunity to enchant your world. How you make it is just as important as why you make it, and thankfully Telesco understands this deeply.

The sections that called to me the most, however, were the sections on culinary astrology. There, not only the character of the sign is explored but also the detailed ways to set the stage, or table, with decoration, crystals, drinks, flowers, and, last but not least, recipes for each sign. Here, the readers can learn more about themselves and those around them in an immersive way. Knowledge combined with expertise will help bring about positive change, and this book will help you get there.

This book doesn't just belong on your bookshelf; it belongs in your kitchen. You should read it, and then you should use it often. There are so many different ways to interact with this book, and I hope you explore all of them. I hope you try every recipe and check out every exercise. This book begs to be utilized in every way. Readers will not only learn something, hopefully a lot of things, but also take all these useful methods to heart.

Lilith Dorsey

preface

A Kitchen Witch's Cookbook has come of age (thirty years as of this writing). Before it hit the press, I was researching and typing up all manner of recipes. The exploration opened whole new worlds in terms of what I cook and how. It was enriching, to say the least.

Our house buzzed with activity. Every week, people came by to test the food. The social nature of cooking was striking and dynamic. People sat at the table and reconnected, without electronics, over a meal. Mind you, that "table" was sometimes a couch and a TV tray or an outdoor lounge chair, but the results were the same. Laughter, love, and a sense of kinship thrived. After the book was published, knowing people used *A Kitchen Witch's Cookbook* for everything from an informal dinner to an after-ritual feast brought great joy and continues to do so.

So why write another cookbook? For one, food changes life, and life changes food. The culinary world is anything but static. It reflects cultural, societal, and global transformations. New techniques and new flavor profiles appear regularly. As someone who has caught the "foodie" bug, those changes are very exciting and motivating. In my home, it is not only okay to "play with your food" but encouraged.

This new book brings you recipes based on different methods of cooking and different topics than the first book offered. Books can take on second incarnations, too. In the process, I owe a sincere debt of gratitude to my readers and Llewellyn for keeping *A Kitchen Witch's Cookbook* in stores and in your home. Thanks to both, the first book will continue to enjoy a long, meaningful life, just as I trust this new one will.

introduction

My mother told me to never cook angry. When I asked why, she said you'd end up with a bunch of antagonistic people at the table. The wisdom in those words came home to roost as Kitchen Witchery came into my life. If there's ever a moment when "you are what you eat" had renewed meaning, it was then. Eating internalizes the energetic signature of the food and the person who makes it.

The beauty of Kitchen Magic and making meals is discovering the power (if you will) that is already in your pantry. All you have to do is to focus, mix it up, activate it, and manifest it! You will not have to jump on one foot while facing north with your wand pointing east under a new moon for metaphysical menus to work correctly. Thank goodness, because I am a *klutz!*

The intent is, as always, the key to success, as is having an honest connection with (and trust in) your components and the process. Otherwise, the magic falls as flat as bread without enough yeast. Why? Because psychology plays a role in edible spells, as with other spiritual processes. If a recipe doesn't quite fit your dynamic, don't use it. Change it so it's more personal.

Think about the potential! Today, Wiccans, Pagans, and Witches like you grew up with the Food Network. These Food Network Kitchen Witches, and often their children, tried new things or spruced up trusted recipes. *Cooking with the Kitchen Witch: Magical Recipes from the Hearth* takes that enthusiasm, adds a pinch of magic, and applies it to everyday meals. How? Your kitchen, when approached mindfully, is a sacred space. Within it, you can experience the joy of concocting recipes filled with a sprinkling of Kitchen Witchery anytime you wish.

Through your culinary efforts, you can cultivate your craft while making good soul food. From choosing symbolic ingredients to serving out sumptuous fare, the entire process for any meal becomes a simple, meaningful ritual. Since people cook all the time, this approach is fantastic for multitasking.

What sort of recipe ideas await you? Well, here's a sneak peek:

- Follow Your Bliss Fusion Gastronomy: Mixing and mingling flavor profiles to suit your spiritual goals
- Slow-Simmered Magic: Your slow cooker is a modern cauldron
- Potluck Possibilities: Get ready for your next post-ritual feast
- The Fire Festival: Barbecue and grilling
- Cooking for Star Signs: Tantalizing the senses using birth sign correspondences
- Edible Petals for Spellbinding Courses

And much, much more.

You'll learn to harmonize with your kitchen while creating enchanted morsels. There are tips for turning your table and serving platter into a symbolic message. After all, we eat with our eyes first. It doesn't have to look like a magazine cover. Instead, you will design imagery invoking subtle vibrations to soothe, delight, inspire hope, bring laughter, and evoke love.

Don't be afraid to get creative. Many recipes offer alternative ingredients to suit your palate. Dig into traditional family recipes and find greater meaning. Compile your successes and start creating new traditions today.

Trust me, it's addictive and functional all at the same time. The transformation in your recipes fills your home with enchantment perfectly timed to meet your goals.

One inspiration for this new edition was some 1920s books I came across. I have a love affair with antique tomes. Inside those homemaker's guides, you can find everything from recipes and gardening instructions to how to milk a cow and darn socks. Along the way, there were all these little tidbits of information to savor and treasure, along with an unexpected (and delightful) surprise in the form of a smattering of dried flower petals.

The charm enticed me, but I was also in awe of how much knowledge these pages contained that focused on helping people daily. The approach was sound, simply presented, and perfectly illustrated. They could have well been the coyly penned works of Kitchen Witches. Who knows? So, the next time you pick up a dainty book, see what wonders it holds for you.

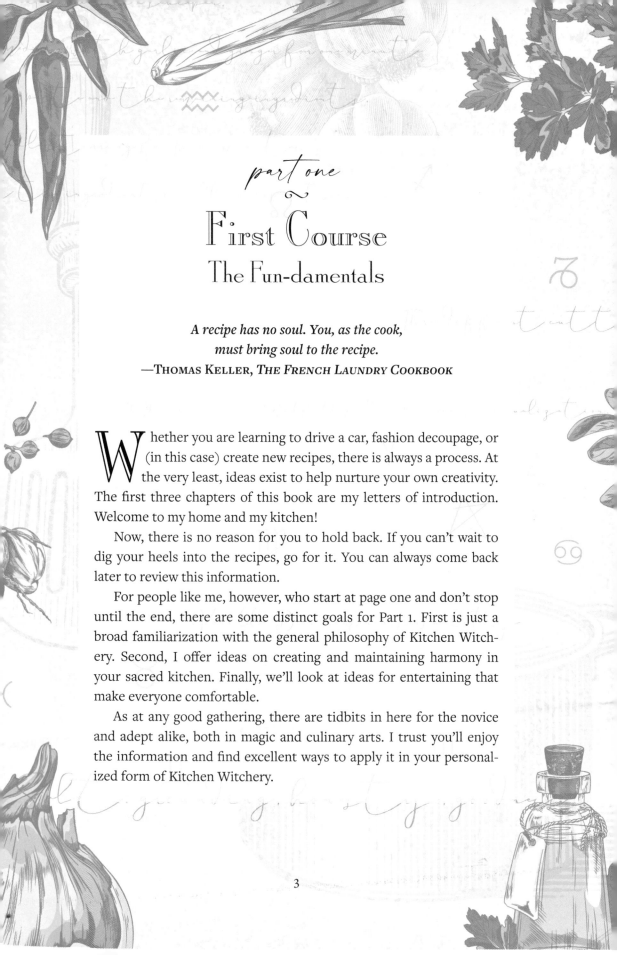

part one

First Course
The Fun-damentals

*A recipe has no soul. You, as the cook,
must bring soul to the recipe.*
—THOMAS KELLER, *THE FRENCH LAUNDRY COOKBOOK*

Whether you are learning to drive a car, fashion decoupage, or (in this case) create new recipes, there is always a process. At the very least, ideas exist to help nurture your own creativity. The first three chapters of this book are my letters of introduction. Welcome to my home and my kitchen!

Now, there is no reason for you to hold back. If you can't wait to dig your heels into the recipes, go for it. You can always come back later to review this information.

For people like me, however, who start at page one and don't stop until the end, there are some distinct goals for Part 1. First is just a broad familiarization with the general philosophy of Kitchen Witchery. Second, I offer ideas on creating and maintaining harmony in your sacred kitchen. Finally, we'll look at ideas for entertaining that make everyone comfortable.

As at any good gathering, there are tidbits in here for the novice and adept alike, both in magic and culinary arts. I trust you'll enjoy the information and find excellent ways to apply it in your personalized form of Kitchen Witchery.

chapter one
edible alchemy: an overview of kitchen witchery

Cooking is like painting or writing a song. Just as there are only so many notes or colors, there are only so many flavors—it's how you combine them that sets you apart.
—WOLFGANG PUCK[1]

If you're unfamiliar with Kitchen Witchery, you're in for a treat. Kitchen Magic is not simply a method; it's a philosophy. Practitioners see the sparkle of life's essence in everything. Every moment presents an opportunity for infusing supportive vibrations into a meal or a chore. Making coffee? Stir it clockwise for positivity!

Examining the symbolism and meaning behind food, and applying it in a spiritual context, extends far beyond the food itself. There's growing the food, harvesting, preparation, and how people serve the food. Some traditions evolved from food availability or ethnic influences.

Culture's role in how and when we consume food (and when we fast) can't be over-emphasized. The simple truth is everybody eats. Readying and enjoying meals are tasks that take up a considerable amount of each person's life.

Food has a social identity; like music, it creates a common language.[2] You can learn much about another person by having them share their food (and how they make it) with you. During the ensuing dialogue, something emerges about how X means Z or why a particular food appears during holidays, festivals, and celebrations. Those little morsels create alchemy between people.

> ## NOTEBOOK FOR YOUR CULINARY ADVENTURES
> I highly advocate for creating a written or cyber notebook for your magical culinary adventures. Think of it like grandma's treasured cookbook. Maintain all your ideas, success stories, and "secrets" in one place for yourself, your loved ones, and future generations.

In the world of the Kitchen Witch, we can find and honor those commonalities. We can return to an item's roots for meaningfulness. Flexibility and ingenuity are two of the cornerstones for successful hearthside magic.

What about Skills?

I want to pause for a minute and talk to those readers who feel uncertain about their culinary skills. I did not know how to cook when I met my husband (yes, it's true). I certainly could manage boxed macaroni and cheese, but I never hit the stove as a kid. It was Mom's sacred space, and I was not about to thwart it. So, what turned me into a passionate home chef? Practice.

My sister, realizing my predicament, sent me a cookbook. I committed myself to preparing a different meal every day for a year. Everyone thought I was weird (okay, they're right), but I had a goal. It could be breakfast, lunch, or dinner, but I vowed to repeat nothing. Some creations flopped (we had the pizza joint on speed dial). Others tasted great. As I found the recipes we enjoyed most, I put a Post-it on the cookbook's page, making it easier to find later.

By the end of the year, I fell in love with food. At a certain point, I didn't need measurements anymore; I could eye it. Once you reach this stage of development, there's a delightful sense of expressive freedom.

A new chapter in our culinary lives started when we moved out of Boston and returned home to western New York. Brewing beer and wine, making barbecue sauce (chapter 7), and mixing gourmet salts (chapter 2) became gastronomic adventures, many of which moved into my repertoire. The only thing I don't do well is baking. To me, baking is chemistry (I blow up the lab).

> **TIP FOR CULINARY SUCCESS**
> Read over your intended recipe. Ensure you have each ingredient and place them on your counter in the order you'll use them. There's nothing more frustrating than realizing you're out of baking powder smack dab in the middle of blending dry ingredients, for example. Placing them in sequence avoids missing an ingredient, too.

I am being long-winded but all that is to say, please be patient with yourself. My journey is still evolving. You won't learn everything overnight. I recommend focusing on one or two recipes; once you master them, go on to more.

Through each effort, you will discover nifty little things (put them in your journal). For example, what constitutes a pinch?[3] Cookbooks disagree, but the generally accepted measure is between $\frac{1}{16}$ tsp and a scant $\frac{1}{8}$ tsp. Thank goodness for internet search engines! As for symbolism? How about economy and carefulness?

Essence of the Kitchen Witch

While it is difficult to define a Kitchen Witch, there are a few common ideals. These create a starting point. When you hear the phrase "fancier doesn't mean better," it may well have been a Kitchen Witch who coined it as a mantra. Culinary wizardry had humble beginnings, and the overall influence of those roots remains firm. The "kiss" philosophy (keep it simple and sublime) thrives in a magical kitchen. Everything begins and ends at the hearth—the heart of the home. In times past, people taught their children here, sewed on buttons, and even dried laundry. It was a practical and meaningful gathering point.

Fast-forward to modern homes. When you have a party, have you ever noticed how many people gravitate to the kitchen for discussion (with appropriate munchables)? It happens organically. From the earliest times to the cutting-edge Kitchen Witch today, that space is unique and, with the proper mindset, even sacred.

If I had to define my vision of a Kitchen Witch, it would be according to my outlook on personal practices. I say this because our community is diverse, meaning my way is certainly not the only way. Take what I share with you and use what works best.

One thing I advocate for is to always lead with your first instinct. Many people second-guess themselves into a pickle.

Second, everything has magical potential, but the meaningful things in your life have a little more oomph. Do you have a treasured wok? Start there. Think about what it represents, then actualize the energy each time you use it.

Third, keep it real. Your Kitchen Witchery should reflect your ethics, principles, and lifestyle. You are the one who has to live with the outcome of your choices. There is no way to accommodate everyone. So, sometimes you just have to say no to well-intended people. By doing so, you say yes to your sacred self. Don't feel guilty about it.

IS KITCHEN WITCHERY RIGHT FOR YOU?

Ask yourself why you think Kitchen Magic appeals to you. What changes can you envision resulting from embracing the Kitchen Witch philosophy? This question is essential. Not every path suits every person. Whatever you choose should motivate you every day to be the best possible version of yourself. If it doesn't work, don't use it. Don't "fancify" or "fix" it if it's working just fine.

Next on the list comes expressing your inner child. Kitchen Magic encourages playfulness with no grand overture. Go ahead and tinker. If you can get someone to join you, all the better. Happiness grows when it's shared. Honoring this aspect of self helps you stay tuned to why you turned to Kitchen Magic in the first place. Children don't get hung up on the process. They just go for it.

Then there's common sense. Practicality goes together with Kitchen Magic. Don't change things just to change them. Have a sound reason. Keep reminding yourself that your efforts need not be fancy to be functional. But (and this is a big BUT), avoid getting stuck in a rut. Let your culinary "mojo" evolve. In this manner, your spiritual side keeps up with changes in the world and inside you.

Finally, your beliefs are personal. Sometimes people ask about matters of faith, seeking some kind of label, making things very uncomfortable. You are under no obligation to answer. Being a Kitchen Witch doesn't require shouting from the rooftops. Just be yourself. Let the example of your life shine through without words.

Focusing on Food

While Kitchen Magic transcends the kitchen, this book's heart is all about food. Eating and drinking tie intrinsically to human socialization. Mealtimes have been essential gathering times for families and communities. It's a moment to share (passing the plate). And astute, wise people assigned each morsel of food a correspondence and recognized energy signature. Okay, it sounds lofty, but it boils down to meaningfulness.

For example, when many people think of an apple, the phrase "an apple a day keeps the doctor away" comes to mind. However, if you are the unfortunate individual hit in the head with an apple while picking them, the symbolic connection doesn't work. So, the recipe calling for apples for health needs a facelift. A suitable alternative is a peach, which has associations with well-being. Make the change; make the magic glow.

Your experiences with (and memories of) food are like secret spices for Kitchen Magic. You add a bit of this, a sprinkle of that, and know precisely what those additions mean to you. You can nearly taste the vibrations merrily rising (think of this the next time you bake bread).

Inspiration from Family and Friends

Have you ever gone to a family dinner or to a friend's house for a gathering and found something you would love to eat repeatedly? Your response to the food gives it excellent potential for Kitchen Witchery. You already appreciate the flavors; you just need to look deeper at the traditional components. Nearly everything in your pantry has interpretive value. You may find you need no further components or feel inspired to make some additions thanks to the goodies you use in everyday cooking.

Some of my perspectives and inspirations about being a Kitchen Witch began, unwittingly, with family trips to the Adirondack Mountains. I vividly remember my grandmother waking long before anyone else and making huckleberry muffins from scratch. The smell was enticing enough to get kids under twelve out of bed and to the table with little fuss. And the deal was, you eat, you clean up. Pretty savvy, right?

Do I still make huckleberry muffins? You bet. Thankfully, they are simple baking at its best. For me, muffins represent being clever. My grandma knew her trick worked every time (you could see a satisfied grin on her face). The aroma while the muffins bake in my kitchen still evokes those cherished memories, which is a type of magic, too.

By way of another illustration, my dad was an army cook. Once married, he brought his knowledge into the kitchen with a plethora of cookies. During the holidays, our kitchen looked like a bakery for days (my sister's kitchen still does). He would fuss and grouse about anise sugar cookies (chapter 6), but ultimately, he LOVED making them because he saw how much people enjoyed them.

When you see a nearly instantaneous outcome of your efforts, it's satisfying right down to your toes. It's one of the fastest quantifiable rewards from Kitchen Witchery. Relish the moment.

Do I think either Grandma or Dad knew anything about magic? Grandma, maybe, but Dad, probably not. But they sure recognized successful results. Their recipes became traditions to which I now bring a twinkle of energy, and you can update generational recipes, too.

Inspiration from TV, the Internet, and Restaurants

Sometimes, my family tried to ban me from bingeing on cooking shows. Inevitably, it resulted in a kitchen with chaos everywhere (eh, hem, *cough*), I mean, a kitchen decorated with spices and other ingredients, along with a fair share of tools. It was enjoyable, but there's only so much a family of five can eat, even when you transform leftovers. Ideas from television, manifested with restraint, can undoubtedly bring out your inner Kitchen Witch.

See, the more you focus your thoughts and attention on making magic, the more you see potential and possibilities. The internet works similarly. Surfing good recipe sites can be addictive. Bookmark the best of the best for future research.

Then there's eating out. I have had some incredible meals at restaurants, some of which inspired a new spell-infused dish. If the restaurant is relatively quiet, the chef may offer insights into some ingredients or methods used for the recipe. Alternatively, go home and look up the name of the appetizer, entrée, or dessert. Search engines are powerful tools. They can transport the information you need in seconds.

One such instance happened when I ordered a nifty twist on pork and beans. It was whole haricot verts (young green beans) with ground pork and Asian-influenced spices. It was so original, with an unexpected flavor profile, that it got me thinking. In magical correspondences, green beans portend joyous occasions. Pork represents longevity and prosperity. All the ingredients were there for a perfect side dish for a birthday party or a seasonal celebration. Look for the recipe in chapter 12.

Now, before you ask, "How does she remember this stuff?" I don't always. When you work with an ingredient repeatedly, its symbolic value becomes part of your knowledge base. I could recite whole dissertations on onions, garlic, ginger, and vinegar. As a backup, I have my Culinary Book of Shadows for reference. My advice? Take a peek at the principal ingredients of a recipe on correspondence lists and see what they have in common. Before you know it, your magical menu is ready to go.

Food's Savory Symbolism

How different eras and cultures integrated food into activities could fill volumes. I look to the Greeks, who were (mashing old and modern terms together) ancient "influencers." The Greeks had dietary laws regarding food that was acceptable to the gods and food suited to people and animals.

They weren't alone. Look at spiritual paths worldwide. You'll constantly find symbolism and meaning in food appearing in rituals, ceremonies, and celebrations. We see this manifest in the broad-based modern-Pagan community, too. People honor the universe or gods with specific foods and use enchanted edibles to inspire luck, a long life, and merriment. Here are some examples of what some foods mean in different settings.

∿ Banana (China): Higher learning; keen-mindedness

∿ Grapes (Peru): Eaten at New Year's for a rewarding twelve months ahead

∿ Ham (Spain): Celebration

∿ Kimchi (Korea): Pride; identity

∿ Noodles (Asia): Longevity

∿ Pretzels (France): Prayer

∿ Turkey (United States): Abundance

China and its festivities are at the top of the ladder regarding using food as a metaphor. The Mandarin language has oodles of homophones. The resulting wordplay is impressive to even the best pun master.

In China, they have a traditional New Year's cake. The name is *nian gao*, meaning "high" or "tall."[4] The symbolism then becomes one of growth, of reaching ever higher. Now, if you are a Kitchen Witch with a funny bone, think about potential culinary witticism. For example, lettuce phonetically becomes "let us." Thus, it could become the foundational ingredient for a salad focused on opening the path or getting a "yes."

Cuisine in Literature

Literature often uses food metaphorically, where it becomes an emblem of something more profound. The emblem could point to cultural identity and preservation. It may allude to relationships, authority figures, and emotions. These ideas come from lore and myth, history, and the author's experiences and knowledge.

When Kitchen Witches come across such concepts, they may find some alluring and try them out. Some may flop, and others may prove triumphant. In either case, there is an educational moment where you can say nope or whoop and write it down in your grimoire.

In my opinion, it doesn't matter where you find inspiration for your culinary efforts. What matters most is how you honor and apply it and (of course) the results. Just keep your eyes and ears open. I like to keep a little notebook where I jot down ideas. They've worked well, mostly. Do not ask about the cream of brussels sprout soup, however (seriously, no).

Tools of the Trade

When you think of magical tools, what comes to mind? A wand? Crystals? Candles, incense, and figurines? Kitchen Witchery is a little different. Everything in your kitchen used for making and serving a meal has symbolism. You just have to be creative about it. Clean out the drawer of mix-and-match items and start hunting for items with symbolic value.

The meaning of a tool is often apparent. A knife cuts away at what we no longer want or need. A food injector (for marinades) allows you to administer a perfect blend of energized herbs and spices into whatever you're cooking.

Just for the fun of it, I went into my "everything" kitchen storage area and made a list of some items there. Next came figuring out correspondences that seemed to make sense (okay, I need to get out more).

ALUMINUM FOIL A possible correspondence I came up with was *protection*. Wrapping aluminum around an item before cooking protects it from too much heat. It also retains (protects) flavor.

BIRTHDAY CANDLES You can use these for making portable altars. Put birthday candles in an old matchbox with a few matches, a stick of incense with a holder, and a tiny quartz crystal. Take it on the road! Alternatively, if you're out of altar candles for your permanent at-home altar, these will suffice. If the candle has a number on it, think about its value in numerology.

BOWL A bowl can be thought of as feminine and receptive. It can safely hold whatever you place within it. White bowls can represent a full moon. Other bowl colors can support the magic you place therein. Fill a yellow bowl with ingredients for creativity and communication, for example.

CAN OPENER What's inside? Getting to the root of a mystery.

CHEF'S KNIFE These are the do-it-all knives of the culinary world. It represents usefulness in a wide variety of situations. You can adapt, turn on a dime, change the "ingredients" of life, and so forth.

COOKBOOKS I like to think of cookbooks as alternative Books of Shadows. The chapters are typically separated by food groups, which will help you determine the best foods suited for your goals.

CUTTING BOARD Cutting boards take a lot of abuse so we can get ingredients cut up while safeguarding the countertop. A good cutting board preserves the edges of your knives. I see them corresponding with safety, upkeep, and defense.

FORK This is a tool for penetrating, for getting to the heart of a matter. Think of the pinpoints left behind in pie dough, for example.

FUNNEL Just as you'd use a funnel to direct your ingredients, I like to think of funnels corresponding to the idea of directing energy where you most need it. Rather than haphazard results, you "funnel" your energy.

MEAT INJECTOR A meat injector gets flavors to marinate from the inside out, helping those flavors stand out. I like to think of this tool corresponding to the interjecting of ideas into a situation where you wish to shift the energy. It may also be helpful to think of it as inserting helpful vibrations.

MICROWAVE Accelerate your manifestation results just as you'd accelerate your cooking time. Use all your traditional ingredients but cook them in the microwave to speed up manifestation.

PEELER You know there's something just beneath the surface of a situation, and you need to know the details before making a choice. Use the peeler to represent your goal. Focus your mind while peeling carrots, potatoes, parsnips, apples, etc. One layer at a time, things clarify.

PLASTIC WRAP This is a good tool to represent the ideas of preserving and sustaining. You can wrap an item representing something you want to protect and add an incantation, for example.

POT HOLDERS Keep yourself from getting "burned." A pot holder is a line of defense from the heat, so perhaps use it as part of a spell intended to get you out of the line of fire.

PROJECT: DISCOVER MAGICAL TOOLS IN YOUR KITCHEN

Reach into any kitchen drawer without looking (avoid the knives). Pull out an item. Now, figure out how to use it to inspire energy in an upcoming menu. Eventually, you'll want to do this with every item in the pantry (depending on your craving for gewgaws, this can take a while). You may even start shopping at the kitchen stores with magic applications in mind (leave your credit card at home)!

ROLLING PIN I think this could correspond to the idea of leveling or evening matters out. Place dough on a floured surface and then use a knife to put a symbol (such as a rune) on it. Now roll out your intent!

SERVING TONGS Think of tongs as tools for portioning energy and applying it wisely. Try using these to pick up your spell components or for mixing so everything evens out. Slotted spoons work similarly.

SQUARE BAKING TIN A square tin represents the four corners of creation and the four winds. In numerology, the number four is dependable and sustainable.

THERMOMETER Just as you'd measure the heat of an edible concoction, think of a thermometer as measuring the figurative climate of a situation or a person. This can be helpful when you're moderating where you should put most of your energy.

TOWEL If you mess up, clean up! Use a towel on your altar in case you spill a libation or incense residue.

WHISK In some recipes, the more you whisk (think: more energy), the stiffer the peaks (the result of raised energy). This is a tool that can correspond to raising energy or enthusiasm. Focus on vibrancy as you whisk a dish you've designed with magic in mind.

WOODEN SPOON A wooden spoon is the wand of Kitchen Magic. Depending on your viewpoint, you can hold the handle, using the spoon portion for meting out your energy. You could also turn it around in order to direct energy.

Ingredients as Spell Components

Eating has a subconscious element beyond just filling our bellies. Each food, each ingredient, has a distinctive nature all its own. It has a specific chemical makeup created by not only genetics but also where it was grown (soil type), how much sunlight it received, the amount of precipitation it absorbed, and how it was processed.

One example is honey. How honey tastes revolves around the flowers bees visit. Orange blossom honey differs from buckwheat or acacia. Homegrown herbs allow for another illustration. If you have a garden, you may have noticed certain herbs taste different from year to year, even if you recycle seeds. Here, all the growing conditions come into play, as well as the time in which you harvest them.

Now think spiritually. A plant getting more sun has more of the fire element within. One getting more rain has more water within. Rich, balanced soil makes for rich, balanced energy. Of course, you won't always know such specifications when shopping, but they add meaningfulness to your spell creation when you do.

Herbs, Spices, and Metaphysical Meanings
Let's look at a few common herbs and spices and their primary vibrational appeal.

ALLSPICE Attracts money

BASIL Luck, love, and prosperity

BAY LEAF Wellness and strength; victory

CHIVES Lessening negativity

CINNAMON High energy; good fortune

DILL Security and warding

GARLIC Deterring spirits; protection

GINGER Strength and warmth

LEMON ZEST Longevity; purification

MINT Communication; virtue

MUSTARD SEED Faith, devotion, humility

ORANGE RIND Vitality; positivity

PARSLEY Festivity; earned honor or acclaim

ROSEMARY Memory; loyalty; friendship

SAGE Wisdom from life's experience

SALT Grounding; honesty; goodness

THYME Gracefulness

VANILLA BEAN Romance; sensuality

PROJECT: MAGIC IN YOUR SPICE RACK

Randomly pick out any herb or spice in your pantry. Does it hold any meaning to you? Do you have memories of someone using it in specific ways? Now, look up the item on a correspondence list and compare. Do the historical and metaphysical connections have any similarity to your own? Can you use what you just learned as an adjunct to personal significance? Make notes of your discoveries.

What you have at home may vary, but you get the idea. There is little (if anything) on this planet that has yet to receive metaphysical classifications at least once. Kitchen Witches have many potential items for the cauldron.

Visualization, Incantation, and Chanting

Spells are just different types of recipes. A Kitchen Witch follows the formula. They may add visualization, incantations, and chants to those instructions. It's easy to see why the careful selection of ingredients matters in making up the total energy-desired profile. But how do incantation, chants, and visualization play into the process?

Visualization ties into the idea of "seeing is believing." Imagination is a powerful tool. In your mind's eye, the results from the project are a "done deal." Alternatively, you might picture sparkling light flowing into your food (the color of the light can be symbolic—hey, multitask!).

Incantations and chanting are similar in some ways. Both are vocalizations, putting words to the winds. They shift the surrounding energies in a room.

You might say an incantation once or repeat it a symbolic number of times. Incantations may be formulaic. They're intended to produce specific magical results. Many of them rhyme for ease of memory.

Chant means to sing. Chanting is one of the oldest spiritual practices. It appears in nearly all spiritual and religious paths. For a Kitchen Witch, chanting repeats continually and rhythmically throughout the preparation. The goal is to deepen the meditative quality of the effort (including focus). Chanting calms lingering doubts, too. You don't have to sing it, but people who enjoy songs will enjoy chanting their personalized tunes.

Food as Spiritual Self-Identification

Before I embraced Kitchen Witchery as my path, I never realized food could become a way of identifying myself. When I cook, I find fulfillment and a sense of actualization. The inspiration grew throughout the years. I am head over heels in love with my kitchen (don't tell my dog).

Just as famous chefs have their signature dishes, there was no reason for me not to have my own, and that goes for you, too. How the dish develops is different for everyone. For me, it was born out of an obsession with onion soup. I tried the dish everywhere, figuring out what I liked best.

So what about the spiritual aspects? Onions represent new beginnings, refreshment, and rebirth. They can also embody health. When I learned these associations, onion soup already appeared as a cure-all, similar to chicken noodle soup! The recipe is simplistic: broth, onions, cheese, and bread. Now it was time to roll up my sleeves and try it differently.

Step one was looking up the ingredients and processes I planned to use for magical equivalencies. Fortunately for me, each worked together beautifully!

～ Five different onions (points of the pentagram)

～ Bone broth (pluck and mettle)

～ Minimally, three different cutting methods (body, mind, spirit)

∾ Fresh French bread (health and sustenance)

∾ Cheese (love and wellness)

∾ Butter (a steady mind)

∾ Worcestershire sauce (preservation)

I confess there were culinary considerations in this whole thing. For example, the onion cuts layered both flavors and textures in the final dish. You can read the details for making it in chapter 5.

The results? This creation became the recipe Mom's (Me) Onion Soup, which is named Oneness Onion Soup for this book. When my kids come home to visit, they always ask for it, as do friends. My sister likes batches for her birthday in place of cake!

I encourage you to find your blissful kitchen blend. It may take time to develop, adjusting here and there. Not everything in the dish has to match your intent perfectly. Ultimately, you will have your spiritual "signature" stamp on something you love to make. It's the best of both worlds.

If You Feed Them, They Will Come

Advertisements often have a jingle or a catchphrase. For Kitchen Witches, it may be "If you feed them, they will come." While somewhat tongue in cheek, people often attend an event they're not thrilled about if food is on the agenda. One would hope Neopagan gatherings and festivities wouldn't require nudging. Nonetheless, people sharing their creations is exciting and a community-building effort.

There are three ways in which food shows up at magical events. One: Kate wanted to bake cookies, so she made more to share. Two: An invitation goes out asking everyone to bring a dish to pass. Three: Pure happenstance.

I appreciate the third the most. Picture this (based on a true story): I am enjoying an event until hurricane rain strikes. The weather passed through with a vengeance. So, people got creative. They found protected areas for grills, electric burners, and anything with a heat source for coffee and tea and went to work. A call goes out for people to bring their food to the kitchen, where they can warm up and find comfort while others cobble the meal together. It was a living example of stone soup. Even if we were wet, chilled, or muddy, it didn't matter because everyone was in the same fix. And food brought us together, offering an edible hug.

Endnotes

1. Perry Garfinkel, "Puck Goes Back to His (Ginger) Roots," *Huffington Post*, last updated February 3, 2012, https://www.huffpost.com/entry /wolfgang-puck-spago_b_1253197.

2. Vatika Sibal, "Food Identity of Culture and Religion," ResearchGate, September 2018, https://www.wathi.org/food-identity-of-culture-and -religion-researchgate/.

3. Lid & Ladle, "How Much Is a Pinch?" *Sur la table*, accessed April 4, 2023, https://learn.surlatable.com/how-much-is-a-pinch/.

4. China Highlights by Cindy, "10 Amazing Chinese New Year's Desserts to Ring in 2023," last updated July 20, 2023, https://www.chinahighlights .com/travelguide/chinese-food/chinese-new-year-desserts.htm.

chapter two

harmonizing with your space

*If you are a chef, no matter how good a chef you
are, it's not good cooking for yourself; the joy is in
cooking for others. It's the same with music.*
—WILL.I.AM[1]

Have you ever walked into a room and felt like something was askew? The ambiance was off. Once you found a way to fix it, that lingering concern disappeared. Move something here, add something there, and it was "right" again. Such "fixing" is the focus of this chapter. You want the created energy to flow effortlessly when making a special meal, not hit a stone wall with a resounding *splat*.

Elements of Design Harmony

Cozy is a word summing up the concept of design harmony for the Kitchen Witch. You work toward managing the energy of your space to make it pleasant and welcoming. You set the items in your kitchen "just so," and wherever possible, you bring in the light!

The spiritual impact of illumination is quite notable. In the temporal sense, light dramatically affects how our minds perceive space. It impacts the way we feel. Strong artificial lights seem harsh and cold because they overpower everything else. In the dining area, dimmer switches are a culinary magician's built-in tool for ambiance—letting the lighting set the mood.

Combine and contrast shapes, textures, and colors in the rooms where you spend the most time. It isn't just your guests who should feel comfortable. You must be at ease with your hearth for the magic to flow correctly. A few guidelines help create a Witchy kitchen that's beautiful and functional.

~ Movement: Add elements into your decorating scheme that take a person's eye from one point to the next through the room. More is not necessarily better here. A couple of symbolic touches will do. For example, you might put a small pot holder hook painted with yellow flowers on a wall for joy and happiness. If there is a window to the right, the flowers on the hook naturally direct your eyes to the window where you have a living plant. Continue this. Put something else on the sill, and so forth, all around your space.

∾ Energy moves, and you are designing an environment with positive movement built right into the whole. It's like a channel through which you can direct your spells and Hearth Magic.

∾ Besides offering movement, your yellow flower hook will engage visitors' eyes. The coy blossom design brings a smile.

∾ Proportions: When you bring new things to your sacred culinary space, one should not overshadow the other. Say you have a tall floor vase you adore. However, when you step back, it looks clunky in a small area with a low ceiling. Scrap the idea and try something else.

MINDFUL MOMENT: FINDING ENERGY BLOCKAGES

Are there any items in your kitchen that seem out of place? Why does it feel askew? Is there anything you'd like to move into your kitchen from around the house? Experiment a little. Take one thing out, bring one item in, and keep your senses open to how each change alters energy patterns.

Throughout your life, you will probably switch out the meaningful items in your kitchen for new ones. The same principles apply.

Measuring Up Your Space

To harmonize with your kitchen, you must take a long, hard look at it first. Do you like the layout? Should you move some things for easier access? A magical kitchen is where everything has a place and there's a place for everything. It should make sense to you and evolve organically. How you work it out is personal, sometimes to the point of becoming protective and defensive about the organizational design.

For example, if you were to walk into my kitchen, you'd find a basket for what I call "smalls." As the name implies, smaller implements, such as a garlic squeezer and bag clips, reside there. If someone uses an item and moves it into the big bin, they will later encounter a disgruntled Witch. I could not find what I wanted when I needed it. Said item had a mindful place.

Throughout the years, we have had people living with us. One of the first things I teach them is "where things live in Trish's kitchen." Part of harmonizing with your space means creating some polite ground rules for others, too. Then, you can set everything up with the proper energetic fluidity without jamming it.

Renovations

A lot can change in most homes where folks have lived for many years. You might tear out the bathroom, repaint everything, put in or take out gardens, and renovate your kitchen. The beauty of renovation is now you can put your entire vision into place rather than cobbling it onto what was there when you moved in. Talk about an opportunity!

If you are fortunate enough to remodel, take your time. Don't just accept the first blueprints you see (or paint palettes or flooring). Renovation is a bit like putting together a puzzle. You're a Kitchen Witch, so start with the hearth and work outward.

Home renewal often becomes a work in progress. You complete the first part, and part two hinges on financing, zoning, or soil tests. Use the pause as an opportunity to refine part one significantly so that when you begin the next step, everything's ready for a perfect fit. You are in the spiritual heart of your home.

We started our adventure in our current home with bright orange 1940s floral flooring (did I mention BRIGHT?). My response upon first seeing this was less than enthusiastic. *Yuck* is not a good word when thinking about your sacred space. I saw my husband also staring at the floor with absolute confusion. Guess what changed first?

Then, the stove was directly in a walking path between rooms (yes, really). There was no way magic could move easily around it. So, moving the stove was the second step in our progression.

Our kitchen isn't large, so the third project was developing creative ways to store things. We noticed our kitchen aisle was hollow in one spot. So, we cut it open, creating a hidden cubby for wraps and bags. Once filled, it fit neatly back into the cutout space with only a little handle peeking out.

The idea of a containment space that was devised to hold household products that, themselves, store foods had a playful air. There was the nifty symbolism of constraint, control, and regulation. Only now, the potential energy would double!

With each revision, the sense of resonating more with my home improved.

Minor Changes

Depending on your situation, you may not have the chance to renovate. Have no worries. There are plenty of ways to express your metaphysical brand in the kitchen. If we return to the idea that bigger is not always better, home remodeling is definitely on the bigger side. But the little details matter.

Perhaps you keep a petite water feature near a window to welcome helpful fairies into your home. Add a little sweetbread, and the Fey will be pleased. This decorative touch brings you into better sync with the Witchy kitchen.

What if there is a mixing spoon given to you by your mother? You keep it in a small assortment next to the stove, where it's handy. Every time you pick it up, a little of Mom remains in the spoon and the memories you have helped create the

Take time in your kitchen when silence settles. Bring a notebook. Sit and look around. Smell the air. Touch the surfaces. Observe placement and color. When ingenious ideas start flowing, capture them via free-flow writing. The proverbial fine print of your kitchen comes alive in your creativity. Trust your instincts. Then, when time allows, implement the concept; manifest the magic.

magic. To anyone else, it's just an everyday item. To you, however, it's a wand of wonder.

Keep Things Clean

Have you ever walked into a dirty church? I haven't. Cleanliness has a feel all its own. It's fresh and unfettered by distractions. Necessary items remain, but all else is out of sight, stored for another day. Kitchen Witches know how important it is to clean up their rooms! It adds to efficiency, not to mention a healthy home.

You don't need a special occasion to cleanse your space. Make it part of your spiritual routine. Wipe down those countertops, clean the sink, put dishes away, sweep up the floor, and try to sort the plastic containers. I say *try* because plastic containers are the "socks in the dryer" of the kitchen. You'll never find matching lids again.

Keeping up with the routine, as practicable, alleviates a certain amount of what I call kitchen guilt. You have a few hectic days, and the sink piles up. Every time you pass it, it bugs you. Dishville is calling out, beckoning…*it needs you*, but you still have other things requiring your time and attention. Ugh! When you finally get to the task, it feels overwhelming. Nonetheless, once completed, you breathe a sigh of relief, and your kitchen space feels, well, cleaner.

Life happens. The need for a bit of cleanup is always around somewhere, especially if you have pets or children. It's okay. Just get back to tidying up before you start your next epicurean enchantment.

Cleansing and Purifying the Sacred Pantry

Beyond keeping everyday energies in balance, formal purification and cleansing are an essential part of the Kitchen Witch's skill set. Using them creates spiritual hygiene and harmonizes with your kitchen. People often use the terms interchangeably because they have a lot in common. There are, however, some nuances setting the two apart.

Cleansing

Cleansing takes place materially. It acts as maintenance, removing lingering energetic residue. Some Witches use salt or sugar to clean and remove any proverbial toxins from tools and components. Cleansing hits an item's exterior (or aura, if you will).

The cleansing process removes excess and unnatural vibrations from an object but will not change the underlying intrinsic value to make it unique. For example, if you buy a quartz crystal from a store and cleanse it, you can rid it of random energy from all the handling. Cleansing will not, however, harm the natural metaphysical patterns in the stone. It doesn't alter the stone's nature.

When something in your home feels heavy, icky, or dramatically different from the norm, stop and think. Has the energy in your home become lifeless? These are the times for cleansing. For many, this happens after visitors come and go. The beauty of cleansing is it does not impact any long-term spells you've cast on your space, such as wards. Instead, cleansing just determinedly goes after whatever causes imbalance.

Purification

Purification goes one step further than cleansing. It isn't a material but rather a spiritual deep-cleaning process. You will notice the difference even if you cannot qualify it in tangible terms. You can purify spaces, altars, or yourself for workings. Essential oils, incense, and smoke cleansing may play key roles, alongside calling on the universe for a little jump start.

Purification has a ritual aspect to it, determined by your practices. When you inherit a family member's home after death, this is the time and place for purification. You want to really penetrate everything.

> ### PUTTING CLEANSING AND PURIFICATION INTO PERSPECTIVE
> To use a mundane example, you cleanse your shower by wiping down the glass. You purify the shower by scrubbing corners and removing all the mold and dirt.

Limitations

Cleansing and purification have limits. They are both energetic processes with energetic outcomes.

Nothing happens on a grand scale. You cannot, for example, use cleansing to "wash" someone out of your life or wipe away your memories. Here, you're dealing with free will. You will always have your past as part of what you are today. Cleansing and purification are not preventive measures. They won't stop you from making poor decisions.

Blessing and Protecting Your Kitchen

Now that you've removed unwanted energy, it's time for a blessing. *Bless* in Greek means "to speak well."[2] Old English embraced *bless*, defining it as "making happy, prosperous, and fortunate." The definition perfectly aligns with the Kitchen Witch's philosophy. Alternatively, the term can refer to invoking God's blessings. Not all Hearth Witches have a designated Divine being with whom they work. So, this section focuses on creating a permanent vibration of felicity in your kitchen.

> **PAUSE FOR CONSIDERATION: THINKING ABOUT KITCHEN BLESSINGS**
>
> What immediately comes to mind when you think of a blessing for something or someone? Are there specific words or components that seem natural? If so, by all means, use these in your blessing rituals.

The kitchen is a common room. Blessing raises positive energy there and creates a protective bubble of sorts. How often you bless your kitchen is up to you. I advise at least once a year, perhaps on New Year's or another date significant to you.

You will find you need to reinforce your blessing periodically. One example is after you've had plumbing work in your kitchen. Wastewater isn't pleasant, and the mishmash of energy it houses isn't spiritually agreeable. So clean things up and bless the space again.

Protection

Let's start with the protective element of blessings. One of the best tools and one familiar to the kitchen is salt. People and priests used salt for eons to banish negativity and safeguard a space. The most significant benefit here is you can use salt in various ways to achieve the same goal, and it's undoubtedly budget friendly. For example:

- Mop the floor with a tincture of salt water. Add in some lemon for a lovely aroma. Lemon purifies and attracts love.
- Place a pinch of salt at the corners of your windows.
- Go outside and sprinkle salt on the ground near the wall closest to your cooking space.
- Keep a mixture of lemon slices and salt in the refrigerator to banish foul odors. (Such odors often indicate spoiled food, so check everything. Safety first.)
- Throw salt out the nearest door, turn your back, and walk away to deter unwanted guests or put negativity behind you.
- Asperge the kitchen with salt water (perhaps use a pastry brush).

FACTOID—THE WORLD OF SALT

Did you know there are different types of salt? You are probably familiar with table salt and kosher salt (which are perfectly fine for magical purposes, by the way). But there's more. Varieties include Himalayan pink or black salt, sea salt, Celtic gray sea salt, red Hawaiian salt, and Hawaiian black salt. I confess when I first discovered them, they piqued my curiosity. I ordered four types to try. And guess what? They have strong potential for various kinds of spells and workings, not to mention unexpected flavors. I used the color for creating basic correspondences that made sense to me:

∾ Pink salt is ideal for blessing your kitchen with friendly, playful vibrations.

∾ Red salt is "active"—it inspires movement, courage, and vitality.

∾ Gray salt invokes balance and neutrality.

∾ Black salt offers grounding, banishing, and improved personal power, and it supports an ambiance of elegance.

Salt isn't the only ingredient in your pantry you can use for protection. Other options include basil, chamomile, mint, sage, rose, rosemary, a broom, a mop, and a dishcloth.

Blessing

Cleansing and purification move out the unwelcome energies, leaving room for everything you wish to attract. Start with a clean slate for your blessing.

Blessing activities should entice the senses as much as possible. Your senses introduce you to all the elements of the world. The more you activate them, the more sensitive you become to changes, good or bad. So put together a blessing kit of sorts. You want everything ready within hand's reach.

∾ Light incense for smell and to symbolize prayers or affirmations moving upward.

∾ Bring eye-catching elements into the space. I like living plants. They give off an aura of well-being and growth. For protection specifically, think about spiny cacti.

∾ Have a specially prepared beverage you drink during the blessing (hey, you need blessings, too!).

∾ Use a crystal singing bowl, play a CD, or sing a song for the sense of hearing. Music is replete with magic.

∾ Texturally, feel your counter surface, the wood on the counters, etc. Then, as you move, envision the radiant light of grace filling each nook and cranny.

Some Witches like to bring small cauldrons to the stove and fill them with aromatics so energy stretches beyond the kitchen. Others add crystals as decorative charms. Examples include amethyst for reduced stress, rose quartz for gentle love, green jade for luck, garnet for hope, and peridot for improved focus. The nicest thing about sacred stones is no one pays much attention to them. So, if you have family members who are squiggly about this "magic thing," they probably just see them and think, "how pretty."

As you move through your kitchen for the blessing, trace runes or sigils on items using rose water (for love). The emblems dry invisible. You can additionally think or speak an incantation for consecrating your space. Here's one example:

Bring blessing and favor to every tool and every pan
Excite the power of herbs and spices, each chosen by plan
Hold tight to the magic in cupboards and drawers
When open, released to each loving endeavor
Bless my kitchen now and forever

Now, as you can see, this isn't exactly elegant poetry à la Frost or Dickinson. It doesn't have to be. The essential elements in any incantation or verbal component to metaphysical workings are:

(a) the words make sense to you,

(b) they're comfortable when you speak them out loud, and

(c) the piece reflects the things lying heavy on your heart and mind, here and now.

ACTIVITY: WRITE A KITCHEN BLESSING

Work on writing one or two blessings for your kitchen. If you don't feel you can come up with anything, there are numerous kitchen prayers and blessings you can find on the internet. Find two (or more) you like and keep them in your notebook for future use.

Ask yourself these questions:

~ What do I want to attract most to my hearth and home?

~ What present needs do I want to include in a blessing rite?

~ Is there something I'd like to add or take away from previous blessings?

They do not have to rhyme. I use a jingle-like format as a mnemonic tool. While you do not have to memorize your blessing, I find doing so helps you really focus on attracting and directing your energy effectively.

Working with Feng Shui Concepts

There is a certain feng shui in the kitchen and dining room. When you see stuff that doesn't belong there, it strikes you immediately. For us, the dining room table often became cluttered with mail, homework, and crafts. It was a situation I had to resolve before making a magical menu.

You want the whipped-up energy to effortlessly flow when making your special meals. Feng shui (the art of placement) is one method you can employ to achieve fluid movement. As a philosophy, it marries with Kitchen Witchery in splendid ways.

Feng Shui Basics

The feng shui I'm using differs from the original Chinese practices. It's more Westernized. When it became popular in the 1970s, inevitably, people tinkered with the idea. For the Kitchen Witch, honoring the concepts of feng shui is natural. We adopt many approaches to energy in our work from all over the world. And we are grateful for every spark of inspiration.

Feng shui has five elements: wood, fire, earth, metal, and water.[3] When you incorporate these elements into your Kitchen Witch plans, you can achieve the design harmony spoken of early in this chapter. Merging feng shui theories with interior design is nothing new. It's a mindful way of creating an environment reflective of your lifestyle, goals, and feelings. Your kitchen becomes experiential.

Each element has a color. Red is in the south (fire). Yellow is in the northeast and southwest (earth). White is in the northwest and west (metal). Blue stands in the north (water), and green lies in the east and southeast (wood).

Each element/color combination presides over specific areas of our lives.[4]

NORTHWEST (WHITE; METAL) Inspirational people and travel; cosmic motivation

NORTH (BLUE; WATER) Career and business; rejuvenation

NORTHEAST (YELLOW; EARTH) Education and knowledge; sweet pleasures

EAST (GREEN; WOOD) Family and health; dynamics; strength

SOUTH (RED; FIRE) Fame and recognition; consistent source of money

SOUTHEAST (GREEN; WOOD) Wealth; creativity

SOUTHWEST (YELLOW; EARTH) Relationships and marriage; sustainability

WEST (WHITE; METAL) Children; synchronicity

CENTER The heart of the home; health

To inspire potential, good fortune, and possibilities, put specific symbolic items in the proper direction in your kitchen. For example, items that could represent earth include ceramics, a salt lamp, or drawings of mountains. Earth covers topics

Go through the house and find a few items you can use to represent each element. Then, write them down in your notebook, using them as needed.

such as your job and recharging. The earth items should be placed in the northwest and southwest.

For wood, add a carved statue (perhaps of a deity with whom you have a relationship) or a money tree (*Pachira aquatica*), which is a "woody" plant, in the southeast or east.

When you want to direct good vibes to your children, put metal items such as a pot or a slotted spoon in the west. You can use the same items in the northwest to attract helpful people into your life. There is no lack of metallic objects in most kitchens!

Moving on to water items, these influence your career and any business decisions you make. Before signing on the dotted line, look for a wine bottle, an aquamarine, or a blue candle (or anything else you associate with the water element). Put what you've chosen in the northern part of your kitchen.

Fire items include anything red (perhaps a pot holder), a microwave, a carnelian, hot spices, lamps, a burning candle, or a sun catcher. When you've worked very hard on a project but feel unnoticed, it's time to engage the fire element in your kitchen. Put any items you've chosen in the south area of your space.

By the way, you don't need a special reason to put representative items in the cardinal directions. You could leave something there year-round to keep the good *qi* ("the vital force") resonating constantly.

Wiccan Twist on Feng Shui

Wicca and many other magical traditions recognize five elements: earth, air, fire, water, and spirit. As you might imagine, the meanings for each differ from the Eastern view. However, there's no reason not to put a spin on things.

Element	Color	Direction	Meaning
Earth	Dark green or brown	North	Consistency; security; growth
Air	Pale yellow; pastels	East	Reason, intellect; inspiration
Fire	Red; orange	South	Power; energy; passion
Water	Blue shades	West	Emotions; calming; health
Spirit	All; white	Center	Origins; manifestation

There are far more meanings and energetic signatures for the elements, but this gets you started. Build on the feng shui idea of placement. Pick an item representing your goal and put it in the corresponding direction in your kitchen (or your home).

Examples of possible placement:

NEEDING TO CALM PEOPLE DOWN IN THE HOUSE Put a chalice filled with water in the western portion of your kitchen.

CREATING FINANCIAL SECURITY Put a container of sunflower or sesame seeds in the northern region of the kitchen.

SEEKING INSPIRATION Set up burning incense in the eastern area of the kitchen.

IMPROVING PERSONAL ENERGY Place a brazier in the southern part of the kitchen.

Spirit gets tricky because putting something smack dab in the middle of your cooking space may confound. One idea is to hang a multicolored ornament off a light fixture to support magical manifestation for a recent spell or ritual.

Ah, but we're not done yet. Why not include an incantation during placement? Give your words to the winds and let them flow outward. Or sit and meditate on your goal before positioning. Want to add a ritual? Go for it! You don't have to plan something if the approach you like is already in your mind and heart.

There's No Place Like Home: Determining Directions in Your House

For this whole concept to work, be it feng shui or modern Neopagan practices, you need to know the facing direction of your home. In ancient days, people built their homes where they could receive the best energy. You wanted more sunlight (yang) than shade (yin). The yang region has the most activity (such as facing a road).

The easiest way to find the facing direction for your home is by using a compass. Stand in your front doorway looking outward. The pointer on the compass will tell you the facing direction and degrees. Once you know the direction, you know the element of your threshold. So, if your house faces east, it is wood in feng shui and air in the classical element array. Move clockwise around the home (or any space) from there to find the other general directions.

Is It *You* or the *Space*?

To round out the exploration of harmonizing with your space, you'll have to ask yourself if what you are sensing is *you* or your *space*. Walls have ears, and some have very vocal, energetic expressions. Those vibes can hit you and send you into a tailwind. Perhaps you have had a particularly crummy day, so your cooking magic doesn't feel right. Your chakras are all mucked up.

If you want harmony with your space, don't work magic when you are ill, out of sorts, angry, or just feeling off. Not only won't you achieve the coveted accord, but the results of your spell or ritual will likely malfunction if they work at all. "Know Thyself" is part of the Kitchen Witch's code. Everything in magic begins from within, in your heart, mind, and soul. Use wisdom in terms of when you work and why. It will take you a long way toward success.

Endnotes

1. IMDb, "Will.i.am Quotes," accessed September 12, 2023, https://www .imdb.com/name/nm1443238/bio/.

2. M. J. Kelly II, "Discovering the True Meaning of Blessing: A Closer Look at the Hebrew and Greek Words," *Medium*, last updated March 20, 2023, https://medium.com/@mjkelleyII/discovering-the-true-meaning-of -blessing-a-closer-look-at-the-hebrew-and-greek-words-e8ff1de56024.

3. Victor Cheung, "A Simple Guide to the Feng Shui Five Elements Theory (Wu Xing)," Feng Shui Nexus, last updated January 16, 2020, https:// fengshuinexus.com/feng-shui-rules/feng-shui-five-elements-guide/.

4. IFSG, "The Feng Shui Bagua," International Feng Shui Guild, accessed October 18, 2023, https://www.ifsguild.org/the-feng-shui-bagua/.

chapter three
entertaining with intent

To me, cooking is an art form, and like any art form, you first
have to learn the fundamentals. And then, once they're there, once
they're just part of you, and you get up and do a little dance or
something, you don't follow somebody else's formula. You can take
off on your own, and you learn through doing. Then you can let
go of some of these strict rules and make your own rules. I don't
even think level measurements are such a big deal these days.
—JUDITH JONES[1]

M uch of Kitchen Witchery is holistic. Of course, a magical recipe will do, but adding plating and serving elements into the picture amps up the energy. Think of how you feel when looking at a feasting space with flowers, fruits, the best tableware, crystal, and runners. I find it awe-inspiring. It definitely has the "wow" factor.

You, too, can create the "wow" factor in your plating and serving methods with little pomp and circumstance. This chapter offers ideas and suggestions you can try. But why?

The Psychology of Magic

Psychology and magic intertwine. You think. You visualize. You weave together a magical idea—these have psychological sources. Our minds recognize and respond to symbols, colors, and smells. Presentations cue associations and emotions. Those relationships pave the roadway for a specific impact.

Here's a straightforward illustration. What do you think of when you see someone sitting at the head of a table? Most people feel

> ### HISTORICAL TIDBIT
> The "head of the table" concept may have originated in medieval times. The only important ornament on the table was a saltcellar. Those who sat "above the salt" held higher ranks or had greater prominence.[2] The tradition has been around so long we barely think about setting up the table just so. It simply happens out of habit.

the individual must be special or an authority figure. So, when working a spell for authority privately, you might sit there to support the process.

Dining Etiquette

Etiquette speaks volumes about cultures and eras. For many, a formal table setting is an art form. Here, manners matter. The Old Testament, documents of the ancient Greeks, and European table customs have profound roots. Some of those customs still happen through repeatedly observed practices, such as the table setting. The Kitchen Witch can create a personal vision or adapt what history provides.

Consider how many stand up to greet a guest at the dining table. Originally, it honored the elderly or dignitaries and reflected humility. Standing affords a way of showing attention and care. You can use such a gesture to integrate intent into your dining experiences. I love the idea of welcoming people to the table and affording hospitality.

I don't dig too deeply into things like table settings, though. Where everything goes makes my head spin. I remember being taught as a child how to set out silverware, and I always put the salad fork in the wrong place! Don't get me started on tea conventions. Now, I'm just happy if I can find a *clean* fork.

More seriously, I wanted to share a little about where things came from and why we still think the way we do about many culinary matters. There's no intent to encourage the creation of a grand, dramatic presence with lavish food (unless, of course, you want to). Instead, return to meaningfulness and intention.

Meaningfulness and intention mean

- Having purpose
- Having aspiration
- Having will
- Stretching out
- Turning one's attention
- Giving heed
- Extending

As you read about plating and serving with intent, remember these words: What is your purpose? To what do you wish to pay attention? How do you want to extend your unique magical energy? The questions aren't difficult to answer, but your answers matter.

Plating and Serving Themes

Choosing a theme around which to build your culinary magic makes the process much more manageable. The theme becomes your starting point and cornerstone for the event. It supports everything from decoration and the components of your dish to the choice of spells.

To illustrate: You want to improve communication between family members at a meal, so "communication" is your theme. Now start building. Yellow creates a happy ambiance, while pale orange improves interaction. Some of your decorating touches could contain either of these colors. If you're working with feng shui, the southwest area of the room is most suited to whatever highlights you choose. From a Neopagan selection, the direction is east.

How do you integrate subtle supporting elements in your room's decor? How about

- Table with or without cloth (or runner)?
- Good china or daily wear?
- Cloth or paper napkins (or none)?
- Flowers?
- Candles?
- A centerpiece?

In thinking about communication, avoid having anything ostentatious in the middle of the table. Making a person crane their head to see someone else kind of defeats the purpose!

While you're at it, present a basket for cell phone collection.

Perhaps have a small rose quartz or amethyst at the center of the table. Oh! How about getting small stones and gift bags for each place setting?

Choose runners and tablecloths for their colors or patterns if you want to use them. You can find options at secondhand stores. The selection of dinnerware depends on the occasion. Some family celebrations mean that the good china comes out of hiding.

Your room is set up. Now it's time to cook. Here is a brief list of ingredients with their magical correspondence:

- Allspice—Kindness
- Anice—Harmony
- Apple—Love

~ Chamomile—Reduces anxiety and anger

~ Ginger—Unity

Putting this list together, your feast might include an allspice-rubbed pork roast, baked apples, and a chamomile-ginger iced tea.

Beyond this, you can bless each item, cast a spell while cooking, or light a candle to the hearth gods. I put on classic rock and dance music to elevate my energy levels.

Holiday Themes

I love holidays. They make a Kitchen Witch's life much easier because they have built-in symbols. Of course, you may not like them all, but if there are a couple to which you respond positively, the solution becomes obvious! No need to reinvent the wheel.

The way in which people observe holidays reveals changes here and there through-out history. There was a lot of "borrowing" going on in earlier times. An idea developed, and when people liked it, individuals put together a test run. Good results meant that idea became part of the holiday repertoire. Easily transferable symbols worked likewise, such as the Yule/Christmas tree.

Yule

Saturnalia was a week-long festival in ancient Rome in which people tried to make the Sun God happy and beneficent. The culmination was December 25. The era of Saturnalia is long past. Today we celebrate Yule.

> **WITCHY TIP FOR YULE**
> A customary gift during Yule is wax candles, celebrating the return of light. Most magical folks adore good candles.

> **WITCHY TIP FOR NEW YEAR'S**
> Romans wore red on 1/1, believing it would attract fertility, luck, and health.[5] The custom is something easily adaptable to a Kitchen Witch's festivities.

New Year's

In 46 BCE, Julius Caesar permanently established January 1 as the official beginning of the year.[3] The date celebrated the two-faced god Janus, whose name means "door" (aptly).[4] The high priest would make offerings to Janus, hoping for blessings in the coming year.

Easter

Easter comes from the name *Eostre*, a goddess of spring. The eggs and the bunny both represented the reborn earth and fertility. In Rome, it was a celebration of Anna Perenna, a mother goddess. Wine was the conveyance of choice in Rome. A person could lengthen their life by a year for each cup quaffed.

WITCHY TIP
FOR EASTER
Mix the best of both worlds. Set up some altar space with colored eggs and a chalice of wine.

WITCHY TIP FOR
BELTANE
There are several charming May Day customs requiring no real tweaking. Hang garlands of flowers. Braid lilies of the valley (being of pure heart), daisies (love and new beginnings), and hawthorn buds (hope and happiness) and place them around the home.

May Day

This was the celebration of the Roman goddess Maia. May bears her name.[6] Modern Witches celebrate May 1 as part of the year's wheel: Beltane.

There are one or more holidays and celebrations worldwide for every day of the year. With some forethought, you can make any day a magical holiday in your home.

Seasonal Themes

The wheel of the year moves ever forward. While holidays occur on one of a few consecutive days, you can use seasonal themes for three whole months. What's nice about this is once you've put everything in place and blessed it, there's no more effort required. Set it and forget it until the next season.

The hemisphere in which you reside shifts things a bit. I live in the Northern Hemisphere, but for those in the Southern Hemisphere, spring comes when we're experiencing autumn (March 1–May 31).[7]

Northern Hemisphere	Southern Hemisphere	Dates
Winter	Summer	December 1–February 28
Spring	Autumn	March 1–May 31
Summer	Winter	June 1–August 31
Autumn	Spring	September 1–November 30

Please keep this in mind when pondering seasonal correspondences.

Spring

There are tons of magical themes tied to spring. The earth is reborn. Set up a blooming plant in your window to represent growth (it's better if the plant blossoms). Open your windows for vital, fresh air.

WITCHY TIP FOR SPRING

Use accents of subtle green in your kitchen. Empower a light green piece of jade and put it in one of your windows. Cook up kale (well-being), spinach (vitality), or avocado (prosperity). Other ideas include lime (imagination), green apple (friendship), green grapes (good luck), and kiwi (happiness).

Come spring, our lives move from the comfort of the inside to going outdoors to enjoy the pleasant weather. Pale green surrounds. It is no surprise to discover pale green corresponds to the energies of calm, renewal, upbeat outlooks, and health.

There are plentiful ideas for creating a spring ambiance. Make a wreath out of seed packs. Glue them decoratively on a form (such as foam). Place the resulting garland over your kitchen entryway. Put out spring-colored candles. Grab a mason jar, tuck a few lemons in it, then add yellow tulips into the jar as a centerpiece.

Summer

When summer arrives, it's filled with potential. It's a great time of year to focus on manifestation. Romance and opportunities to let your inner child play are in the air. For colors, the sun rising high in the sky makes yellow the predominant hue for simple touches. Think dandelions (personal power), sunflowers (optimism), pansies (secret love), and primrose (optimism).

As for food, make a fruit bowl with summery options. Use bananas (desire), honey (sweetness), and lemon (uniqueness). Alternatively, put out yellow grapefruit (spirituality), pineapple (hospitality), and yellow pear (comfort).

Couple this decoration with an aromatic herb presentation center stage. Basil is one choice, representing good wishes (can anyone say pesto?). This would be a lovely dish to share with friends you haven't seen in some time.

To top it all off, have happy, bold accents around your kitchen. Put up fairy lights and set up a wishing tree outside.

WITCHY TIP FOR SUMMER

Since summer is a fire season, complete with summer solstice celebrations, don't forget the incense. Keep it light. You don't want to overpower people. Jasmine might be one choice, representing beauty and love.

WITCHY TIP FOR FALL

Combine carrot or sweet potato with orange juice and minced apple. Use it as a colorful side dish. The carrot and orange juice provide bountiful energy. Sweet potatoes are for hope and faith. Finally, apples round out the plate with the quest for future happiness.

Fall

As we move into fall, harvest images and freshly harvested foods are plentiful. The colors orange and red come into play, with orange representing determination and practical expression. Red is a little more active, symbolizing energy and courage.

For your decorations, there's no reason not to use gourds, fall leaves, and small pumpkins made into votive holders. Other ideas include pine cones, grapevine wreaths with orange flowers, pomanders, Indian corn, and begonias. There are orange-colored carrots, oranges, sweet potatoes, and apples for edibles.

Winter

The colors for winter are white and silver. The earth sleeps, but there is so much potential beneath the surface. Winter reminds spiritual people there is more to life than what meets the eye. Just because we do not see progress doesn't mean it's not happening.

Winter completes the seasonal round. We talk about "old man winter," whose breath freezes the grass. It's dramatic. If there's something you need stilled, slowed, or immobilized, winter is an excellent time of year to focus on those goals in spells or rituals.

WITCHY TIP FOR WINTER

Discovery! Bananas, pears, and coconuts are white when peeled! Those three fruits taste yummy together. Bananas inspire financial growth, pears are for prosperity, and coconut lends a little good luck besides!

Because winter often rotates around the solstice with culturally specific decorations, lean into it. You can add touches of white and silver elsewhere, such as spraying some "snow" on your windows and putting up white string lights. White food options are abundant. They include onions, cauliflower, turnips, white beans, white potatoes, rice, scallops, mushrooms, and tofu.

Family Traditions

From birth to death, some moments mark important transitions in our lives. Be it a birthday, a wedding, a graduation, an anniversary, or a reunion, such times give a Kitchen Witch pause for gratitude and remembrance. Honor your traditions with decorations, food, rituals, and prayer. Then you too could start making traditions (something new families often consider).

What type of new traditions could you make? Here are some ideas:

Activity	Magical Correspondences
Annual volunteering	Community; kindness, compassion
Weekly neighborhood grill-outs	Think globally, work locally
Bonfires at the end of school	Fire element; revelry; liberation
Fall hiking	Transformation, changes
Summer sunrise observation	Manifestation; new beginnings; hope

By remaining alert and aware, you can create many meaningful activities for you and/or your family to do annually. Think about the edibles you want included, how you will prepare them, and ultimately how to serve them to loved ones.

Moon Phases

A Witch recognizes the moon as a source of spiritual connection and intuition. Each phase of the moon creates a different magical dynamic you can use for Kitchen Magic. By remaining aware of the lunar influence, you can give your meal an energetic boost as you cook with focus and serve from the heart.

New Moon

The new moon is a time of reflection when you can do inner work. Take one day to fast and cleanse while setting your intentions and goals for the rest of the month. It's an excellent framework within which to cleanse the dinner table. Keep the rest of your fare healthy and light, and don't forget to hydrate!

Serve your dish on dark-colored salad plates. Create a vision board on which everyone can write their spiritual strategy for the month. Add affirmations! Leave it up for the remainder of the moon phase or all year round. Decorate with fresh flowers in a pale-colored vase.

Waxing Moon

The waxing moon is about slow, mindful growth. Are you taking the proper steps to achieve your goals? Time for follow-through!

With the theme of maturing, find the foods to feed your soul and renew your sense of self. Edibles with heady herbs and spices work well for this lunar phase. Colorful vegetables, seeds (chia, flax, sunflower, etc.), and many proteins (fish, chicken, meat, eggs, and dairy) are all good choices for a waxing moon cycle.

Trying something new and exciting, be it a method, a recipe, or an ingredient.

Full Moon

The nearly perfect white circle in the sky represents clarity and fulfillment. Take pride in your progress. Put things that no longer serve you in the past so you can keep moving forward and welcome blessings.

> ### TRIVIA: THE MAN IN THE MOON IS A RABBIT[8]
> In Chinese folklore, there is a hare on the moon (the Jade Hare) that creates herbs for immortals. There are many versions of this myth, focused on the rabbit's willingness to give its life for another. As a reward, its likeness remains on the lunar surface. Art sometimes illustrates the rabbit as a companion to Lady Moon. With this in mind, images of a rabbit could become part of your waxing moon decorations.

Since the moon is full, why not your table, too? Treat yourself to something lavish and luscious. Full-bodied food is perfect for this phase, and having a decadent dessert is definitely okay! Make it look like a feast.

Focus on edibles for filling people, such as pasta and chili. Ingredients suited to the full moon include cabbage, potato, oregano, garlic, nuts, cinnamon, and chocolate. Use round serving plates. Charge up some lunar-influenced crystals and bring them to the table for decoration.

Waning Moon

Visually, the moon appears to shrink during this phase. If you want to break a bad habit or cycle, focus your spells on that intention. Any leftovers from the full moon have a new incarnation now (where's the soup pot?). Look for lighter fare filled with vegetables and fruits.

Serve crescent-shaped items such as cookies, croissants, Chinese dumplings, cashews, and citrus slices.

On the Go

A lot of meals in our lives are informal. We grab a snack here, hit the drive-through, make a sandwich, and so forth. As a result, it's unusual to have special plating or decorations. You can still work with intention.

One of my favorite magical components for easy fare is condiments. You have a hamburger, so why not decorate the bun with a ketchup rune for luck (*Fehu* or *Wengo*)[9] and family happiness? Make a ham sandwich and draw a dollar sign with the mayonnaise for financial enhancements.

Any condiment with a dispenser is a boon for Kitchen Witches like me who lack artistic ability (I do words, not pictures). You can think of your meaningful emblems as a substitute for fanciful plating.

Here are fifteen condiment examples and potential magical uses:

AIOLI The show's stars are olive oil and garlic paste, a combination idea for strengthening friendships.

AU JUS Typically made from beef drippings, you could use this for strength and virility.

BALSAMIC Balsamic vinegar comes from aged grapes. Grapes represent fortune and abundance.

BARBECUE SAUCE While barbecue sauce can contain many things, one predominant ingredient is Worcestershire sauce. Worcestershire has a complex flavor with notes from molasses and anchovies for energy and endurance.

CHIMICHURRI The primary components in chimichurri are parsley and oregano, which have energies for festivity and joy.

CRANBERRY SAUCE Cranberry sauce symbolizes peace, abundance, and the attitude of gratitude.

FISH SAUCE Fish exude fertility and vibrations for renewal. Psychologically, fish represent the depths of the unconscious.

MUSTARD Mustard is the seed of faith and growth. Wear a bundle of mustard seeds as a reminder of your potential growth.

OYSTER SAUCE Oyster sauce promotes love and pleasure. It is a sacred food for Athena and has associations with Dionysus.

RANCH DRESSING Homemade ranch has two key components, depending on how you make it: buttermilk and egg yolks (which blend into a mayonnaise consistency). The buttermilk represents sustenance and abundance. Eggs support both with the characteristics of promise and potential.

SOUR CREAM As the name implies, sour cream is cream based. Cream characterizes sophistication and elegance. Since there's a slightly tart edge here, you can add some sass to the profile.

SOY SAUCE Made from soybeans, this sauce bursts with spiritual and magical energy.

SRIRACHA A hot sauce made with chili peppers having protective attributes.

TAHINI Tahini comes from sesame seeds, symbolizing endurance and permanence.

WASABI A hot horseradish from Japan, wasabi has a kick. Horseradish comes under the dominion of Mars and fire. It repels the evil eye and mal-intended spells.

I looked at the ingredients making up the condiments to discover their energetic imprints. Thanks to the internet, it's not hard. You never know how you might be able to use the odd thing lingering in the back corner of your pantry!

Altars

The word *altar* comes from a Latin term meaning "a high place" or a place of worship.[10] In Kitchen Magic, altars can be formal or informal, serving as part of the decorating scheme and filled with symbolic energy. For me, my kitchen countertop becomes an altar while I cook.

When you set up a magical recipe, each piece has significance and purpose. Order your ingredients as a progression of intent. Each component adds another layer of magical nuance. Put leafy vegetables in the east. Use barbecue (chapter 7) or other "fiery" foods in the south. Place apple yogurt in the west and root vegetables such as yams in the north. Each of these choices reflects the elemental correspondence for the cardinal direction.

EARTH (NORTH) Alfalfa, avocado, barley, bread, buckwheat, butter, carrots, cheese, corn, potatoes, radishes, rice, salt, spinach, tea, wheat, yams

AIR (EAST) Almond, amaretto, anise, bamboo shoots, baking powder, banana, celery, dandelion, dill, figs, hazelnut, honey, lavender, leafy vegetables, lemongrass, pine nuts

FIRE (SOUTH) Barbecue sauce, cayenne, chili pepper, chives, cinnamon, clove, garlic, ginger, mint, mustard, onion, rum, tarragon, tequila

HOMOPHONE WIZARDRY

The words *altar* and *alter* sound exactly alike. To my mind, the meaning of *alter* can correlate with *altar* spiritually. *Alter* means to change or make different in some manner. Isn't that precisely what magic does? Your *altar* changes or "alters" the energies of the space, supporting your goals.

WATER (WEST) Beer, cherry, coconut, cranberry, cucumber, lemon, orange, passionfruit, strawberry vanilla, water, wine

You can think of your table as an altar too. Set out your platters of food in the cardinal directions. Put one edible in the center, revealing the core theme of your efforts.

Do Altars Need Divine Associations?

If you follow a god or goddess (or several), including them in your kitchen altar seems natural. But people whose spiritual path does not include this construct should decorate a space with sacred intent. For example, create an all-purpose space in your kitchen where you swap out candles, crystals, incense, and decorations regularly.

My kitchen has little room for a designated altar, so it's in my living room. The Kitchen Witch in me wants simplicity. When people visit my home, they notice it and ask about the items, but it never seems off-putting. When I create a special meal, something goes on the living room altar, reflective of my goals. It is simply a way of showing the universe my heart's desire without bells and whistles.

People with more room and who like more expansive expressions of their path can get as complex as they wish. There are no hard and fast rules about how you present your home and feasts to others. My rule of thumb? If I step back, look around, and smile approvingly, all is good.

Prayers

The word *pray* is derived from the Latin word *precari*, meaning to "ask earnestly, beg, or entreat."[11] For metaphysical practitioners, affirmations and spells both fit this category. Pausing to hold hands and share words stressing love, understanding, communication, remaining flexible, staying aware, acting mindfully, and offering gratitude has somewhat gone out of "style." Yet, for the Kitchen Witch, it creates another opportunity to set intentions with everyone!

Why has prayer become less prominent than before? In part may be because of the hectic pace of life. Families don't gather around their tables because of work schedules and other responsibilities.

Then too, if people don't see prayer working, they may stop altogether. The effort didn't "pay off." Prayer and its equivalents don't work that way. What you desire may not always be in your best interests. Plus, rote prayer isn't a great idea. It's better to use ten words reflecting your heart than one hundred rattled off with little thought.

For magic, prayer should be wise and well-considered. Focus on a keyword (or words). You can direct it to the Divine or the universe at large. Prayer is personal to you or to all who attend. The attitude with which you enter prayer or meditation changes everything.

If we liken this to spell craft, what happens when you work with anger in your heart? What happens when you're ill or lack focus? It is no surprise the results are less than stellar.

When you decorate, plate, and serve with intent, it is a moving meditation or prayer. As you move, breathe. As you breathe, focus. Walk clockwise around the spaces you're preparing. Repeat a mantra.

I realize I am repeating myself, but I cannot stress how important it is to personalize your Hearth Magic and let your soul lead you. The more you listen to your instincts, the better the results.

The Pesky Guest List

My mother stressed the importance of hospitality in our home. She showed me how politeness and manners matter. In heated moments, carefully choosing words can build bridges and promote emotional healing. In my home, we have a "no drama" agreement. Whatever has been going on, it goes on the back burner. We focus on family and activities that improve bonding. Visitors know this before coming to our home, too. This is part of my intent for peace and playfulness.

When you entertain with intent, a new dynamic comes into view: the interaction between you and your guests. Unfortunately, you can be the best Kitchen Witch in the world and have group dynamics muck things up. It is not the fault of your magical efforts.

The struggle for civility grows more pronounced during the holidays. You plan a fantastic meal lush with flavor and energy, and an argument erupts. The anger tosses the overall ambiance you lovingly created into chaos. Don't just let it build.

It's time for you to become a diplomat (or appoint someone to step in). The goal is to make the day memorable for everyone in a good way. The sooner you can fix things, the better.

If need be, I will ask people who fight in my home to step out. They can take their harsh words and cynicism past my threshold. Once done, I ask them to please wipe their shoes. Leave the negativity outside where it belongs. Now, not everyone appreciates this suggestion. But it's my home, and I don't want harsh energies "sticking."

Your home is a sacred space, no matter the day or who is present. It's your haven. People should not abuse your warm, welcoming atmosphere with their behavior. There's always one guest who lingers for hours past my bedtime. (Hey, I'm an old lady. My days of midnight festivities are long gone.) I'll hand them their coat as a "subtle" hint.

Then, too, some folks don't know they're carrying spiritual baggage and unwittingly leave it on your couch. Clean up in aisle eleven! It's time to have a helpful discussion about magical hygiene. The subject is terribly under-recognized.

Throughout your entertainment, you remain the maestro. Direct your orchestra with savvy. Don't be afraid to stand firm in your place of power when necessary for the sake of all in attendance.

The Kitchen Witch's "Church"

From finding your goal to serving and internalizing your food, the art of Hearth Magic becomes a ritual where your kitchen is the proverbial church. You don't have to use every step or suggestion for impressive outcomes. Not every idea works for every setting, let alone your lifestyle.

There is absolutely *nothing* in this book carved in stone. Change it. Adapt it. Toss it. What doesn't work for you requires no space in your life. Treasure what does work instead. Create your beauty and blessings every day. It is a gift to yourself and everyone around you.

Endnotes

1. Charlotte Druckman, "Judith Jones In Her Own Words," *Eater*, September 23, 2015, https://www.eater.com/2015/9/23/9355183/judith-jones.

2. TIME staff, "A Brief History of Salt," TIME *Magazine,* February 8, 2021, https://time.com/3957460/a-brief-history-of-salt/.

3. History.com editors, "Julian Calendar Takes Effect for the First Time on New Year's Day," *History,* July 21, 2010, https://www.history.com/this-day-in-history/new-years-day.

4. Collins Dictionary, "Janus Definition in American English," Collins Dictionary, accessed October 18, 2023, https://www.collinsdictionary.com/us/dictionary/english/janus.

5. Milano Style, "Wear Something Red on New Year's Eve," *Milano Style*, December 21, 2010, https://milanostyle.com/wear-something-red-on-new-years-eve/.

6. Adrianne Ross, "What's in a Name? Months of the Year," The British Museum, December 29, 2017, https://www.britishmuseum.org/blog/whats-name-months-year.

7. Amy McKeever, "Every Season Actually Begins Twice—Here's Why," *National Geographic*, May 31, 2003, https://www.nationalgeographic.com/environment/article/history-science-of-meteorological-astronomical-seasons.

8. Elizabeth Choi, "Moon Rabbits, Leaping Hares, and Emblems of Rebirth in Art," Sothebys, September 13, 2019, https://www.sothebys.com/en/articles/moon-rabbits-leaping-hares-and-emblems-of-rebirth-in-art.

9. Edred Thorsson, *Futhark: A Handbook of Rune Magic*, Newburyport, MA: Samuel Weiser, Inc., 1992.

10. Collins Dictionary, s.v. "altar," accessed November 22, 2023, https://www.collinsdictionary.com/dictionary/english/altar.

11. Online Etymology Dictionary, s.v. "pray," accessed April 18, 2024, https://www.etymonline.com/word/pray#etymonline_v_18618.

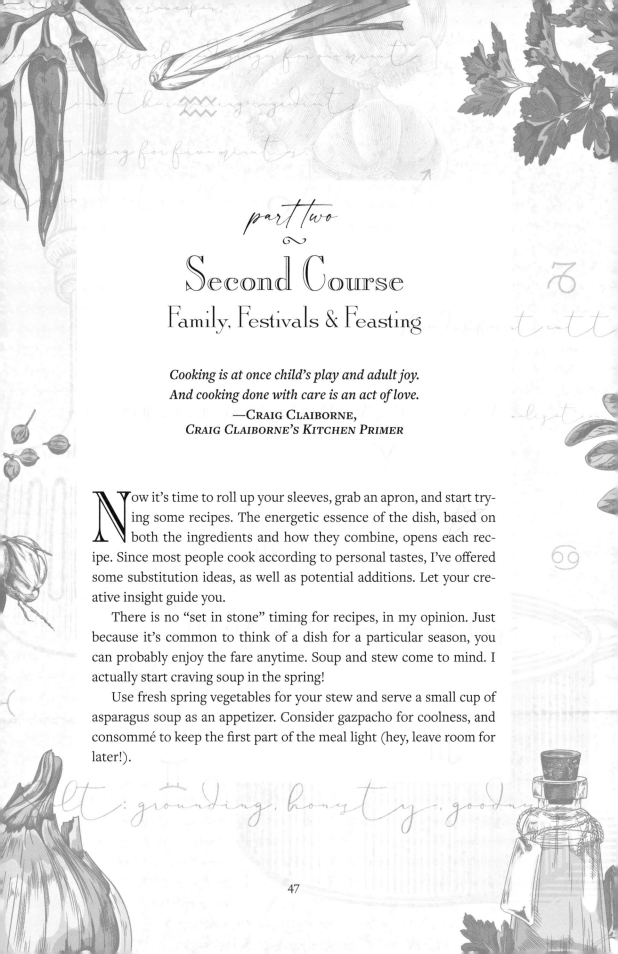

part Two
~
Second Course
Family, Festivals & Feasting

Cooking is at once child's play and adult joy.
And cooking done with care is an act of love.
—CRAIG CLAIBORNE,
CRAIG CLAIBORNE'S KITCHEN PRIMER

Now it's time to roll up your sleeves, grab an apron, and start trying some recipes. The energetic essence of the dish, based on both the ingredients and how they combine, opens each recipe. Since most people cook according to personal tastes, I've offered some substitution ideas, as well as potential additions. Let your creative insight guide you.

There is no "set in stone" timing for recipes, in my opinion. Just because it's common to think of a dish for a particular season, you can probably enjoy the fare anytime. Soup and stew come to mind. I actually start craving soup in the spring!

Use fresh spring vegetables for your stew and serve a small cup of asparagus soup as an appetizer. Consider gazpacho for coolness, and consommé to keep the first part of the meal light (hey, leave room for later!).

chapter four

follow your bliss
fusion gastronomy

The only real stumbling block is fear of failure. In
cooking, you've got to have a what-the-hell attitude.
—Julia Child[1]

The world's history exhibits "borrowing" and "adapting" in every segment of society. One of the best illustrations is the spice trade. People carried their religions, folklore, and superstitions about herbs as they traveled. They would share this information with potential buyers. A little showmanship and pizzazz went a long way then, even as it does now. Some sojourners bought the product and left. Others enjoyed what they heard, retained some ideas, and gave it a go.

Wherever cultures mix and meld, fusion cooking becomes inevitable. You get to know the people in your village. One comes over and asks about what's on the stove. A taste test proves impressive. The guest suggests adding a pinch of this (or a dab of that), explaining why. *Ta-da*, fusion is born. No one had a fancy name for it then, but it's a social phenomenon, and it continued moving forward.

Regions meld with subregions, East meets West, Mexican shakes up American, or Italian and French combine. The potential types of fusion cooking are nearly as limitless as your imagination. Consider how Filipino cuisine hardily embraced the tastes of Spain, China, and Latin America. Malaysian menus may combine Chinese, Indian, and Javanese influences. A casual pizza tossed together for a fast meal transforms with the choices made in cheeses and toppings.

Wolfgang Puck garnered high acclaim as the pioneer and face of modern fusion cooking.[2] In the 1970s, he melded Chinese and French influences into what would soon become a formalized global shift in the culinary world. The wonders home cooks and chefs have created since then are too numerous to mention.

For a Kitchen Witch, concocting something new, reflective of a merged family, group, or community, is enticing. What better way to honor unity in diversity? When people recognize the effort, it's a happy surprise, showing how much you care.

Secrets to Successful Fusion

As you might expect, there are a few tips for making fusion food work. Even with Hearth Magic, a little finesse goes a long way. What are the secrets?

KNOWLEDGE To create something new, first have a sound understanding of culinary methods or the willingness to learn them. You want to navigate your kitchen deftly and understand the flavor profile of your ingredients.

RESEARCH AND TESTING Kitchen Witches enjoy trying new things, so this element of fusion cooking is right up our alley. You are putting together a puzzle. Taste each piece and figure out what feels great in your mouth. Texture matters, too. Connect the first piece to the next and watch your vision evolve.

PREPARE FOR FAILURE Some of your attempts are going to be inedible. Flops in fusion cooking are just part of the undertaking. I sometimes *think* a mixture will pair well, only to discover it's terrible.

Early on, I became frustrated with myself. Don't follow in my footsteps. Instead of being upset, figure out what went wrong. Was it the spices? The cooking times? Too much or too little liquid? This is a teachable moment.

There are various options in highly recognized fusion cooking from which to choose. In this chapter, I'm introducing you to Tex-Mex, Hawaiian Fusion, and Asian Fusion.

Tex-Mex

The United States is called a melting pot for a good reason. It is unsurprising to see two adjacent areas creating a tasty fusion. Tex-Mex began with the mixing of Texan and Mexican cuisine (they share more than 1,200 miles of border). Warm, rich seasonings act as a keynote in these recipes. They tap at the heart of our spirit. Hot herbs and spices rev up passion and energy. You'll discover a hearty portion of the fire element in these foods.

One-Skillet Opportunity Beef and Rice

Energetic Essence: Rice provides a foundation of providence and joy. Beef tops it all off with financial stability.

Ingredients

1 lb 80/20 ground beef

1 tbsp oil

1 cup white onion, diced

1 medium sweet green pepper, diced

1 cup corn kernels (fresh
    off the cob is best)

10 ozs enchilada sauce (your choice)

1 oz package taco seasoning

3 cups white rice, precooked

1 cup shredded Mexican cheeses
    (such as asadero, queso blanco,
    Monterey jack, and sharp cheddar)

1 tbsp fresh cilantro, chopped

Red pepper flakes (optional)

Lime wedges (optional)

Substitutions

Asadero: Mozzarella or provolone

Queso blanco: Farmer's cheese

Instructions

1. Use a large Dutch oven, if possible, to cook beef until browned.

2. Drain all but 2 tsps of the fat rendered from the beef, leaving the 2 tsps in the pan.

3. Add oil (vegetable is acceptable), then sauté the onion, pepper, and corn. Stir regularly for about 6 minutes. This is an excellent opportunity to add a mantra, a blessing, or a spell.

4. Stir in the enchilada sauce, taco seasoning, and rice until well incorporated.

5. Top the meal with cheese and cilantro when serving (and red pepper flakes if you're feeling adventurous).

~ **TIPS** You can use any leftover rice (no waste) in another dish. Have lime wedges on the side.

CHICKEN SALAD FOR ABUNDANCE

Energetic Essence: Lettuce is associated with cash, but you must not cut it to maintain the energy. Black beans provide peace and ensure better days are ahead. Cilantro is a magical herb for prosperity.

Ingredients: Tex-Mex Dressing

1 cup ranch dressing

2 tbsps taco seasoning (any
  level of heat)

Ingredients: Salad

3 boneless, skinless chicken breasts

Salt and pepper

6 cups romaine lettuce, torn

2 Roma tomatoes, diced

1 cup corn kernels, fresh

4 green onions, sliced

15 oz can black beans, drained and rinsed

½ cup cheddar cheese, shredded
  (mild or sharp)

¼ cup chopped cilantro (less
  or more to your taste)

½ of a fresh lime, juiced

1 cup corn tortilla chips, crushed

Substitution

Cilantro: Parsley (joy, victory),
  dill (luck and wealth), or
  Thai basil (good wishes)

Instructions

1. Prepare the Tex-Mex dressing first by mixing the ranch dressing and taco flavoring. Chill.

2. Chop the chicken into bite-sized pieces.

3. Cook the chicken over medium heat for about 12 minutes (until cooked through to 165°F).

4. Sprinkle lightly with salt and pepper while the chicken sautés.

5. Toss the remaining ingredients in a bowl.

6. Let the chicken cool.

7. Mix it into the salad along with the dressing.

8. You can enjoy the salad as is or wrap it in a large soft fajita shell. Think of wrapping as a way of "tucking in" your magical energy.

Promising Vibes Cheese Enchiladas with Savory Gravy

Energetic Essence: Dream books say that seeing cheese in your night vision portends something good as well as happiness, especially in your love life. Chili brings passion and spice into the equation.

Ingredients: Gravy

⅛ cup vegetable oil

⅛ cup unsalted butter

¼ cup flour

2 tbsps chili powder

1 tsp garlic powder

1 tsp onion powder

½ tsp each salt and pepper

½ tsp oregano

2 cups broth (beef, chicken, or vegetable)

Substitution

Chili powder: Chipotle (warmth), 2 tsps paprika (festivity) with 1 tsp cilantro (peace and love)

Instructions: Gravy

1. Begin by assembling the gravy. Heat the oil and butter over medium heat.

2. When the butter melts, whisk in the flour, stirring for about 30 seconds (effectively, this is a roux).

3. Add the spices, mixing thoroughly.

4. Slowly pour in the broth, continuing to whisk. Be patient; you don't want lumps. Stir clockwise to attract positive energy.

5. When the sauce thickens, taste-test it. Adjust the spices as desired.

6. Simmer for 15 minutes over low heat. If the sauce gets too thick, add a small amount of broth.

PROMISING VIBES CHEESE ENCHILADAS WITH SAVORY GRAVY
∾ CONTINUED ∾

Ingredients: Enchiladas

2 tbsps vegetable oil
8 flour tortilla shells
3 cups Colby jack cheese
1 medium white onion, minced
Pickled jalapeños (optional)

Substitution
Colby jack cheese: Monterey
   jack or mild Gouda

Instructions: Enchiladas

1. Preheat the oven to 450°F. Pour the oil into a baking pan, covering the surface evenly.

2. Lay the tortillas in the oil. Warm in the oven for 5 minutes.

3. Remove the tortillas from the pan and pour in half of the gravy.

4. Once you can handle the tortillas, put ¼ cup of cheese and 1 tbsp white onion in the middle of each.

5. Roll them and put them back into the pan with the gravy.

6. Repeat with all eight shells.

7. Cover the enchiladas with the remaining gravy, followed by extra cheese.

8. Bake uncovered for 10 minutes.

9. Serve with pickled jalapeños if desired.

IN A PICKLE (PICKLED JALAPEÑO PEPPERS)

You can make pickled jalapeños at home in under 15 minutes. In a small pot, combine 10 sliced jalapeño peppers with 1 cup white vinegar, 1 cup water, 2–3 cloves mashed garlic, 2 tbsps white sugar, and 1 tbsp salt. Bring this mixture to a boil. Remove the pot from the heat. After about 10 minutes, use a fork to move the jalapeños from your boiling pot into a glass jar. Pour the brine over the top, then close the lid. Refrigerate. When you open the jar and remove a few jalapeños, you are symbolically getting "out of a pickle!"

Tex-Mex Breakfast Burritos for Grounding

Energetic Essence: Potatoes come from the earth, making them a natural aid for keeping two feet on the ground. From your new roots, the egg's hopeful quality grows.

Ingredients

½ lb 80/20 ground beef

1 tbsp Spanish onion, minced

2 tsps salt, split according to directions

⅛ tsp garlic powder

½ tsp onion powder

½ tsp chili powder

½ tsp oregano

½ tsp cumin (optional)

1 tbsp extra virgin olive oil

1 cup white potatoes, diced

8 large eggs

½ cup water

½ cup cheddar or Cotija cheese

Pico de gallo

½ avocado, diced

4 burrito shells (large)

Refried beans (optional)

Cilantro lime crema (optional)

Instructions

1. Sauté the ground beef and drain off excess fat.

2. Add the onions, ½ tsp salt, and other seasonings. Stir and break apart the meat so it's flaky.

3. Transfer to a bowl.

4. Add a tbsp of oil to a frying pan. Sauté the potatoes and season with 1/2 tsp salt until brown.

5. Remove them to a second bowl.

6. Whisk eggs with water and 1 tsp salt.

7. Pour them into the pan and cook until they firm up. Stir occasionally. Place in a third bowl.

8. Create an assembly station with beef, eggs, potatoes, cheese, pico de gallo, and avocado.

9. One at a time, lay out a tortilla. Put a quarter of the ground beef in the center of the shell. Follow with a quarter each of the eggs, potatoes, cheese, pico de gallo, and avocado.

10. Fold the shell over the short side.

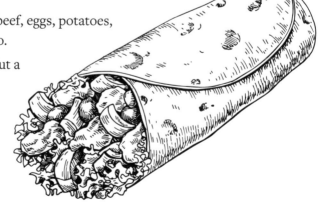

TEX-MEX BREAKFAST BURRITOS FOR GROUNDING
~ CONTINUED ~

11. Rotate the shell and tuck the burrito ends as you roll it up.

12. Gently warm each in the frying pan, until they are a light golden brown.

13. Serve with a side of refried beans and cilantro lime crema if desired.[3]

A PEEK AT PICO (PICO DE GALLO)

You can buy pico premade, but homemade ensures a crisp texture. Assemble your own using 1 cup of chopped red onion, 1 finely chopped serrano pepper (seeded), ¼ cup lime juice, ¾ tsp sea salt, 4 large, ripe diced tomatoes, and ½ cup chopped cilantro. Chill overnight.

If you feel adventurous, add some mango. Pico brings energy into your day. Mango supports happiness and prosperity.

HAWAIIAN FUSION

As Asians immigrated to Hawaii, they met with a rich culture. Plantation workers came from China, Korea, Japan, and the Philippines. When people cared for the land together, they might sit down for a communal meal, everyone getting new tastes from other cultures. Over time, Asian-Hawaiian Fusion took root and shows no signs of slowing in popularity. You can even find innovations in high-end restaurants.

Unifying Plate Lunch

Energetic Essence: The plate lunch is an ideal symbol of harmony and acts like a twist on a "potluck" meal. Depending on what each person brings, it could include everything from barbecue, macaroni salad, and sushi to Asian noodles or rice. The chosen components go into sectional containers, piled together, and remain ready to enjoy.

There are no exacting ingredients for the Unifying Plate Lunch. To be honest, it's a great way to use up leftovers. What's most important is that people want to be involved and give their hearth-centered cooking talents to friends and neighbors.

Composition of the Unifying Plate

These ideas come from native edibles in Hawaii, pairing them with a Far Eastern flair. Some promising potential dishes for the Unifying Plate include:

- Button mushrooms, tempura style
- Macaroni and cheese
- Fried mahi-mahi
- Kalua Pig with mirin
- Lettuce-wrapped seafood
- Poke with sea salt and soy
- Sweet potato with miso
- Teriyaki chicken
- Tokyo banana pie
- Wild rice with herbs

Have segmented bowls available and fill them clockwise, focusing on generating the vibrations of accord. If people are serving themselves, have everyone create a card describing the dish and its meaning.

RELIEF RICE BUNDLES (SPAM MUSUBI)

Energetic Essence: Both rice and spam are comfort foods in Hawaii. Spam arrived in the islands at the end of World War II.[4] This is a humble dish for contentment and satisfaction, to which you can bring extra flavoring by adding herbs, spices, or broth to the rice (while it cooks).

Ingredients

12 oz can Spam
¼ cup oyster sauce
¼ cup dark soy sauce
¼ cup white sugar
¼ cup brown sugar
1 tbsp mirin (rice vinegar)

1 tbsp toasted sesame oil
6 cups cooked sushi rice (no vinegar)
Nori

Substitution
Oyster sauce: Fish sauce,
    teriyaki, or hoisin

Instructions

1. Remove the Spam from the can.

2. Segment it into ten equally thick slices.

3. Place it into a food storage bag with the oyster sauce, soy sauce, white and brown sugar, mirin, and sesame oil.

4. Turn the bag several times so the slices get coated and the sugar dissolves.

5. Leave to marinate for 20 minutes.

6. Drain.

7. Fry the Spam on both sides until it's lightly crispy. You do not need oil, as it was in the marinade.

8. Shape ten firm bundles of rice into oblongs about 1–1½ inches thick. Some people use an empty, clean sardine can with both the bottom and top cut out as a form.

9. Put the nori shiny side down on a cutting board. Cut it into the same size as the rice bundles.

10. Lay down one bundle of rice with a matching size piece of spam on top.

THE SCOOP ON SUSHI RICE

When shopping, you are looking for short-grain white rice from Japan or medium-grain California rice. The bag typically says, "sushi rice" (easy, right?). Avoid jasmine and basmati rice, as they're simply not sticky enough for sushi. Sushi rice holds form, making it an excellent vehicle for 3D symbolism.

Relief Rice Bundles (Spam Musubi)

∽ CONTINUED ∽

11. Use the nori to wrap the bundle up, using just a little water on your fingers to secure it.

12. If you want to add a dip, how about wasabi mayonnaise?

Side Dish Suggestions

Pineapple slaw (warm welcomes)

Hawaiian sweet rolls (calmness)

Miso soup (family pride)

Spinach with sesame dressing (wellness)

Spring Season Curried Shrimp with Mushroom Cucumber Relish

Energetic Essence: This dish is a perfect companion for spring observances. The combination of shrimp, mushroom, and cucumber provides the support you need for positive changes. Those transformations lead to liberation and reconnection with your inner child.

Ingredients: Marinade

3 tbsps curry powder

1 tbsp minced ginger

1 tbsp garlic

½ tbsp lemongrass, minced

½ cup olive oil

1½ tbsps light soy sauce
(preferably Yamasa Brand)

1¾ lbs extra-large shrimp (about 30),
peeled and deveined

Ingredients: Relish

1 cup Japanese cucumber,
seeded and diced

⅓ cup Maui onion, finely diced

4 ozs enoki mushrooms, base removed

½ tbsp grated ginger

2 tbsps soy sauce

2 tbsps spicy sesame oil

2 tbsps unseasoned rice vinegar

1 tsp toasted white sesame
seeds for garnish

Substitutions

Enoki mushrooms: Cremini
mushrooms are best, with beach
mushrooms as a second option

Maui onion: Walla walla or Vidalia onion

Instructions

1. Combine all the ingredients for the marinade in a mixing bowl.

2. Let this set for 15 minutes.

3. Place all the relish ingredients in a mixing bowl and toss well.

MAKING HOMEMADE TOASTED SESAME SEEDS

Toasted sesame seeds absorb negativity and attract luck. You can make them at home with little fuss. Begin with 1 cup of sesame seeds. Bake them in a 350°F oven on parchment paper for about 10 minutes until golden. Alternatively, fry them in a skillet over medium heat for 5 minutes. Cook up large batches and freeze them in portion-sized bags for up to a year.

SPRING SEASON CURRIED SHRIMP
WITH MUSHROOM CUCUMBER RELISH
∾ CONTINUED ∾

4. Heat a heavy, dry sauté pan or skillet. Remove shrimp from the marinade and sear over high heat for 30 seconds per side or until cooked.

5. Garnish shrimp with the sesame seed, and add salt and pepper, if desired. Serve with the relish.

Asian Fusion

In the 1970s, Asian food with other cultural influences became popular. In America, fusion flavors appeared between China and the United States in the late 1800s.[5] Among the first dishes on the fusion menu were chop suey mixes (meat, eggs, and vegetables).

Thai Chicken Tostada Treasure

Energetic Essence: In China, peanuts often represent honor, wealth, and vitality. Coconut milk brings abundance and sustenance. Consider making this dish on a waxing moon so your energy grows.

Ingredients

6 flour tortillas

Vegetable oil

1 tbsp coconut cream

2 cloves minced garlic

1 tsp fresh minced ginger

1 tbsp curry paste

⅓ cup peanut butter (smooth or crunchy)

1 tbsp white sugar

1 tbsp fish sauce

1 tbsp toasted sesame oil

6 ozs coconut milk

2 cups diced chicken, cooked

Serving cups with red lettuce, bean sprouts, shredded carrots, diced onion, chopped parsley, and chopped peanuts

Substitution

Coconut milk: Soy milk, almond milk, cashew milk, oat milk, rice milk, evaporated milk, heavy cream, or Greek yogurt

Instructions

1. Set the oven to 375°F.

2. Gently coat the tortillas on both sides with vegetable oil.

3. Put them on a baking sheet, bake for 5 minutes, and turn. Bake for 5 more minutes.

4. Put coconut cream in a saucepan. Heat on medium with garlic and ginger for 1 minute.

5. Add the curry paste, peanut butter, sugar, fish sauce, sesame oil, and coconut milk.

6. Simmer while stirring for 5 minutes. You want the ingredients well incorporated.

7. Spread sauce on one side of each tortilla.

8. Top with chicken.

9. Allow guests to add vegetables to their liking.

Asian-Style Prosperity Cabbage Rolls

Energetic Essence: This dish is perfect for improving your bottom line. In Chinese, the ideogram for cabbage is a pun for "100 wealth."[6] Pork is a prosperous food, and ginger adds lively vibrations.

Ingredients

2 tbsps sesame oil

2 tbsps fresh ginger, minced

3 cloves garlic, peeled and minced

1 cup shiitake mushrooms,
  tops only, sliced thin

1 lb ground pork

¾ cup precooked rice

2 sliced green onions

1 medium-sized carrot, shredded

¼ cup cilantro leaves, minced

½ tsp red pepper flakes

1 tbsp dark soy sauce

3 tsps rice vinegar

1 head napa cabbage

¼ cup hoisin sauce

Substitutions

Shiitake mushroom: King oyster,
  portobello, button, enoki,
  or porcini mushrooms

Cilantro: Parsley

Instructions

1. Set the oven to 375°F.

2. Heat the sesame oil over medium heat. Add ginger, garlic, and mushrooms.

3. Sauté for 5 minutes until the mushrooms caramelize.

4. Cool and transfer into a large mixing bowl.

5. Add pork, rice, green onion, carrot, cilantro, red pepper flakes, and soy sauce to the ginger mix.

6. Add 1 tsp rice vinegar.

7. Mix until everything is well blended.

8. Core the cabbage and separate the leaves.

9. Lay single cabbage leaves down with the stem nearest you.

10. Put ¼ cup of the pork mixture near the stem of each leaf.

11. Fold the stem upward, then fold the leaf inward.

12. Roll from the bottom up tightly.

13. Repeat until you've used all the filling.

14. Spray a 9x9 pan lightly with oil.

15. Lay each leaf, seam side down, into the baking dish.

16. Mix the rest of the vinegar with the hoisin sauce.

17. Brush this blend over the cabbage rolls.

18. Bake for 30 minutes (until pork reaches 160°F internally).

19. Serve over rice or as a side dish.

STUDYING SHIITAKE MUSHROOMS

Shiitake mushrooms come from East Asia, where they are central to the cuisines of China and Japan. Shiitake remained a dietary staple among the working class for some two thousand years (representing providence). Where many mushrooms are best fresh, shiitakes get better as they age. Their umami flavor grows, so people serve these mushrooms in lieu of meat, particularly in vegetarian cooking.

Spicy Bok Choy Roasted for Health

Energetic Essence: This dish supports overall wellness. Bok choy is an excellent source of vitamins C and K. One cup of bok choy has only nine calories. Tamari is high in protein and antioxidants.

Ingredients

3 heads baby bok choy

2 tbsps olive oil

2 tsps sesame oil

2 tbsps tamari oil

2 cloves garlic, minced

1½ tsps red pepper flakes

½ lemon, juiced

Salt crystals

2 tsps toasted sesame seeds (garnish)

Substitution

Tamari: Soy sauce, fish sauce

Instructions

1. Set the oven to 425°F.

2. Slice the bok choy in halves lengthwise.

3. Place the halves on a baking sheet.

4. Mix the olive, sesame, and tamari oils, garlic, red pepper flakes, and lemon juice.

5. Brush this blend evenly over the inside of the bok choy. Take a moment to separate layers so the spices get into the cabbage leaves.

6. Sprinkle salt crystals on top.

7. Roast for 12 minutes. The bok choy will wilt and feel between tender and crisp.

8. Serve garnished with sesame seeds.

Side Dish Suggestions

Eggplant

Grilled shrimp

Stir-fried beef

Stuffed mushrooms

BOK CHOY COMMENTARY

Bok choy is a Chinese white cabbage that initially grew wild in the Yangtze River Delta. When bok choy arrived in Korea in the 1400s, it became the primary ingredient in kimchi. Fresh, unwashed bok choy keeps in the refrigerator for up to six days. It has a flavor similar to Swiss chard (mild and mustardy). You can braise, steam, or grill it. If steaming bok choy, you know it's done when the stems are fork-tender.

Sticky Finger Spareribs

Energetic Essence: The sticky component in this recipe is honey, which has a strong historical and ancient presence. Honey represents life's sweetness, pursuing truth, and growing knowledge. It makes a suitable "sending off" dish for students moving away from home. This recipe serves two, but you can easily increase it for a crowd.

Ingredients

2 tbsps clover honey

5 cloves fresh garlic, minced

1 tsp sesame oil

1 tbsp coconut aminos

8 spareribs

Sesame seeds and green onion (garnish)

Barbecue or soy sauce (optional)

Substitution

Coconut aminos: Soy sauce, tamari

Instructions

1. Combine honey, garlic, sesame oil, and aminos.

2. Put the ribs into a food storage bag with the honey mix and refrigerate.

3. Let them marinate for at least 4 hours.

4. Mix them once an hour or so.

5. Preheat the oven to 325°F.

6. Remove the ribs from the bag and transfer them to a baking dish.

7. Cover the ribs completely with foil and cook for 1 hour at 325°F.

8. After 30 minutes, apply some of the marinade to the ribs, then close the foil again.

9. Return the ribs to the oven.

10. Open the foil.

11. Change the oven setting to low broil.

12. Place the ribs under the heat so the marinade caramelizes.

13. Put on a plate, garnish with sesame seeds and green onions, and serve with some type of dipping sauce, such as your favorite barbecue blend or soy sauce.

Side Dish Suggestions

Cole slaw

Fried rice

Stuffed baked potato

Tomato cucumber salad

CURIOUS ABOUT COCONUT AMINOS?

Despite the name, coconut aminos come from fermented coconut plant sap, not coconuts. It tastes a bit like soy sauce and is an excellent substitute for soy among people with food allergies.

Gatherings with Friends and Family

Anytime you get together with other people, you have the opportunity for fusion dishes. Of course, everyone has favorite foods they like to share. Ask your guests for three options for recipes they might want to bring. Review the lists along with your own and see what combinations come to mind. Fusion food does not have to be culturally driven. It often arises when you have two great recipes and want to marry them.

For example, I love potato salad. I have a friend who makes hot German style that's very high on my yummy scale. In looking at the ingredients she uses, I saw celery seed, mustard seed, and vinegar. So, we created a cold version using mayo, celery seed, mustard seed, vinegar, chopped celery, onions, and cucumbers. The tasty result became part of our household repertoire.

Fusion Findings

As you probably expect, I spend many hours in my kitchen. It is my haven and playground. Sometimes I just go there to think (I call it cooking therapy). The emerging ideas are sometimes intriguing, and I'd like to share this one with you.

At the outset of this chapter, I mentioned people traveling and sharing their recipes to achieve a whole new edible. However, fusion goes deeper into every component in your pantry. Whenever you grab "this herb" and add it to "that ingredient," it is, essentially, fusion cooking. The herbs have roots in various parts of the world, and their symbolism includes those influences.

Let's use dill as an illustration. Dill originated in Egypt, moving into Greece and Rome.[7] It pairs well with both garlic and parsley. Garlic had its beginnings in China and parsley in the Mediterranean. Using these together, you blend each herb's origins into harmony. It's fusion, baby!

THREE'S (NOT) A CROWD BEAN SALAD
(FOR FRIENDSHIP)

Energetic Essence: First, the number three. Described as a perfect number, three takes one (the individual; oneness) and adds it to two (partnership; duality) for the sum of three, a magic number. The number three symbolizes harmony, wisdom, and understanding. Each comes in handy when building and maintaining friendships.

Next come the components. In India, basil represents good wishes to others. First cultivated in Asia, it became a bush of love and comradery when it reached Italy.

Red is the color of enthusiasm, yellow is fondness, and green is a better future. Green and red beans come from Peru; yellow beans started in South America.

Ingredients

14.5 oz can green beans (cut)

14.5 oz can yellow beans (waxed)

15–16 oz can red beans

1 cup white vinegar

1 cup sugar

1 tbsp mustard seed

1 tbsp celery seed

1 tbsp basil

Salt (optional)

Instructions

1. Pull out a large mixing bowl and spoon.

2. Add all the ingredients and mix well.

3. Place a small plate on top of everything to keep the beans submerged.

4. Leave at room temperature overnight.

5. Taste-test for sweet/sour levels. Add salt if you wish.

6. Place in the refrigerator overnight before serving.

Potential Additions

Garbanzo beans

Great Northern beans

Onion, thinly sliced

White corn (frozen or canned)

Cucumber, chopped

Endnotes

1. Julia Child, *People Who Love to Eat Are Always the Best People and Other Wisdom*, New York: Alfred A. Knopf, 2020.

2. Perry Garfinkel, "Wolfgang Puck Fusion Veteran," *Wall Street Journal*, February 1, 2012, https://www.wsj.com/articles/BL-SJB-8547.

3. Sam Sifton, "Crema," *New York Times Food*, accessed September 26, 2023, https://cooking.nytimes.com/recipes/1018885-crema.

4. Olivia Waxman, "Spam Is Turning 80. Here's How the Canned Meat Took Over the World," *TIME*, July 5, 2017, https://time.com/4827451/spam-history-80th-anniversary/.

5. Natasha Gelling, "Sorry, Wolfgang, Fusion Foods Have Been with Us for Centuries," *Smithsonian Magazine*, July 24, 2013, https://www.smithsonianmag.com/arts-culture/sorry-wolfgang-fusion-foods-have-been-with-us-for-centuries-17238814/.

6. Nations Online, "Food Symbolism During Chinese New Year Celebrations," accessed September 22, 2023, https://www.nationsonline.org/oneworld/Chinese_Customs/food_symbolism.htm.

7. Janeen Wright, "The Herb Society of America Essential Guide to Dill," The Herb Society of America, accessed September 26, 2023, https://www.herbsociety.org/file_download/inline/0191822e-0527-4cac-afb6-99d2caab6b78.

chapter five
slow-simmered magic

*The table is a meeting place, a gathering ground, the source of
sustenance and nourishment, festivity, safety, and satisfaction.
A person cooking is a person giving: Even the simplest food is a gift.*
—Laurie Colwin[1]

Look at your Crock-Pot or slow cooker. Now imagine it made from cast iron. While smaller in stature, your slow cooker is an effective cauldron, simmering your magic to perfection.

While you can use a microwave for fast results, there is a distinct difference in how your food smells and tastes. When you check and stir the slow cooker, you can add spells, incantations, or direct energy into each bite. Your spoon acts as a wand at the ready.

Slow cooking creates a cumulative affect, shifting the energy to a higher *altitude* thanks to your determined *attitude*.

LOW AND SLOW COOKER

Around the world, you'll find Indigenous groups slowly cooking various edibles. One example is barbacoa in the Caribbean. People gradually cooked meat on racks over small fires producing smoke. This process preserved the meat. And while it didn't happen in a pot, the idea is the same: taking your time, imparting flavor, and for the Kitchen Witch, amping up energy. By the way, this process is now called barbecue.

In more recent history, the first slow cooker appeared in the 1930s. An inventor, Irving Nachumsohn, sought to create traditional Jewish stew on the sabbath when prohibited from cooking.[2] In 1940, Nachumsohn took out a patent. In the 1970s, the market witnessed the birth of the Crock-Pot.

Benefits of Using a Slow Cooker

Besides the spiritual benefits, there are many practical benefits of using slow-cooking methods or machines. For example, if you're working a long day, your meal is ready when you get home. Put it in; let it go! Other advantages include:

ONE-STOP SHOP Most slow cooker prepa-
rations take three steps—putting all the
ingredients in simultaneously, setting
the temperature, and putting on the lid.

CLEAN UP Besides the serving dishes,
you'll have only one pot to wash.

YEAR-ROUND FUNCTIONALITY Slow cookers do not heat the kitchen like an
oven, meaning you can use them in hot
months. Similarly, you can make low
and slow barbecue in winter when you
don't want to be outside at the grill.

BUDGET FRIENDLY You can buy less-
expensive cuts of meat. They'll tender-
ize and become more flavorful thanks to extended low-temperature cooking.
Also, you'll use less electricity than in an oven preparation.

SIZE-SMART You can buy a small slow cooker (3–4 quarts) for four or fewer
people. A 5–7-quart machine is best for more people or when you want to
make extra to freeze.

Tips and Tricks

Like any other tool, there are ways to make your slow cooker work better for you
(work smarter, not harder!).

~ When you pull out your slow cooker, spray the inside with oil so it will clean
up more quickly. Metaphysically, the spray is a protective element, holding the
energy you generate neatly in place.

~ Avoid filling the machine over two-thirds full. Otherwise, the suggested cooking time won't be accurate.

~ If meat is part of the recipe, let it thaw in the refrigerator and leave it until
you're ready to prepare everything. This is a safety-first step based on USDA
food preparation guidelines.

~ Layer the ingredients in the pot in order of cooking time. Hard vegetables
such as carrots go in the bottom, with the meat following, and "soft" components including grains, pasta, tomatoes, mushrooms, and celery go on top.
Putting soft components in the bottom creates mush. The neat thing here is
you're also layering your magic.

~ Don't open the pot a lot. It increases cooking time and releases some good vibrations you've carefully created. Avoid the temptation.

For a Kitchen Witch, one enjoyable aspect of one-pot wonders is the ability to pick and choose components that mix and mingle energetically and in their flavor profile. There are thousands of recipes out there you can use for inspiration. Here are just a few of my favorites.

Apple Cider Pot Roast

Energetic Essence: Apples represent sweetness, beauty, and hope. The fruit is hardy, providing the additional symbolism of strength and growth. In Jewish tradition, dipping apples in honey encourages a delightful new year. Parsnips and potatoes promote grounding.

Ingredients

1 tbsp butter

2 lbs rump roast (serves 4–5)

1 cup Honeycrisp apple cider

2 tbsps Worcestershire

2 tbsps all-purpose flour

¼ tsp each fresh ground salt and pepper

4 small parsnips, halved

2 medium white potatoes, quartered

1½ cups pearl onions, whole

4 cloves garlic

Substitutions

Cider: Applesauce with water, apple wine, or apple juice

Parsnips: Carrots

White potatoes: Sweet potatoes

Worcestershire: Spicy Shiraz, soy sauce

Instructions

1. Set the slow cooker to low.

2. Melt the butter in a sauté pan.

3. Gently brown the roast on all sides.

4. Meanwhile, place the cider, Worcestershire, flour, salt, and pepper in the slow cooker.

5. Place the parsnips, potatoes, onions, and garlic in the slow cooker.

6. Add the roast on top.

7. Cook for 8 hours.

8. Transfer the meat to a cutting board and let it rest for 10 minutes.

9. Slice the meat and enjoy with some vegetables!

Side Dish Suggestions

Apple biscuits

Braised brussels sprouts

Popovers

Spiced green beans

CIDER CHRONICLES

Greek stories recount a beverage called *sikera*, devised from fermented apples.[3] It was a drink suitable to the gods because of the fruit. Romans documented cider around 55 BCE. Julius Caesar discovered Celtic Britons making it from crab apples. After the Norman Conquest in 1066, many apple varieties became available. Cider nearly replaced ale as the most favored beverage.

CURRIED BUTTERNUT SQUASH

Energetic Essence: Squash is one of the three sisters in the Iroquois and Cherokee tradition: corn, beans, and squash. These vegetables support each other's growth. Here, squash represents nurturing and harmony.

Ingredients

15 ozs coconut milk

1–2 tbsps vegetable soup stock

4 cups water

3 tbsps fresh ginger root, grated

1 tbsp curry powder

1 tbsp turmeric

½ tsp cardamom

½ tsp salt

15 oz can diced tomatoes

4 cups butternut squash, cut into ½ inch pieces (no skin)

1½ cups yellow split peas, rinsed

1 medium Spanish onion, chopped

¼ cup extra virgin olive oil

1 small lemon, juiced

1 tsp lemon zest

2 scallions (green onions), diced

4 cups cooked wild rice

Substitutions

Butternut squash: Spaghetti squash, acorn squash, buttercup squash

Yellow split peas: Green split peas, lentils

FEATURING: BUTTERNUT SQUASH

Butternut squash is a winter vegetable that's sweet and nutty. Its orange color deepens as it ripens, and the flavor grows richer. Surprise! While used as a vegetable, butternut squash is a berry. Butternut squash appears typically in savory recipes, but you can use it for cakes, similar to carrots.

Instructions

1. Set the slow cooker to high.

2. Pour the coconut milk into the slow cooker, then add the soup stock, water, 1 tbsp ginger, curry, turmeric, cardamom, and a pinch of salt.

3. Whisk thoroughly.

4. Add tomatoes (including juice), squash, peas, and onion.

5. Cook for 5 hours (the liquid should nearly absorb).

6. Remove the lid; turn the pot to low.

7. Make a sauce from the olive oil, lemon juice, lemon zest, scallions, rest of the ginger, and ¼ tsp salt.

8. Serve squash over rice with sauce trickled on top.

Side Dish Suggestions

Grilled chicken

Ham with honey sauce

Sausage

Shrimp with lime

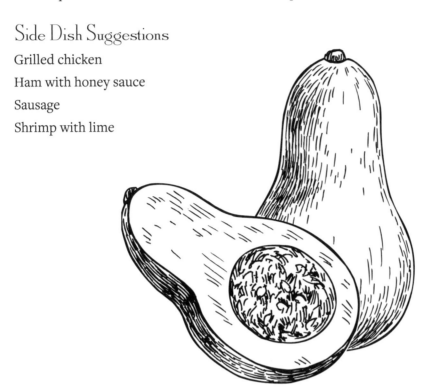

MAGIC MEATBALLS

Energetic Essence: This is one of my favorite party recipes because you can play with the flavor profile, and it's nearly effortless. The magical signature of this dish changes depending on the type of jelly you use. For example, grape jelly generates energy for abundance, fertility, transition, luck, and well-being. Other options include:

Apricot: Happiness; elegance; hope

Blackberry: Protection (the bramble); loyalty

Orange marmalade: Optimism; energy; creativity; determination

Pineapple: Hospitality; celebration; warm welcomes

Ingredients

12 ozs chili sauce

10 ozs jelly of your choosing

2 lbs frozen mini meatballs (Larger meatballs don't fit well in a slow cooker unless you have a large-sized one. Or make your meatballs from scratch in any size you want.)

Substitution

Chili sauce: Ketchup with cayenne pepper, spicy ketchup, chili garlic paste

Instructions

1. Set the slow cooker to low.

2. Put a little of the chili sauce and jelly on the bottom of the cooker (1 tbsp should do).

3. Pour in half the meatballs.

4. Add half of the remaining chili sauce and jelly over the top.

5. Repeat with the remaining meatballs, sauce, and jelly.

6. Cook for 5 hours with the first hour on high and the last four hours on the low setting. Stir once an hour to coat the meatballs evenly.

7. By the end of cooking, the sauce will be a glaze.

8. Serve with toothpicks, over rice, on submarine rolls, or with a side of roasted vegetables.

TWELVE GRAPES [4]

Also called the twelve grapes of luck in Spain, there is a New Year's tradition of eating grapes as the clock strikes midnight. As you hear each chime, eat one grape, representing the twelve months ahead. Doing so brings prosperity and good fortune.

ONENESS ONION SOUP

Energetic Essence: Onion *comes from the Latin word* unio *that means "unity."*[5] *Egyptians saw the onion as representing eternal life—so much so that they buried pharaohs with onions.*[6] *Other magical vibrations in the onion include health and protection. I chose the idea of accord because this recipe mixes and mingles a variety of onion types.*

Ingredients

1 medium red onion

1 large white onion

1 large Spanish onion

1 medium Vidalia onion

1 medium sweet (Bermuda) onion

½ stick butter

6 cups water

2 packs of beefy onion soup mix

1½ tbsps beef stock base

1 tbsp onion powder

3 tbsps Worcestershire

French bread

Provolone cheese slices

Green onions, minced (garnish)

Substitution

Onions: You may only have access to some of the onions listed in this recipe. If that's the case, just use another type you can find at the market. Make sure you have the same number of onions, though.

 ∾ **TIP** Add pearl onions for a whole onion bite.

Instructions

Note: There are four types of onion cuts in this recipe, representing the four quarters of creation. The first (using the food chopper) produces very small pieces and juice. The second is dicing (¼- to ½-inch cuts). Third is slicing. For this, follow the lines appearing lengthwise, slicing from top to bottom. Finally, you'll do a rough chop (¾-inch pieces).

1. Quarter each of the onions.

2. Take 1 quarter of each and run them through the food chopper until very tiny.

3. Take the second quarter of each and dice them.

4. Take the third quarter of each and slice them.

5. Finally, use the last quarter for rough chopping.

6. Put these into a frying pan with the butter.

Oneness Onion Soup
∽ CONTINUED ∽

7. Brown the onions over medium heat until they're soft and fragrant (get them as brown as possible without burning, about 15 minutes).

8. Transfer them to a slow cooker.

9. Add the water, soup mix, stock base, onion powder, and Worcestershire.

10. Cook for 2 to 3 hours on high until it reduces by 1 cup.

11. Taste-test. Add more seasoning at this point if you want a bolder flavor.

12. Turn off the pot and let the soup rest overnight in the refrigerator.

13. Reheat the next day, serving it in a bowl with a slice of toasted and buttered French bread, a slice of provolone, and a sprinkle of green onions. If you have ovenproof bowls, put the soup under a low broil until the provolone melts and gets a light brown color around the edges.

LAYERING FLAVORS, TEXTURES, AND RESTING FOOD

Different cuts of onion in this recipe result in layered textures in the finished product. You'll get a bite of each type of onion from mincing in every spoon. You'll then experience different mouth feels from the other cuts. Resting the soup overnight lets the flavors marry. You'll find any leftover soup improves in flavor after another day. I use the resting method with many recipes, including chili, hash, and sauces.

Side Dish Suggestions

Baked potato

Buttered noodles with parmesan

Caesar salad

Glazed carrots with bacon

Grilled sandwiches

AUSPICIOUS SLOW-COOKED ASIAN RIBS

Energetic Essence: Pork encourages good health, wealth, and improved serendipity. If you choose beef ribs, they resonate with masculinity, strength, power, and affluence.

Ingredients

4 lbs baby back ribs (serves 4)
½ tsp cracked pepper
⅓ cup teriyaki sauce
⅓ cup mirin sauce
1 tbsp rice vinegar
3 cloves garlic, finely minced

1 tsp fresh ground ginger
Sesame seeds (garnish)

Substitution
Rice vinegar: Apple cider vinegar,
    balsamic vinegar, champagne
    vinegar, white vinegar

Instructions

1. Carefully remove the silver skin from the back of the ribs. It's easiest to loosen all sides and then pull it off from one end to the other.

2. Cut the ribs into pairs.

3. Sprinkle the ribs on both sides lightly with pepper.

4. Put the ribs into the slow cooker with the teriyaki and mirin sauces.

5. Cook on low for 7 hours (if you're in a hurry, put it on high for 4 hours).

6. Make a finishing sauce by simmering the vinegar, garlic, and ginger for 8 minutes.

7. Remove the ribs from the cooker, and brush on the vinegar sauce.

8. Sprinkle with sesame seeds.

> ∽ **TIP** If you have a kitchen torch, you can create a browned crust. Alternatively, briefly put the ribs under the broiler, making them more like barbecue.

SOY SAUCE VS. TERIYAKI VS. MIRIN

Teriyaki starts with a soy sauce base, adding mirin, ginger, garlic, and brown sugar. Some brands exclude mirin, but both versions have a sticky finish with a hint of sweetness and tang. Mirin has a bold flavor, and because of the sugar content, it gives food a shiny finish, ideal for glazing. All three can, when necessary, substitute for each other with minor changes in the flavor profile. Always taste-test first before switching out ingredients.

Side Dish Suggestions

Dim sum (pot stickers)
Sesame-braised brussels sprouts
Shiitake mushrooms with garlic and
    peas
Stir-fried rice
Udon noodles

STICKY STUFFED PEARS OF POISE

Energetic Essence: Depending on the culture, the symbolism of the pear changes. Because of its shape, it alludes to the Sacred Masculine. Others feel that this fruit represents longevity, grace, comfort, and nobility.[7] Since the pears are "sticky," your energy likewise "sticks" where you want it.

Ingredients

4 plump green or red Anjou pears

½ cup walnuts, finely chopped

1 cup dates, chopped

2 tbsps butter (unsalted)

¼ cup brown sugar

1 tbsp vanilla extract

Pinch of salt

¾ cup pear, apple, or pineapple juice

Vanilla bean ice cream

Instructions

1. Slice the pears in half lengthwise.

2. Use a melon scoop or a small spoon to clean out the center (you want an indentation for the filling).

3. In a small bowl, mix the walnuts, dates, butter, brown sugar, vanilla, and salt.

4. Lay each pear half with the skin down in the slow cooker.

5. Fill the hollow with the nut mix.

6. Pour the juice around the pears.

7. Turn the cooker to low for 4 hours (check for tenderness).

8. Top with ice cream when serving.

VEGETARIAN CHILI: BEANS OF BLESSING

Energetic Essence: There are numerous superstitions about beans, but one of the most prevalent is they bring improved luck.[8] Artisans made bean charms and talismans during the Victorian era for fertility, growth, and happy new beginnings.

Ingredients

15 oz can fire-roasted diced tomatoes

28 oz can fire-roasted crushed tomatoes

½ tbsp chili powder

½ tbsp chipotle powder

1 tsp cumin

1 tsp coriander

1 tsp smoked paprika

3 cloves of garlic, finely minced

1 medium white onion, chopped

1 medium green pepper, chopped

1 stalk of celery, chopped

1 large carrot, chopped

1 large Anaheim pepper, chopped

¾ cup wheat berries

¾ cup water

Salt and pepper to taste

30 oz can red kidney beans

Sour cream, grated cheese, lime wedges, and green onion (garnish)

Substitutions

Anaheim pepper: Poblano pepper, ancho chili pepper, jalapeño pepper

Fire-roasted tomatoes: Regular canned tomatoes plus a pinch of smoked paprika, sun-dried tomatoes, tomato purée

Instructions

1. Put all the ingredients except the garnishes in a slow cooker (you'll need a 5–6-quart machine).

2. Set the slow cooker to high for 4 to 5 hours for a fast cook.

3. Set the slow cooker to low for 6 to 7 hours for slow cooking. Watch for the vegetables to be fork-tender.

4. Place the garnishes on the table so people can help themselves.

~ **TIP** Consider serving with pita, naan, or sourdough bread slices.

WHAT ARE WHEAT BERRIES?

Wheat berries are the whole edible part of wheat kernels. They have no outer shell. Wheat berries are healthy, containing iron, fiber, and protein. The berries taste somewhat earthy with a nutty texture. You can use wheat berries in cereal, stew, salads, bread, and soups, and more.[9]

NUTTY SLOW COOKER CHICKEN WITH CUCUMBER SALAD

Energetic Essence: Chicken represents contemplation, confidence, divination, and community. The underlying vibrations can change if you swap out nut varieties. Walnut pairs perfectly here, symbolizing intelligence and wisdom. If you use pecan, the recipe supports conscious efforts to improve your financial stability. Cashew represents having time to enjoy the rewards of hard labor and succeeding in a goal. Consuming almonds helps you better understand your purpose and place.

The cucumber salad is a refreshing side dish, representing luck and success.

WHAT IS GARAM MASALA?

Garam masala is a staple in Indian cuisine. It comes in both powder and paste form. *Masala* translates aptly as "spices," while *garam* means "hot." [10] Mind you, not all spice blends with this label are overly piquant. Northern India's fare features mild garam masala mixes, while southern India adds the heat, usually by adding red chilies.

Many households have their own "secret" blend. Some underlying commonalities exist, including the use of black pepper, cardamom, cinnamon, cloves, coriander, cumin, and nutmeg. Other popular spice additions include garlic, ginger, bay, and star anise. The resulting flavor is slightly sweet and fragrant with just a hint of heat.

Ingredients: Chicken

1 large Vidalia onion

2 tbsps olive oil

1 tsp garam masala

4 lbs chicken (whole)

Salt

⅔ cup walnuts

¼ cup fresh mint leaves

¼ cup fresh basil leaves

1 tsp oregano

1 tbsp lemon juice

Substitution

Garam marsala: Curry powder, cumin with allspice (4:1 ratio)

Instructions: Chicken

1. Slice the onion into ¼-inch pieces.

2. Lay the onions in the bottom of an oiled slow cooker so they cover it evenly.

3. Combine the oil and garam masala and rub the entire chicken with it (inside and out).

4. Sprinkle all sides of the chicken evenly with salt (approximately ¾ tsp).

5. Tie the drumsticks of the chicken together.

6. Place the chicken in the middle of the slow cooker.

7. Cover and cook on high for 4 hours.

8. While the chicken cooks, purée the walnuts, mint, basil, oregano, and lemon juice. Set aside.

9. When the chicken is done (165°F internally), remove it from the pot and let it rest for 10 minutes.

10. Remove the onions from the pot and blend them into the nut mixture.

11. You can either drizzle the sauce on the chicken at service or put it in a gravy tureen.

> ∾TIP Serve with warm flatbread, lightly coated with olive oil, garlic powder, onion powder, dill, and basil.

Ingredients: Cucumber Salad

1 lb English cucumber
1 white onion
2 tbsps white vinegar
2 tbsps white sugar

1½ tsps sea salt
1 tsp celery seed
1 tsp mustard seed

Instructions: Cucumber Salad

1. Thinly slice the cucumber and the onion using a mandoline (if you have one; otherwise a knife is fine).

2. Put the slices in a coverable bowl.

3. Add all the remaining ingredients.

4. Mix thoroughly.

5. Place in the refrigerator for 15 minutes or more before serving.

6. Stir again.

7. Place on the table and let people serve themselves (pass clockwise for positive energy).

> ∾ TIP Make this salad the night before. The flavor improves with time.

Potential Additions

Cucumber salad: Cherry tomatoes, feta, olives, chickpeas, lemon zest

MANDOLINE MAGIC

One of the tools that took a while before it came into my kitchen was a mandoline. I tried to make even slices of onion for soup or pickling and potatoes for German potato salad. It did not work well. Enter stage right: the mandoline.

A mandoline slices ingredients so they're uniform. It's also much faster than hand slicing. There are different kinds, but I highly advise finding one with some type of hand protection or a feeding tube. Both protect you from razor-sharp blades, which come in various sizes from thin to thick.[11]

COLOR MAGIC: PORK, WHITE BEANS, AND WINE

Energetic Essence: You get to play with color symbolism for this recipe. White beans represent faith, peace, wisdom, and destiny. However, this recipe could use several other beans based on your needs. Here are some color correspondences for different beans:

Black beans: Mystery; power; sophistication

Cranberry beans (cream and red): Elegance; reliability; calm

Mung beans (green): Beginnings, growth; well-being

Pinto (rust-colored flecks): Pride; vitality; optimism; warmth

Red beans: Luck; love; faithfulness

Ingredients

6 ozs smoky bacon, thick cut

2 cups chicken bone broth

1 cup white zinfandel wine

8 cloves garlic, smashed

1 cup Great Northern beans, drained

15 oz can small white beans, drained

15 oz can petite diced tomatoes
   (Italian style)

1 large Spanish onion, chopped

2 lbs pork butt (lean), cubed

Substitution

Zinfandel: Riesling, pinot
   grigio, pink Moscato

Instructions

1. Crisp up the bacon, let cool, and crumble.

2. Place the broth, wine, and garlic in the slow cooker.

3. Whisk them all together.

4. Add the beans, tomatoes, and onion to the wine mixture.

5. Mix again.

6. Place the pork butt on top.

7. Turn the cooker to low and cook for 7 hours.

8. After 2 hours and after 4 hours, baste the pork with the juices in the bottom of the pot.

9. Remove the pork from the slow cooker. Pull the pork using a fork.

10. Serve the pork with the beans.

Serving Suggestion

If you want the dish a little hardier, serve it over egg noodles.

Side Dish Suggestions

Brats (or hot dogs)

Fried chicken

Macaroni salad

Potato wedges

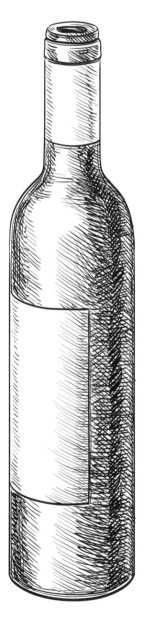

BOON BRISKET

Energetic Essence: Brisket is a favorite holiday food in Jewish households. It's served, typically, during the holidays of Rosh Hashanah, Passover, and Hanukkah. The meat is easy on the budget, but when cooked slowly, it tenderizes. Overall, brisket represents celebrating (without breaking the bank).

Ingredients

3 lbs beef brisket (trimmed)
Salt and pepper
1 red onion
1 yellow onion
1 medium green pepper
14 oz can chopped tomatoes
    (Italian style), drained

3 cloves of garlic, smashed
1 tbsp extra virgin olive oil

Substitution
Brisket: Chuck roast (also known
    as poor man's brisket)

Instructions

1. Pat down the brisket with paper towels. Lightly season all sides with salt and pepper.

2. Coat the slow cooker with cooking spray.

3. Put the brisket in the middle.

4. Turn the setting to low and let the meat cook for 10 hours.

5. About 30 minutes before the brisket comes out, slice the onions and peppers and preheat the oven to 425°F.

6. Mix the onions, peppers, tomatoes, and garlic with the olive oil.

7. Roast on a baking sheet in a 425°F oven for 20 minutes.

8. Use onions and peppers on top of the brisket for garnish.

BASIC GUIDE TO BRISKET

Brisket comes from the pectoral muscles of a cow, meaning it's full of connective tissue. This trait is why brisket suits slow cooking. A whole brisket is huge (10–14 lbs). Unless you have a lot of hungry guests, look for something precut.

There are two cuts of brisket. The flat cut (first cut) is larger than the second cut. A thin layer of fat covers one side, making it ideal for braising. The deckle point (second cut) has good marbling, so you can smoke it and keep it juicy.

Side Dish Suggestions

Cole slaw
German potato salad
Mexican corn salad
Rolls

SWEET SISTER'S SAUSAGE SOUP

Energetic Essence: My two sisters and I love soup year-round. I thought of them being ever tried and true when putting together this recipe. This meal represents my wish for their lasting happiness. Spiritually speaking, seeing a pale-colored sausage in a dream portends joy on the horizon. It may be a gift, a letter from someone special, or a pleasant gathering with family or friends.

Note: Bratwurst is naturally white when you buy it!

Ingredients

1 lb bratwurst
1 tbsp olive oil
½ cup Riesling
1 onion, chopped
2 celery stalks, sliced
3 garlic cloves, minced
6 cups chicken bone broth
   (or vegetable stock)
2 tsps Italian seasoning

1 bay leaf
4 cups spinach
9 ozs cheese tortellini
   (defrosted if frozen)

Substitutions
Bratwurst: Sweet Italian sausage
Riesling: Zinfandel, pinot grigio
Spinach: Arugula, escarole, radicchio

Instructions

1. Remove the casings of the bratwurst and crumble.
2. Place in a skillet with oil, browning for 6 minutes.
3. Transfer the sausage to the slow cooker.
4. Deglaze the skillet using wine, mixing in all the brown bits.
5. Pour this into the slow cooker.
6. Add all remaining ingredients except the spinach and the tortellini.
7. Cook on low for 5 hours (the vegetables must be fork-tender).
8. Add the spinach and tortellini, cover the pot, and cook for 15 minutes.

Side Dish Suggestions

Grilled cheese
Flatbread
Pear salad with walnuts and gorgonzola
Stuffed potatoes
Sweet potato fries

WINDS OF CHANGE CORN CHOWDER

Energetic Essence: In many Native Indigenous cultures, the Great Spirit gifted corn to human-kind.[12] It is a source of sacred wisdom. Some tribes use corn pollen to bless people. It represents providence, prosperity, faith, and joy and appears in rituals for growth and transformation.

Ingredients

3 small red potatoes, cut in eighths (sized for easy eating)

2 cups frozen corn

1 tbsp garlic

1 Vidalia onion, chopped

2 carrots, chopped

2 stalks of celery, chopped

4 ozs kielbasa, cut into ¼-inch pieces

2 tbsps flour

Salt and pepper to taste

4 cups chicken broth

⅓ cup heavy cream

1 tbsp butter

Oyster crackers (optional)

Instructions

1. In a 6-quart cooker, place the potatoes, corn, garlic, onions, carrots, celery, half the kielbasa, flour, and salt and pepper.

2. Stir, making sure the vegetables become evenly coated with flour.

3. Add the chicken broth. Cook on low for 5 hours until fork-tender.

4. For a textural element, take the remaining kielbasa and brown it up on the stove.

5. Add this to the chowder with heavy cream and butter.

6. Top with oyster crackers, if desired.

Side Dish Suggestions

Crusty bread

Fried calamari

Green salad

Ham and cheese sandwich

CHOWDER IN HISTORY

Chowder began on immigrant ships from England and France to North America. The first published notation about chowder appeared in "American Notes and Queries" in 1890. The French settlers in Canada used clams and bacon in their brew. In the United States, chowder started in New England. There, a pot sat simmering at the seaside where people could put their extra fish and add potatoes and seasonings.[13]

Like many beloved recipes, families had their own special chowder, often appearing at family gatherings. It was a common dish that, when eaten, brought comfort and a sense of nostalgia. Some chowders use milk and roux to create thickening. And, like this dish, not all chowders have fish in them.

Kindred Spirit Red Sauce

Energetic Essence: A little background here. I have had a best friend since college. I remember visiting her while she made jar after jar after jar of red sauce to put up for the coming year. Interestingly enough, dreaming of red sauce means you have a "charming friend" (wink, wink). Our lives have remained intertwined like spaghetti noodles, and the sauce binds our love altogether. This one-pot recipe isn't exactly like hers. I prefer chunky, whereas she likes smooth, but the symbolism remains.

Ingredients

1 lb 80/20 ground beef

1 lb ground Italian sausage (hot or mild)

½ large white onion, chopped

1 medium green pepper, chopped

1 tbsp fresh garlic, minced

4 15 oz cans crushed or diced tomatoes
(Some varieties of crushed and diced tomato have seasonings like basil and garlic if you want even more flavor)

3¾ cups tomato sauce

¾ cup tomato paste

2 basil leaves, chiffonade (see page 200)

2 bay leaves

1 tbsp Italian seasoning

1½ tbsps sugar

½ cup bone beef broth

Salt and pepper to taste

Instructions

1. Sauté the ground beef and sausage together.

2. Drain off the fat and move the meat into the slow cooker.

3. Using the drippings from the beef/sausage, fry the onions, green pepper, and garlic until the onion is translucent.

4. Move the vegetables to the slow cooker.

5. Pour all other ingredients into the pot and stir them well.

6. If you're in a hurry, cook on high for 3 to 4 hours, but this benefits from slow cooking (low for 6 to 8 hours).

7. Serve it on your favorite pasta with garlic bread, or can it to be used later.

Endnotes

1. Laurie Colwin in Whitney Hopler, "Famous Quotes on Cooking and Wellbeing," *University News*, accessed September 28, 2023, https://wellbeing.gmu.edu/famous-quotes-on-cooking-and-well-being/.

2. Marjorie Ingall, "Meet the Jewish Inventor of the Slow Cooker," *Tablet Magazine*, last updated August 5, 2017, https://www.tabletmag.com /sections/food/articles/jewish-inventor-of-slow-cooker-irving-naxon.

3. Annalise Jolley, "Basque Cider Houses," *National Geographic Travel*, accessed September 9, 2023, https://www.nationalgeographic.com /travel/article/basque-cider-houses-keep-cultural-and-culinary-history -alive.

4. Lauren Frayer, "In Spain New Year's Is All About the Grapes," *Morning Edition*, NPR, December 27, 2016, https://www.npr.org/sections /thesalt/2016/12/27/506484561/in-spain-new-year-s-eve-is-all-about-the -grapes-save-the-bubbly-for-later.

5. EtymOnline, "Onion," accessed November 22, 2023, https://www.etymonline.com/word/onion.

6. New Mexico State University, Onion Breeding Program, "History," accessed September 12, 2023, https://onion.nmsu.edu/history.html.

7. Brittany Wilmes, "Pear Symbolism for the New Year," USA Pears, accessed December 30, 2010, https://usapears.org/blog/pear-symbolism -year.

8. Jacqueline Simpson, *A Dictionary of English Folklore*, Oxford: Oxford University Press, 2003, https://www.oxfordreference.com /display/10.1093/oi/authority.20110803100117959.

9. Jenny Smith, "Wheat Berries: A True Whole Grain," University of Illinois Extension, January 10, 2018, https://extension.illinois.edu/blogs /simply-nutritious-quick-and-delicious/2018-01-10-wheat-berries-true -whole-grain.

10. Santha Rama Rau, *Cooking of India*, Foods of the World, Chicago, IL: Time Life Education, June 1969.

11. Karla Walsh, "How to Use a Mandoline Slicer," *Better Homes and Gardens*, September 5, 2022, https://www.bhg.com/recipes/how-to /food-storage-safety/a-mandoline-saves-time/.

12. Jack D. Forbes, "Indigenous Americans: Spirituality and Ecos," *Daedalus: American Academy of Arts and Science*, Fall 2001, https://www.amacad.org/publication/indigenous-americans-spirituality -and-ecos.

13. Jake Walker and Robert S. Cox, *A History of Chowder*, Charleston, SC: The History Press, 2011.

chapter six

potluck possibilities

Cooking is all about people. Food is maybe the only universal thing that really has the power to bring everyone together. No matter what culture, everywhere around the world, people get together to eat.
—GUY FIERI[1]

Potluck dinners are one way of alleviating stress in order to free the host up for enjoying more time with their guests. As much as a Kitchen Witch loves the pantry, good company and conversation prove just as enriching. Plus, the recipes people bring may inspire future magical meals.

Potluck Planning: Tips and Tricks

There are no hard-and-fast rules about potluck other than the shared dishes are large enough for all guests to receive a portion. While some people just put out the call for any fare, others plan a little more, assigning categories to avoid three bowls of potato salad. I like the second approach; adding a spiritual theme to the process makes it even more special.

Hosting

If you are hosting, think about beverages. Ensure there's a mixture of drinks (alcoholic and nonalcoholic) and enough for everyone. If someone brings a beverage, it's icing on the cake. You also want to provide cutlery, plates, bowls, napkins, and glasses.

POTLUCK ETYMOLOGY

The first appearance of the term *potluck* occurred in the sixteenth century (the Tudor period) in a work penned by Thomas Nashe, an Elizabethan playwright and poet. He used it to describe food a person provides to unexpected guests. They received the "luck of the pot."[2] Fast-forward to the 1930s, people began having communal meals as a way of easing the financial constraints of the Great Depression and keeping people fed.[3]

There is a possibility the term *potluck* in Canada and the United States came from Indigenous people of the Pacific Northwest. They had a tradition of "potlatch," or giveaway. At the potlatch, people shared items freely.[4] While this took place, there were rituals honoring spirits and the recitation of oral histories.

Now comes the tricky part, envisioning where everything will go in your space. You could just let guests "have at it," but the way you lay things out can cause disasters if you're not thinking. Have you ever tried to reach over a bowl of dip for a salad? Check your sleeve!

Find ways to stage similar items together. Have a drink station, snacks, appetizers, casseroles, desserts, etc. Plan for slow cookers (find your outlets!). Pull out extra spoon holders for serving. Inevitably, people forget them. Have some take-home bags and containers (you cannot get everything in your fridge).

And finally, prepare for messes. I create a plastic bin with paper towels, stain remover, cleaning necessities, etc. Knowing where everything is when you need it is nice. Now, I confess I'm a terminal planner, but trust me when I say you'll be glad you did. Plus, you have a head start on items for tidying up after the potluck.

Attending

I was out of my element the first time I received an invitation to a potluck. I'd only really started cooking. The choice? A humble salad. Yeah, not thrilling, but it suited the moment. Over the years (thankfully), I learned a great deal about attending potlucks.

When I cooked beans and transported them in the slow cooker, the first pothole my tire hit taught me to do things differently. Bring food that travels easily. Use secure, covered containers. Assemble after your arrival. Pack serving utensils.

> ∼ **TIP** Line a cardboard box with a plastic garbage bag
> and transport your goods inside. It's a "just in case"
> maneuver.

Next, other people are bringing grub, too. So, you don't have to make a large portion. If your offering feeds five people, you're in good shape. Tell the host beforehand if you need a prep space, oven time, or an outlet. They'll appreciate it.

Speaking of appreciation, bring a little something to honor your guest's hospitality. A bottle of wine, flowers, napkin rings, agate coasters, scented candles, and nifty cooking gadgets all fit the situation.

Potluck has a very social nature. No matter who you gather with, work toward having a fun time together. Whip up those positive vibes. What do you bring? This chapter gives you some ideas to get those creative juices flowing.

∼

Because there is such a broad range of potential offerings, I stress one thing about potluck meals. Take a moment to write an ingredient list and leave it with your contribution. It may seem trivial, but it alleviates the chances of allergic reactions since guests can see the components. It is a gesture of mindfulness.

ANTIPASTO SKEWERS

Energetic Essence: Antipasto is colorful and creative. It has roots in Medieval Italy, where savory and sweet finger foods appeared on a platter.[5] This course aims to excite the palate in preparation for the main course. There's no reason you can't use it as an energizing prelude, setting the magical tone for your meal to come.

Ingredients

9 ozs tortellini (meat, cheese, or spinach; if you can find colored tortellini, it's very festive)

½ cup Italian dressing

1 tbsp Worcestershire sauce

1 tbsp red vinegar

Pinch brown sugar

1 tsp minced garlic

30 cherry tomatoes

15 each black and green olives

30 small basil leaves, fresh

30 slices salami or prosciutto

30 mozzarella balls (small)

15 pieces of artichoke hearts

15 long skewers (you may have some leftover)

Substitutions

Artichoke hearts: Broccoli stems, bamboo shoots, brussels sprouts, hearts of palm

Italian dressing: Vinaigrette, Greek dressing

Mozzarella: Feta squares, Monterey jack, Gouda

Instructions

1. Cook the tortellini as instructed on the package.

2. Drain and rinse with cold water to stop the cooking.

3. Put the tortellini in a food storage bag.

4. Pour in the Italian dressing, Worcestershire, vinegar, sugar, and garlic.

5. Refrigerate for 4 hours, then drain.

6. Set out the remaining ingredients in front of you like an assembly line.

7. Start threading the skewers, mixing up the colors (tortellini, tomato, olive, basil, salami, mozzarella, artichoke, etc.).

8. Chill briefly before serving.

Potential Additions

Cubes of cooked chicken, beef, or ham

Lettuce as a bed for the skewers (have some extra dressing on the side)

Pineapple

Shrimp

Tofu

White pearl onions (lightly grilled)

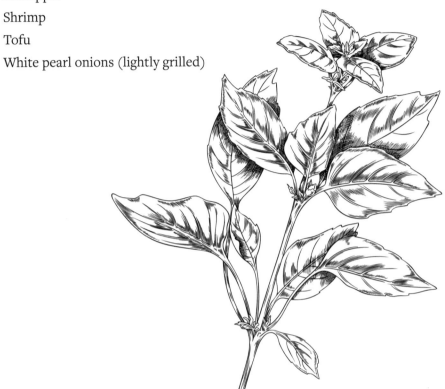

CHAMPAGNE PUNCH

Energetic Essence: If everyone else is bringing food, why not bring a beverage? The bubbles in the champagne lift everyone's mood. Cranberries inspire peace between people, strawberries evoke love, and raspberries contribute kindness.

Ingredients

1 gallon pitcher (allows room for the fruit)

¼ cup Grand Marnier

½ cup vodka

¼ inch slice of fresh ginger

1 cup pomegranate juice, frozen into ice cubes

2 cups ginger ale

1 750 ml bottle (3 cups) of rose champagne, cold

1 seedless orange, sliced thin

1 lemon, sliced thin

1 pint raspberries

Substitutions

Fruit (any): Maraschino cherries, pineapple chunks

Ginger ale: Flavor-infused sparkling seltzer, lemon-lime soda

Grand Marnier: Cognac, Cointreau, Chambord

CHAMPAGNE DEBATE

In France, the lore claims Dom Perignon invented champagne in 1697. However, an English scientist found winemakers having a sparkle in their wine some thirty years earlier.[6] They used extra sugar or molasses to evoke the bubbles. Take any wine, add special yeast and sugar, cap it, and fermentation does the rest.

Instructions

1. Bring the ingredients with you and assemble them on-site. Make sure they're all thoroughly chilled.

2. Put the Grand Marnier, vodka, ginger, and pomegranate ice cubes into the pitcher. (Having the pomegranate juice in ice form keeps the punch cold when left out for serving.)

3. Add ginger ale, champagne, fruit slices, and berries about 15 minutes before serving. You're good to go!

METAMORPHOSIS CHEESE-STUFFED MUSHROOMS

Energetic Essence: This is a marvelously simple dish. Mushrooms represent transformation and rebirth. Make this the appetizer of choice during times of change, resulting in spiritual and mental growth.

Ingredients

12 large mushroom caps

¼ cup pizza sauce

1 cup mozzarella cheese, shredded

12 slices pepperoni

Extra virgin olive oil

¼ tsp each salt, pepper, and sugar

1 basil leaf, coarsely chopped
   or parsley (garnish)

Substitutions

Mozzarella cheese: Fontina,
   provolone, Edam

Pepperoni: Sliced shallot, sliced
   olive, minced sweet pepper

Pizza sauce: Sweet chili sauce, pesto,
   barbecue sauce, marinara

Instructions

1. Set the oven to 450°F.

2. Spray a cooking pan (with sides), then lightly arrange the mushrooms in the pan so they don't touch each other (this improves even cooking).

3. Put 1–2 tsps of pizza sauce in the bottom of each mushroom.

4. Follow with 1–2 tbsps mozzarella.

5. Top each mushroom with a pepperoni cap.

6. Drizzle lightly with olive oil.

7. Bake for 15 minutes or until the cheese lightly browns.

8. Transfer to a serving platter.

9. Sprinkle with salt, pepper, sugar, and garnish.

Rainbow Pasta Salad

Energetic Essence: If there were ever a symbol for diversity, it would be the rainbow. The harmony of colors brings a smile when you see it. When looking at a rainbow, it appears as an arch. In truth, it's a circle representing the spheres of people with whom you travel and trust. It may prove challenging to find all the visible colors of the rainbow for your dish. Just aim for as much variety as possible.

Ingredients: Pasta Salad

1 lb rotini

1 each green, yellow, and red peppers, chopped

2 cups blue bayou tomatoes, halved

1 cup indigo carrots, shredded

1 seedless cucumber, chopped

3 violet-colored basil leaves, chiffonade (see page 200)

½ cup black olives, sliced

1 cup garbanzo beans

1 cup feta cheese, crumbled

Substitutions

Basil leaves: Oregano leaves, spinach leaves

Garbanzo beans: White kidney beans, cannellini beans

Instructions: Pasta Salad

1. Cook the rotini according to the box directions.

2. Cool.

3. In a large mixing bowl, combine the rotini and all other ingredients.

4. Add dressing (recipe on next page) and chill before serving.

5. Include a long-handled spoon for portioning.

6. Let the salad chill overnight so the flavors marry.

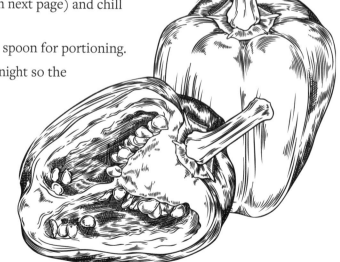

Ingredients: Salad Dressing

½ cup extra virgin olive oil

3 tbsps red wine vinegar

2 tbsps lemon juice, freshly squeezed

½ tsp onion powder

1 tsp garlic powder

2 tsps garlic, minced

2 tbsps each parsley, oregano,
and basil, freshly chopped

1 scant tsp honey or white sugar

¼ tsp red pepper flakes

Substitution

Red wine vinegar: Balsamic vinegar,
white wine vinegar, raspberry vinegar

Instructions: Salad Dressing

1. Mix all the ingredients in a cruet with a top.

2. Shake liberally, then chill for one day.

3. Shake again before using (shaking energizes your magic).

~ **TIP** If you cannot get fresh herbs, 1 tbsp of fresh translates into 1 tsp dry.

RAINBOWS CONNECT THE HEAVENS AND THE EARTH

Greek mythology tells us rainbows were the personification of a goddess named Iris.[7] She is the messenger between the firmament and Earth, the rainbow bridging the two. Her presence symbolizes hope. Similar beliefs about dragons exist in China as they, like the rainbow, exist between the cosmos and the land.

FOR YOUR HONEY: HONEY NUT BRIE

Energetic Essence: Cheese symbolizes opportunity, especially in relationships. In this case, you're using warm, soft cheese to keep those feelings intimate and cozy. Pistachios bring happiness, almonds bring sweetness, and figs bring wisdom.

Ingredients

8 ozs brie (your choice of brand)

⅛ cup pistachios

⅛ cup almonds, sliced

¼ dried figs, rough-chopped

3 tbsps orange blossom honey

¼ tsp orange flower water

¼ tsp fresh thyme

Crostini or sliced strawberries, peaches, or apricots for serving

Substitutions

Almonds: Hazelnuts, Brazil nuts

Fig: Pears, apricots, dates

Pistachios: Pine nuts

Instructions

1. Set the oven to 375°F.

2. Line an ovenproof dish with parchment paper.

3. Bake the brie for 10 minutes (you want the cheese soft, not melted).

4. While the brie cooks, mix the pistachios, almonds, figs, honey, water, and thyme to create a honey nut mixture. Warm the mixture slightly.

5. Spoon the honey nut mixture over the top when the brie comes out of the oven.

6. Serve warm with crostini or fruit.

BRIE BEGINNINGS

Brie is among the most famous cheeses to come out of France. Monks in the area of Meaux created it around the seventh century.[8] Various historical accounts mention cheese, including, most notably, a story recounting how Charlemagne described brie as one of the most delicious things (774 CE).

The basic flavor profile for brie is the same across the board, but for minor flavor variations arising from the grasses and flowers the cow eats. It's comparable to Camembert but with a higher butterfat content. Over time, varieties of brie came into the market, some of which have herbs, use other types of milk, and still others are smoked.

Amity Olive Tapenade

Energetic Essence: Tapenade sounds fancy, but it only means a spread with three key ingredients: olives, capers, and anchovies. In ancient Greece, the olive branch represents peace, particularly toward people of power and influence.

Ingredients

1 cup black olives, pitted
1 cup green olives
¼ cup sun-dried tomatoes
¼ cup fresh parsley
8 basil leaves
1 clove garlic, minced
½ lemon, juiced
Salt and pepper to taste
1 tsp onion flakes

½ tsp anchovy paste
2 tbsps capers, rinsed
½ tsp chipotle or red chili flakes
¼ cup olive oil

Substitutions

Green or black olives: Kalamata olives
Onion flakes: Onion powder,
    chopped green onions
Sun-dried tomatoes: Fresh tomatoes

Instructions

1. Finely mince the olives, tomatoes, parsley, and basil.

2. Place them in a mixing bowl.

3. Add the garlic, lemon juice, salt, pepper, onion flakes, anchovy paste, capers, and chili flakes.

4. Stir.

5. Slowly pour the oil into the olive blend.

6. Taste-test.

7. If you have a blender or food processor, use it to make the tapenade smoother.

~ **TIP** Be careful with the salt. Olives
    are already salty. Taste-test often.

Amity Olive Tapenade
∽ CONTINUED ∽

Potential Additions

Balsamic vinegar

Feta cheese

Oregano

Sliced red onion

OLIVES IN ANTIQUITY

In Greek mythology, Zeus promised whoever brought the most useful invention to him would become the god or goddess of Attica. Athena brought the olive tree and planted it on Acropolis Hill. The local belief is the olive tree remaining there came from Athena's original gift.

Olive is one of the oldest cultivated trees (3000 BCE, Crete) because its oil has many uses, including light, heat, medicines, and the base for perfume.[9] Archaeologists found olives in Egyptian tombs dating to 2000 BCE. Once olives reached Rome, soldiers and traders alike brought olives with them as the Roman domain expanded.

Propitious Pineapple Pico with Chips

Energetic Essence: The Chinese word for pineapple sounds similar to the phrase "luck coming your way."[10] *Bring a little serendipity into your life. Share it with friends. Besides this, the Chinese say that the pineapple spikes symbolize the ability to see into the future.*

Ingredients: Pico

1 ripe pineapple

¼ cup each yellow, green, orange, and red peppers, finely chopped

1 cup of tomatoes, diced

¼ cup cilantro, chopped

⅓ cup red onion, minced

Juice from 2 limes

1 tbsp jalapeño pepper

1 tbsp garlic, minced

1 tbsp vinegar

1 tbsp brown sugar

Substitution
Pineapple: Mango, peach, papaya, guava

Instructions: Pico

1. Lay the pineapple on its side and remove ⅓ of the pineapple top, leaving the stem leaves attached.

2. Cut all around the pineapple inside, close to the skin.

3. Now, make cuts across the middle.

4. Take out the chunks of pineapple and set aside. Retain juices.

5. Finely dice up 1 cup of the pineapple.

6. Finely dice up the peppers (you want them close to the same size as the pineapple).

7. Combine the pineapple, pineapple juice, and all the other ingredients in a mixing bowl.

8. Store in the fridge overnight before serving.

9. Put the salsa in a nice dish at the gathering.

  ∽ **TIP** You will have pineapple leftovers. For future use, freeze the individual chunks on a cookie tray (so they don't touch). Once they're frozen, transfer them into food storage bags. They're safe in the freezer for six months.

> ## KING OF FRUIT
> In sixteenth-century Europe, the pineapple received the honorable title "King of Fruit." There was a high demand for pineapples. Supplies ran out periodically.
>
> When hosting a gathering, it was imperative to have a pineapple present on the table. If one could not afford one, shopkeepers rented them!

Propitious Pineapple Pico with Chips
∾ CONTINUED ∾

Ingredients: Chips

Large tortilla or burrito shells
  (number depends on how many chips you want)
1 cup vegetable oil
Coarse salt

Instructions: Chips

1. Slice the tortilla shells into 8 wedges shaped like a triangle.

2. Leave the tortilla pieces out overnight. It will dry them out and help them fry better.

3. Heat the oil to 350°F. It's great if you have a deep fryer (you'll need more oil), but you can do this in a stovetop pan.

4. In small batches, fry the chips to golden brown.

5. Transfer the fried chips to paper towels.

6. Salt them lightly.

Potential Additions

Add chipotle and honey powder to your finishing sprinkle for a kick.

Progressive Pork and Beans

Energetic Essence: This is a great recipe choice when working toward more significant accomplishments in any field. Beans represent growth, success, and precision. Pork and bacon symbolize positive forward movement and resourcefulness.

Ingredients: Base

1 lb thick-sliced smoky bacon, cubed

1½ lbs pork butt, cubed

1 white onion, diced

4 lbs mixed Great Northern beans, navy beans, and cannellini beans

Instructions: Base

1. Cook the bacon and cubed pork. Add the onion and keep sautéing for 7 minutes.

2. Transfer the pork mixture to the slow cooker.

3. Add the beans (if canned, use the liquid too).

4. Mix the sauce (recipe follows) with the beans.

5. Stir until everything is coated.

6. Cook on low for 4 to 6 hours.

Ingredients: Sauce

2 cups ketchup

¼ cup brown sugar

¼ cup molasses

2 tbsps stone-ground mustard

1 tsp garlic powder

1 tsp salt

1 tsp fresh ground black pepper

1 tsp kosher salt

1 cup beef or chicken stock

Substitutions

Ketchup: Tomato sauce

Molasses: Maple syrup, honey

PORK AND BEANS BEGINNINGS

Pork and beans is an elusive dish when you trace its history. Most people believe Native American cuisine in the Northeast had similar dishes. A second theory says it originated with a French concoction. Cassoulet is a slow-cooked recipe with beans and meat, having a slightly sticky appeal. Recipes came with English travelers to America.[11]

Progressive Pork and Beans

~ CONTINUED ~

Instructions: Sauce

1. Put all the sauce ingredients into a pan.

2. Warm over medium heat, stirring regularly.

3. Remove from the heat after 10 minutes (it should thicken some).

4. Pour onto bean mixture.

Potential Additions

¼ cup dark beer (reduce the stock by ¼ cup)

Visionary Anise Sugar Cookies

Energetic Essence: Anise encourages an awareness of your spirit guides and teachers. It supports the growth of your psychic gifts, especially clairvoyance.

Background: This was my father's favorite holiday cookie. My sister keeps the tradition alive, and I can tell you people fight over them when they get into the house. I hide some just for me (don't tell).

Ingredients

1 cup unsalted butter, room temperature

1½ cups sugar (you can remove ½ cup of white sugar and replace with brown)

2 large eggs, room temperature

½–1 tsp anise extract (NOT flavoring)

¼ tsp vanilla extract

3 cups flour

1½ tsps aniseed

1 tsp salt

1 tsp baking powder

1 tsp baking soda

Substitution
Aniseed: Orange zest

Instructions

1. Set the oven to 375°F.

2. Put the butter and sugar in a large bowl.

3. Beat them together for 6 minutes (you want them fluffy).

4. Blend in eggs and extracts.

5. Mix the dry ingredients (flour, aniseed, salt, baking powder, and baking soda).

6. Slowly combine the dry ingredients mixture into the butter/sugar blend.

7. Shape the dough into 1-inch balls.

8. Grease a cookie sheet.

9. Lay each ball down one at a time and flatten them with a glass bottom dipped in sugar.

10. Leave room between the cookies, as they will spread.

11. Put in the oven for 8 minutes. Give them 1–2 more minutes if they don't seem done.

12. Cool before decorating.

VISIONARY ANISE SUGAR COOKIES
∽ CONTINUED ∾

Decorating Idea

Use a white frosting first, then use a different color glaze for patterns like the eye of Horus or a pentacle.

MAGICAL USES FOR ANISE

Magicians classified anise as a masculine herb with an elemental correspondence to the air element. It's under the rule of Jupiter, the planet of plenty and wisdom. Spiritually, the usefulness of anise goes far beyond cooking and baking. Here are some ideas you can try.

GOOD DREAMS Keep star anise under your pillow at night.

HEIGHTENED AWARENESS AND POSITIVITY Carrying star anise promotes heightened psychic awareness and improved outlooks.

HOUSEHOLD HARMONY Add anise to boiling potpourri. The aroma spreads happiness and peace throughout your home.

LUCK AND CULMINATION When preparing your altar, add anise for improved fortune and to open your connection to the universe. If your ritual is during a new moon, anise promotes manifestation.

UNCOVERING ANSWERS If you are doing a reading, keep the star anise nearby to reveal previously hidden matters.

CHAKRA PINWHEELS

Energetic Essence: The clockwise spin of pinwheels lends itself to expanding energies. It represents open, healthy chakras. The word chakra *comes from Sanskrit, meaning "wheel."[12] Chakras appear in the Vedas as energy fields throughout your body. Make these so you are likewise "clear" in body, mind, and spirit.*

Ingredients

1 lb Italian sausage (without casing)
½ cup sweet pepper, diced
1 small bundle of green onion, chopped
2 cloves garlic, finely minced
3 12-inch tortilla shells (spinach or garden herb)

8 ozs cream cheese, room temperature
Spicy mayo

Substitution
Italian sausage: Bratwurst (remove from casing), hamburger, ground chicken

Instructions

1. Crumble the sausage into a skillet. Turn the heat to medium and fry for 5 minutes (there should be no signs of pink).

2. Add the pepper, onion, and garlic.

3. Cook for another 2 minutes.

4. Place the sausage blend into a mixing bowl.

5. Leave it to cool for 15 minutes.

6. Cover each tortilla with a ½ tbsp cream cheese (more if you wish).

7. Put equal amounts of filling on each one.

8. Roll them tightly, securing them in saran wrap.

9. Refrigerate for 3 hours.

10. Just before serving, cut the tortillas into 1-inch slices.

11. Drizzle a little spicy mayo over the pinwheels as garnish.

~ **TIP** You can use pre-flavored cream cheese here, such as dill, garlic and herb, or sun-dried tomato.

Potential Additions

Bacon bits (sacral chakra)

Green chilis (root chakra)

Olives (heart chakra)

Shredded cheese (solar plexus chakra)

CONTEMPLATING CHAKRAS

There are seven main chakras in the body. When one is out of balance, it may manifest as illness or weakness, or other ongoing maladies:

ROOT CHAKRA Located in the tailbone region. Houses stability and grounding.

SACRAL CHAKRA Near your belly button. Houses pleasure, inventiveness, and sexual identity.

SOLAR PLEXUS CHAKRA Position is in the upper abdomen. Houses personal power, confidence, self-worth, and well-earned pride.

HEART CHAKRA Stationed just above your heart. Houses compassion, love, tenderness, and empathy.

THROAT CHAKRA As the name implies, this chakra swirls energetically in the throat. Houses communication, finding your voice, expressing your truth.

THIRD EYE CHAKRA Between your eyes. Houses instinct, intuition, seeing the whole picture, and imagination.

CROWN CHAKRA On the top of your head. Houses intelligence, connection with Spirit, guides, and awareness.

ELDERFLOWER MANUSCRIPT MUFFINS

Energetic Essence: This recipe is ideal for summer solstice and for writers looking to get past blockages to pen fresh ideas. Summer solstice unlocks your inner fire and positivity. Elderflower blooms in early summer and has a magical profile matching the summer solstice perfectly. This edible flower helps you look at things with fresh eyes so creativity flows. Share these at your next writer's seminar or brainstorming session.

Note: You can find several sources of fresh elderflowers online.

Ingredients

½ cup unsalted butter, melted

2⅓ cups flour, sifted

2 tsps baking powder

¼ tsp baking soda

¼ tsp kosher salt

½ cup wildflower honey

½ cup plain yogurt

¼ cup sourdough starter

2 large eggs

1 tbsp fresh orange juice

1 tbsp orange zest

1½ tsps vanilla extract

3 tbsps fresh elderflowers

Substitutions

Honey: Maple syrup, molasses, brown sugar

Orange: Lemon

Instructions

1. Coat a muffin tin with butter or spray oil.

2. Set the oven to 350°F.

3. Put out two mixing bowls.

4. Put flour, baking powder, baking soda, and salt in one.

5. In the other, stir together the honey, yogurt, sourdough starter, eggs, juice, zest, and vanilla.

6. Whisk until smooth.

7. Slowly fold the dry ingredients into the wet.

8. Fold the elderflowers into the batter (gently fold, as the flowers are delicate).

9. Put equal amounts of the batter into the treated tin.

THE FLAVOR OF ELDERFLOWER

The art of cooking with flowers was out of fashion for some time, but thankfully it's being reintroduced to the culinary scene. Elderflower, when used correctly, is very delicate. Its taste is subtle, somewhat fruity (similar to apple and pear), and defined by floral notes.

10. Bake for 20 minutes. They should be golden brown and a toothpick placed in the center of the muffin should come out clean.

11. Cool and transfer to a serving tray.

12. Sprinkle fresh flowers all around on top.

Potential Additions

¼ tsp ginger

¼ cup raspberries, crushed

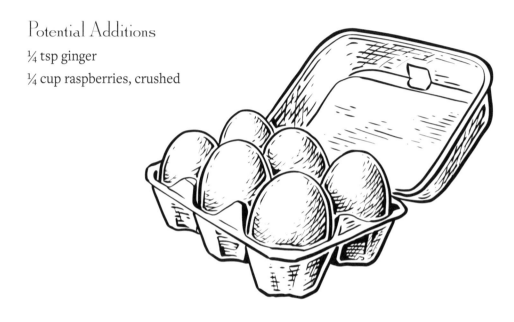

"MIXER" BEER DIP

Energetic Essence: A Sumerian proverb says, "He who does not know beer, does not know what is good."[13] *Beer is the commoner's drink, shared with friends. It's unpretentious, everyday, and ordinary. Mind you, early beer wasn't wimpy. A Trappist monk said (or at least gets credit for the quote), "Beer should be liquid bread, not colored water."*[14] *Overall, beer represents happy (sometimes exuberant) socialization and hospitality.*

Ingredients

2 8 oz packages of cream cheese

⅓ cup IPA beer or Belgian ale

1 tsp Worcestershire sauce

¼ tsp dill

¼ tsp garlic powder

1 oz envelope of ranch dressing mix

2 cups cheddar cheese, shredded

Soft pretzels, crackers, or tortilla chips

Substitutions

Cheddar cheese: Havarti, baby swiss, or Colby jack

Ranch dressing: Use Greek, Italian, or garlic and herb powder mix

Instructions

1. Simply mix everything but the pretzels in a bowl until thoroughly integrated. Some people serve it as is. I like heating it for the ooey-gooey appeal.

   ∾ **TIP** Use this as a sandwich spread. It's great under the broiler.

BREWER'S YEAST BASICS

While beer may be liquid bread because of having many ingredients in common, you cannot use baking yeast to make beer. It will come out tasting like a liquid version of a bitter-flavored loaf (trust me, I tried). Brewer's yeast, water, and carbohydrate are necessary for beer recipes. Beer masters treasured the yeast because of its remarkable fermenting characteristics. When you introduce sugar, the brewer's yeast transforms the carbohydrate into sugars, thus bubbles.

Endnotes

1. Michael Mooney, "Guy Fieri Shares What Feeds His Appetite for Life," *Success*, May 19, 2016, https://www.success.com/guy-fieri-shares-what -feeds-his-appetite-for-life/.

2. Thomas Nash, *Strange Newes, of the Intercepting Certaine Letters and a Convoy of Verses*, National Library of the Netherlands, 1870, https://www .google.com/books/edition/Strange_Newes_of_the_Intercepting _Certai/L55TAAAAcAAJ.

3. Martin Flora, "Potluck Meal Innovation Due to Depression: Guests Chip in With Part of Dinner," *Chicago Tribune*, January 27, 1933.

4. New World Encyclopedia writers and editors, "Potlatch," *New World Encyclopedia*, accessed September 12, 2023, https://www.newworldencyclopedia.org/entry/Potlatch.

5. Carlotta Panza, "How Italians Eat: Explore the History of a Meal," Italy Segreta, September 2021, https://italysegreta.com/exploring-the -history-of-a-meal/.

6. Nick Higham, "Did the English Invent Bubbly before Dom Perignon?" *BBC News*, May 20, 2017, https://www.bbc.com/news/uk-england -gloucestershire-39963098.

7. Liana Miate, "Iris," *World History Encyclopedia*, April 5, 2023, https://www.worldhistory.org/Iris.

8. V. M. Traverso, "The Catholic Monasteries that Invented Our Favorite Cheeses," Aleteia.Org, April 6, 2022, https://aleteia.org/2022/04/06 /the-catholic-monasteries-that-invented-our-favorite-cheeses/.

9. World Archeology, "Crete: Olives," *World Archeology* issue 48, July 7, 2011, https://www.world-archaeology.com/features/crete-olives/.

10. Mandy Lim Beitler, "Why We Eat Pineapple Tarts During CNY and the Meanings Behind Other Goodies," AsiaOne, January 23, 2017, https://www.asiaone.com/food/why-we-eat-pineapple-tarts-during -cny-and-meanings-behind-other-goodies.

11. Felicity Cloake, "Deconstructing Cassoulet, the Classic French Stew," *National Geographic*, March 15, 2023, https://www.nationalgeographic .com/travel/article/deconstructing-cassoulet-classic-french-stew.

12. Britannica, the editors, "Chakra," *Encyclopedia Britannica*, August 7, 2023, https://www.britannica.com/topic/chakra.

13. Joshua Mark, "The Hymn to Ninkasi, Goddess of Beer," *World History Encyclopedia*, November 11, 2022, https://www.worldhistory.org /article/222/the-hymn-to-ninkasi-goddess-of-beer/.

14. Gregorio Sorgi, "Leicestershire Monks Brew UK's first Trappist Beer," *The Tablet*, June 29, 2018, https://www.thetablet.co.uk/news/9331 /leicestershire-monks-brew-uk-s-first-trappist-beer.

chapter seven
the fire festival:
barbecue and grilling

*There is no real need for decorations when throwing
a barbecue party—let the summer garden, in all its
vibrant and luscious splendor, speak for itself.*
—PIPPA MIDDLETON[1]

Barbecue is genuinely a global tribal affair. Americans alone grill more than three billion times a year. When people are staying closer to home, the number continues to grow. If you own a grill (or are thinking of buying one), you will join 75 percent of all American households.[2] Grilling offers the perfect opportunity to work with the fire element.

I cannot help but wonder about the first person eating flame-grilled meat. Did it land on the fire accidentally? Was it a purposeful experiment? We will probably never know, but I am forever grateful for that moment. Barbecue is at the top of my favorite cooking methods.

Putting together your grilling or barbecue project is like figuring out a riddle. There are several parts involved. Solving the riddle means the parts come together harmoniously. Your well-considered choices make it happen. But first, you have to know what options are available. This chapter provides an overview to get you started, along with some of my favorite recipes.

Blazing through History

The word barbecue likely comes from *barbaco*, a term used in the Caribbean for food, specifically meat, cooked over an open flame on a raised wooden grate. The *Smithsonian* reports barbecue was present in the colonial era, with the colonists learning from the Native Americans.[3] Those who were British settlers tinkered with the concept by basting the food with vinegar or butter, so it didn't dry out.

PRESIDENTIAL APPROVAL

GEORGE WASHINGTON avidly loved barbecues. He hosted many, one of which took place over three days.

LYNDON B. JOHNSON was the first president to host a barbecue at the White House. It featured ribs.

JAMES MADISON hosted several grilling events. A recent excavation at his plantation reveals what archaeologists believe was a barbecue pit, complete with charred wood.

GEORGE H. BUSH hosted annual barbecues on the South Lawn of the White House. They were called "a Congressional Picnic." The attendees were senators, representatives, and their families.

BARACK OBAMA took steak-grilling lessons from Bobby Flay, who described the president as a "medium-well guy."

With this history in mind, the art of barbecue can represent leadership, good choices, and community engagement.[4]

Grilling vs. Barbecue

People frequently use grilling and barbecue in the same context. But, they are different in timing and treatment. Barbecue uses the "low and slow" approach, often using marinades, rubs, and smoking wood.

By comparison, grilling is often quicker to make things crispy or create a caramelized surface, which looks good and tastes great. It's feasible to barbecue first, and finish on the grill for searing.

Gas vs. Wood vs. Charcoal

Barbecue has grown in popularity with the modern food culture. As a result, you have many options for your fire festival, each instilling a unique flavor. The processes have advantages and disadvantages. For example, charcoal takes a long time to heat up. Once ready, maintaining even temperatures isn't easy. It's still worth the effort. There is a distinct succulent, smoky flavor from charcoal that neither wood nor gas can provide.

Wood creates layers of flavor (have you ever seen a smoke ring in meat?). Many cooks say wood imparts the best flavor profile for food. The trick is managing and manipulating the wood throughout the process, avoiding over-smoking. Even in Hearth Magic, there can be too much of a good thing.

Complicating things a little further, you can choose from various smoking woods for your cookout. Always avoid softwood (such as pine). Instead, focus on hardwoods and fruitwoods. Hardwoods have an intense flavor. Be careful with the

MAGICAL QUALITIES OF SMOKING WOOD AND USES

ALDER Qualities related to harnessing elemental power. It's delicately sweet and fantastic with seafood.

APPLE Qualities related to health and prosperity. You can smoke nearly everything with apple wood, but pork, poultry, and vegetables accept the flavor more readily.

CHERRY Qualities related to sweetness and grace. Cherry delivers medium smoke. Try it with game meats and vegetables.

HICKORY Qualities related to patience and strength. A very popular smoking wood with a spicy-smoky flavor. Hickory is used commonly with beef and chicken.

MAPLE Qualities related to love and future telling. Subtle and sweet. It's great with any dish with cheese (such as burgers or roulades). Ham *loves* maple smoke.

MESQUITE Qualities related to sustenance and provision. Mesquite is one of the most intense smoking woods, so only use it when you want your recipe *really* smoky. Large cuts of meat work well.

OAK Qualities related to justice, honesty, and might. This is a medium wood with an earthy taste. Try it with turkey.

amounts. Fruitwood works well with delicate proteins, such as fish. Each type of wood has a metaphysical correspondence.

What about using a gas grill? Because of the control these grills offer, many families choose a gas grill for their yard. You have a starter, temperature dials, and drip pans to make things easy. If you want fancy, some models offer add-ons, such as a rotisserie. The caution with gas grills is that they tend to overheat. Keep an eye on your food.

Tools of the Trade

Any type of specialized cooking typically has tools to help create the perfect feast. Your basic barbecue set should include a grill thermometer to monitor the dish's internal temperature. The thermometer improves food safety and lets you know when your meat is at your preferred doneness (a medium steak is 140°F, for example).

Other functional utensils for your master grilling kit include a grill fork, a long-handled spatula, a basting brush, tongs, and heavy-duty oven mitts. I added a meat injector and an outstanding set of cooking knives (a 6-inch chef knife, an 8-inch chef knife, and a paring knife) to my kit. The cutlery was a multi-task investment since I use them in the kitchen.

Basic Multipurpose Barbecue Rub

Energetic Essence: With barbecue rub, you can whip up tons of magical energy designed with your goal in mind. Think about the tastes you love, then check out their correspondences to see which one(s) can "star" in your rub. In this recipe, I've included the ingredient's energetic signatures. In looking at the list, several items pair together for unity, balance, and diversity, a perfect mix for any group gathering.

Note: Barbecue rub can be used as a stand-alone flavoring, or you can combine it with marinade. Both infuse your dish with flavors and can help make meat more tender.

Ingredients

¼ cup packed brown sugar (overcoming)

¼ cup paprika (youth, femininity)

1 tbsp sea salt (truth, honor, loyalty)

1 tbsp cracked pepper (masculinity, ambition)

1 tbsp chili powder (luck, protection from evil)

2 tsps garlic powder (repel bad spirits)

2 tsps onion powder (unity, of one mind)

1 tsp mustard powder (creativity, diversity)

½ tsp chipotle pepper (passion, healthy living)

Instructions

Note: Because of the brown sugar, which absorbs moisture, this dry mix may clump a bit over time. Just loosen it up using a spoon or a butter knife.

1. You can't get easier than this. Just mix everything together thoroughly.

2. If you know you'll have more than you need, store it in an airtight container out of sunlight and in a cool part of the pantry.

3. Coat room temperature meat with the rub thoroughly at least 30 minutes before grilling.

   ∾ **TIP** If you're in a pinch for barbecue sauce, you can turn the rub into one by adding liquid (broth, wine, beer, juice) slowly into a cup until you reach the consistency you prefer.

BASIC MULTIPURPOSE BARBECUE RUB
~ CONTINUED ~

Possible Additions

Cumin: Fidelity, good fortune

Oregano: Joy, love

Parsley: Festivity, esteem

Thyme: Praise, courage

Vinegar powder: Preservation, longevity

Worcestershire powder: Propriety, wholesomeness

SEASONING VS. RUBS

Seasonings blend herbs and spices into small particle mixes intended as a gentle highlight for natural flavors. Season your food before barbecuing and grilling. Rubs are similar to seasonings but use larger pieces of herbs and spices. A rub instills flavor and a surface texture, namely the coveted crust! Apply the rub with a binder, such as mustard, hot sauce, honey, mayonnaise, ketchup, steak sauce, or olive oil.

SHHH, IT'S A SECRET: BARBECUE SAUCE

Energetic Essence: The spiritual intent behind this barbecue sauce is either keeping secrets or revealing them (be careful with both options). Everyone who loves to grill has a "secret sauce," hoping to create something different and irreplaceable unless you know the mystery ingredients or order of preparation (and all the essential steps).

This is very close to the blend I use. I will share my "secret" (without measurement, of course). I like adding fresh ground ginger, powdered vanilla, and lemon or orange zest. It yields just under 2 cups.

Ingredients

⅔ cup ketchup

½ cup wine vinegar

¼ cup brown sugar

¼ cup black strap molasses

2 tsps smoked paprika

1 tsp garlic powder

1 tsp onion powder

1 tsp fresh ground salt

1 tsp fresh ground pepper

1 tsp liquid smoke

Substitutions

Brown sugar or molasses: Honey

Vinegar: Wine, beer, juice

Instructions

1. Place all the ingredients into a saucepan.

2. Simmer over low heat for 10 minutes.

3. Do NOT boil. The brown sugar and molasses burn easily.

4. Follow the recipe to determine the timing for applying the sauces you create. Some recommend applying throughout cooking, and others only at the end.

> ∽ **TIP** Don't drown the protein or vegetables. You don't need much barbecue sauce for it to succeed. If you like a lot of sauce, just set yours aside and add more as desired. You can put out small glasses filled with extra sauce, and people can help themselves.

SHHH, IT'S A SECRET: BARBECUE SAUCE
∽ CONTINUED ∽

Side Dish Suggestions

Grilled watermelon

Mexican street corn

Pork and beans

Spicy fried okra

Steak fries (dip 'em!)

Potential Additions

Basil

Dill

Marjoram

Parsley

DIFFERENT BARBECUE SAUCES

The world of grilling and barbecuing has passionate (and sometimes a little peculiar) individuals. To come up with a great sauce takes creativity, curiosity, and a lot of patience. Writing down precise measurements and methods is essential for repeating your favorite recipe. If you're lucky, you can stumble on a blend by chance (by dropping more of an ingredient than intended into the sauce, for example). Some of the most popular sauce blends include

ASIAN Keynotes are hoisin, rice vinegar, five-spice powder, and ginger

BOURBON, WHISKEY Similar to the base one here, with the addition of ¾ cup bourbon or whiskey

CHINESE Keynotes: Oyster sauce, soy sauce, Chinese wine, garlic

CIDER VINEGAR (NORTH CAROLINA) Often blended with mustard

CITRUS JUICE (FLORIDA) Orange, lemon, lime, and even grapefruit

FRUITED Blackberry, mango, cherry, pineapple, peach, passionfruit, and the surprise contestant: prickly pear

HONEY The beauty of honey is it makes a great binder, too. You can use raw honey, clover (most popular), wildflower, summer flower, honeysuckle (YUM!), buckwheat (bold), and orange blossom, just to name a few.

HORSERADISH (MARYLAND) Horseradish, mayo, lemon zest, salt, and pepper

HOT SAUCE Base of habanero, vinegar, garlic, salt

Mystical Marinade

Acid-based marinades containing things such as lemon, wine, vinegar, tomato juice, and orange loosen the proteins in meat for flavor and tenderness. Some fruit-based marinades (mango, pineapple, kiwi, papaya) are natural tenderizers. It took me years to convince a friend of mine that fruit and meat do, indeed, go together. That first mango rib he smoked made mama proud. (I avoided the temptation to say, "I told you so.")

Just be careful. The meat becomes mushy if it stays too long in a marinade. Shrimp will actually start cooking!

Buttermilk and yogurt are other options. The natural calcium in them activates meat enzymes, similar to what happens when you age meat. Buttermilk and yogurt bring mild acid to the marinade.

Marinating Cautions and Guidelines

- ⁓ Use a sealable container for marinating. Ensure it's properly closed (if using a bag, get all the excess air out). You'll be shaking and turning it, and without closure, you're in for a mess.
- ⁓ Do not use aluminum foil for marinating. It creates an odd flavor, putting the whole taste profile off.
- ⁓ Different edibles require different marinating times. For example, bone-in chicken or a whole fish requires 3–6 hours, approximately. Meanwhile, a boneless chicken breast only needs 1 hour (a little more if it's thick).
- ⁓ Marinate mild fish and vegetables for 15 minutes. A rack of lamb and tenderloins needs 6 hours (even greater after 12 hours). Finally, marinate large pieces of meat, such as a whole roast or a pork shoulder, for a full day. If you're in a time crunch, you can take them out at the 12-hour mark.

LOVEBIRD DRUNKEN STEAK

Energetic Essence: Savor whiskey and bourbon slowly, in pleasant company, with light-hearted conversation. Gradually relax and listen to what each drop tells. In the 1800s, Paul Jones tried to appropriate the creation of bourbon for himself, but he failed.

There is a folktale about how Four Roses received its name and signature imagery.[5] Jones wooed a beauty from the Southern United States, wishing for her hand. Not wanting to rush to a decision, the Southerner promised to answer him at the next ball. As an indication of a positive answer, she flaunted a boutonniere of four scarlet roses. Jones had a happy ending. To illustrate his feelings, he allegedly called his bourbon Four Roses. As a symbol of love, this beautiful legend flourishes to this day. Therefore, in love, men and women often choose this drink as a gift to a partner.

Ingredients

¼ cup extra virgin olive oil

1 tsp mild vinegar (sherry or rice, optional)

1 tbsp Worcestershire sauce

1 tbsp Dijon mustard

1 shallot, sliced

2 cloves garlic, smashed

5–6 sprigs of fresh thyme, leaves picked

1 tsp paprika

1 tsp sea salt flakes

Red pepper flakes to taste (optional)

6 ozs bourbon

2 lbs steak

Salt and pepper to taste

Substitution
Bourbon: Whiskey, beer

Instructions

1. Find a plastic food storage container or bag large enough to house the steak.

2. Put all ingredients up to the steak in the container to form the marinade. Give it a whisk, stir, or shake until everything's mingled.

3. Put the steak into the container.

4. Marinate in the refrigerator for 24 hours. Periodically turn the steak so it marinates evenly.

5. Remove it from the refrigerator and bring it up to room temperature.

6. Meanwhile, bring the grill up to 450°F.

7. Remove the steak from the marinade and pat it dry.

8. Sprinkle it lightly with salt and pepper on both sides.

9. Sear for about 4 minutes per side until you reach the desired doneness (internal temperature for rare is 125°F, medium-rare is 135°F, and medium is 145°F).

10. Let the steak rest for 10 minutes before serving. All beef steak cuts can benefit from this marinade, especially skirt steak, flat iron steak, hanger steak, sirloin, and flank.

Potential Additions

Purchase and apply a brown sugar-bourbon barbecue rub before grilling

STEADFAST TRI-TIP

Energetic Essence: In physics, the Delta (triangle) represents change. When the triangle points up (a symbol of the fire element), it is stable and filled with power. With this in mind, choose tri-tip (a cut that looks like a triangle) for spells focused on staying the course. As a bonus, tri-tip is one of the easiest types of beef to cook successfully.

Ingredients

Tri-tip steak (½ lb per person; half the amount for sandwiches)

Spices—Stick to flavors you enjoy. Traditional herbs and spices for beef include onion, garlic, basil, oregano, curry powder, thyme, salt, and pepper

Substitution
Mixed seasonings: Barbecue rub

Instructions

1. Preheat the grill to 300°F. Make sure you areas for direct and indirect cooking.

2. Remove any silvery skin from the back of the tri-tip. Loosen it around the edges, then pull it back using a paper towel for a good grip.

3. Pat the steak dry.

4. Season the steak. Go easy. You want the meat to shine.

5. Put the tri-tip on the indirect heat side.

6. When the internal temperature of the meat is 110°F, increase the grill's temperature to 500°F.

7. Sear on both sides.

8. Remove when the meat is at the desired doneness (suggested: medium-rare at 135°F).

9. Rest the steak for 10 minutes before service. If you look at a tri-tip, you'll notice it has two grains—one running vertically and one horizontally. Make the first cut to separate the tri-tip where these two grains meet. Once separated, slice each section against the grain for the most outstanding amount of tenderness.

WHAT IS TRI-TIP?

Tri-tip is sometimes confused with brisket. However, this cut of beef comes from the bottom of the sirloin, and it packs a ton of flavor. You may see the names California Cut, Newport Steak, and Santa Maria Steak on menus. They are all tri-tip. Until the nineteenth century, tri-tip became hamburger meat. It took until the 1950s for a chef and restaurant owner, Bob Schultz, to try preparing it as a steak. It became a favorite.[6]

PLEASANT PESTO CHICKEN LEGS

Energetic Essence: In the Victorian language of flowers, sweet basil represented good wishes to whoever received it.[7] Should a man accept sweet basil from a woman, it was a sign the two would eventually wed. Magically, basil bears the vibrations of prosperity, success, peace, and tranquility. Sounds pleasant to me! You can burn a little basil just as you would sage for smoke cleansing your kitchen.

Ingredients

Plump chicken drumsticks
    (2–3 per person)
Olive oil spray cooking oil
Lemon pepper seasoning
2 whole heads of garlic

½ cup pine nuts
2 cups fresh basil
1 cup parmesan cheese, freshly grated
¾ cup extra virgin olive oil
Fresh ground salt and pepper

Instructions

1. Prepare the charcoal (you're looking for 500°F).

2. Carefully butterfly the chicken drumsticks.

3. Spray them lightly with the cooking oil spray.

4. Dust the surface of the chicken with lemon pepper and set aside.

5. Slice off the top of the garlic heads. Place them into an iron pan and place on the grill, heating until softened.

> ### WHAT IS BUTTER-FLYING MEAT?
> Butterflying is nowhere as technical as it sounds. You simply split a cut of meat into two sections still connected to each other. The visual appeal is similar to (wait for it) a butterfly. The meat cooks more quickly and evenly this way.

6. Add the pine nuts to the iron pan.

7. When the garlic is soft and the pine nuts toasted, remove them from the heat.

8. Place the chicken on the grill.

9. While the chicken is cooking, press the garlic out of the skin into a blender, mixing it with the pine nuts, basil, cheese, olive oil, salt, and pepper, and you have pesto.

10. Brush the pesto on the chicken as it finishes cooking.

SWEET SUCCESS SMOKED CHICKEN BREASTS

Energetic Essence: The key component in this dish is mustard, used here as a binder for spices. Mustard seeds represent growth and fruition. They are so tiny yet mature into spectacular plants. Your goals are like that seed. All it takes is sticking to your true north and having faith in yourself.

Ingredients

Cherry and apple smoking wood

1 chicken breast per person

3-4 tbsps honey or Dijon
   mustard per breast

¼ tsp each mixed dry seasonings
   (use all or only your favorites):
   onion powder, lemon pepper, ginger,
   smoked paprika, garlic powder,
   thyme, celery powder, dill, etc.
   If you have leftovers, you can store
in a glass airtight container with
your other spices for future use

Substitution

Honey or Dijon mustard: Yellow
   mustard, spicy brown mustard,
   hot mustard, beer mustard

Instructions

1. Set up the smoker with cherry and apple smoking wood.

2. Heat it to 225°F.

3. Pat the chicken breasts dry.

4. Lather the mustard evenly all over each chicken breast.

5. Sprinkle with your chosen spices. Make sure to apply the dry seasonings evenly.
   Place the breasts into the smoker.

6. Check the internal temperature of the chicken after 90 minutes
   (you want 160°F).

7. Tent the breasts with aluminum for 10 minutes.

8. Serve whole or sliced.

∽ **TIP** If you decide to marinate the chicken, loosen the skin. All those flavors will slip in and make the chicken tastier. You can put a dab of compound butter under the skin for flavor and moisture.

Side Dish Suggestions

Glazed parsnips
Smoked mixed vegetable platter
Spiced potato wedges
Tomato-onion salad

∽ **FACTOID** It takes approximately 750 mustard seeds to make up 1 ounce.

GOLDEN GRILLED COD—PROSPERITY

Energetic Essence: If you travel to Massachusetts, you may see images of golden cod-fishes in various unexpected places. One place is the State House in Boston and another is Old North Church.[8] It is the symbol of the state because the cod made the Massachusetts Bay Colony thrive and profit. People placed golden cod artwork in their homes to attract wealth. Eventually, the pineapple replaced the fish emblem.

Ingredients

Cod filets (6–8 ozs per person)

Sea salt

Coarse ground pepper

Butter Baste for 2 Servings (Double if Necessary)

1 tbsp butter

1 tsp lemon pepper

1 tsp fresh garlic, minced

Pinch of sugar

Chives, diced

2 lemons, sliced

Substitutions

Charcoal: Seasoned charcoal (garlic paprika, Memphis barbecue, bourbon, basil with sage and thyme)

Lemon pepper: Cayenne pepper, dried oregano, and basil

Instructions

1. Start the charcoal.

2. While the coals get white, salt and pepper the cod on both sides.

3. Prepare the butter baste. Squeeze the juice of one lemon into the blend.

4. Put the cod skin-side down once the charcoal is hot (white). The skin keeps the soft meat from overcooking.

CLOSE-UP WITH COD

From a culinary standpoint, cod is a lean white fish. It can act as a good stand-in for salmon, being meaty and mild. It has a slightly sweet flavor profile, like tilapia. Ecologically it is an intelligent choice in seafood because wild Pacific cod is sustainable. You'll find cod very versatile for your menus. Bake, broil, sauté, steam, or roast it. You can even put it into a stew.

When shopping for your fish, there are specific rules to follow. Look at the fish's skin. Does it look dry? If so, it's old. The smell of fresh fish should be something like the sea, not "fishy."

5. Baste the top of the cod liberally with the butter mix.

6. After 2 minutes, flip the cod to the other side.

7. Butter again.

8. When the fish reaches 135°F, it's fully cooked.

9. Serve with a sprinkling of sea salt and lemon wedges on each plate.

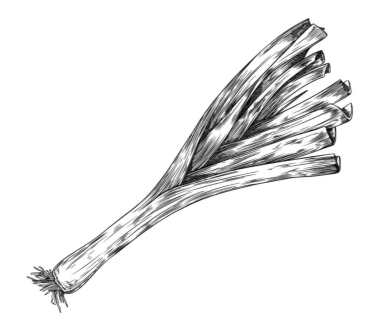

White Fish for Love and a Windfall

Energetic Essence: Dreaming of white fish ensures a good love life. It also symbolizes divine blessings, faithful friends, improvements at work, and meeting helpful people.

Ingredients

Tilapia filets (6 ozs per person)

1 tbsp olive oil

¼ tsp sea salt

¼ tsp fresh ground pepper

1 cup white corn

1 cup chickpeas

¼ cup sweet pepper, chopped

½ seedless cucumber, chopped

¼ cup red onion, chopped

¾ cup Italian dressing

Feta cheese or goat cheese

Substitutions

Italian dressing: Greek dressing, raspberry vinaigrette,

Tilapia: Atlantic cod, striped bass, rainbow trout

SEASONING FROM ABOVE

When you watch chefs, salt is one of the critical components to making a well-seasoned dish vs. one that's bland. One method cooks use to bring out the perfect flavor in their dish is salting from far above the food. At first, it looks like your favorite culinarian is trying to be showy. While the effort certainly has pizzazz, it also has a purpose. When falling from above, the salt spreads out uniformly.[9]

You can try an experiment. Grab your salt grinder and a dark piece of paper. First, grind salt from about 3 inches above the paper. Note the distribution. Now, grind the salt from about 12 inches over the paper. It naturally distributes itself over a larger area, thanks to gravity.

Instructions

1. Set the grill to medium-high and oil the grates.

2. Treat the filets with olive oil on both sides.

3. Sprinkle salt and pepper on the filets.

4. Place the fish on the grill for 4 minutes.

5. Test the fish by gently lifting one end with a spatula. Let the fish cook for 1–2 minutes more if it sticks.

6. Rest the fish for 5 minutes.

7. Mix all the remaining ingredients in a large serving bowl.

8. The salad can go on the side or on top of the tilapia.

∾ **TIP** When the fish is flaky, you know you know it's done. Test this with a fork at the thickest part of the filet. You're looking for an internal temperature of 145°F.

Prudent Pork Burnt Ends

Energetic Essence: The pig is the twelfth sign in the Chinese animal zodiac. People born in this year are mindful of their means. They balance enjoyment of life with security. Pig-born individuals aren't afraid to work hard for pleasurable goals but always have something for a "rainy day."

Ingredients

Pork belly (½ lb per person)

Sweet barbecue rub (see page 124 or use your favorite from the store)

2 cups smoky barbecue sauce (see page 125 or use your favorite from the store)

1 tbsp honey

3 tbsps light brown sugar

5 tbsps butter, cubed

Instructions

1. Preheat the smoker to 250°F. Use maple or cherry smoking wood.

2. Cut the pork into 1-inch x 1-inch pieces.

3. Sprinkle the cubes with barbecue rub; coat on all sides.

4. Transfer the pieces to a disposable aluminum pan.

5. Smoke for about 3 hours (they will have a nice bark).

6. While the pork smokes, mix the sauce, honey, and brown sugar. Toss the pork cubes with this sauce.

7. Add cubes of butter on top of the mix.

8. Cover with aluminum.

9. Smoke for another 1½ hours (stir three times).

10. When the meat reaches 190°F internally, it's ready.

11. Remove from the smoker.

12. Have toothpicks and napkins handy!

Suggested Timing

Share it at summer rituals and events.

Peachy Keen Pork Roll-Up

Energetic Essence: Peaches are an iconic sign of spring with connotations of renewal and fertility. In China, peaches represent luck and are often aptly present as decorations at spring weddings.[10] Peaches inspire joy, pleasure, and good spirits to everyone at the table.

The presentation for this dish looks like a lovely spiral, so perhaps serve it at an event with a spiral dance!

Ingredients

2 fresh peaches

2 tbsps peach brandy

3 lbs pork loin

Sweet and smoky barbecue rub (see page 124 or use your favorite from the store)

Brie (onion or mushroom flavor optional)

Peach preserves

Substitutions

Brie: Camembert cheese

Peaches: Apricots or plums (you can mix the three, which is tasty, and three is a number of good fortune)

Instructions

1. Preheat the grill to 225°F.

2. Rinse the peaches (leave the skin intact).

3. Slice them thinly (about ¼-inch thick).

4. Put them in a small bowl with the brandy to soak.

5. Butterfly the pork loin (you can ask your butcher to do this for you).

6. Use a meat mallet to hammer it (you're looking for evenness).

7. Sprinkle the barbecue rub all over the meat.

8. Lay the peaches fat side down along the length of the pork loin.

9. Follow with thin slices of brie.

10. Place the long edge of the loin near you.

11. Roll the meat into a tight round.

12. Secure the meat in place with a butcher's string.

13. Grill on an indirect heat burner for 3 hours.

14. Brush peach preserves on the meat every hour it grills.

15. The meat should be 140°F internally.

16. Rest the pork loin for 10 minutes. DO NOT rush this.

17. Slice into ½-inch pieces.

Side Dish Suggestions

Butternut squash

Cheese grits

Farro with walnut and green apple

Fried cabbage

FULL MOON CAULIFLOWER STEAK

Energetic Essence: When you slice a cauliflower into steak form, it has the shape and color of a glorious full moon. Spiritually, cauliflower emphasizes the Sacred Feminine, ideal for post-lunar ritual feasting.

Ingredients

Large cauliflower heads
3 cloves garlic, minced
⅓ cup extra virgin olive oil
½ tsp kosher salt
¼ tsp fresh ground pepper
½ tsp chipotle powder
¼ tsp smoky paprika

Substitution
Cauliflower: Cabbage

Possible Sauces
Chimichurri, avocado, Greek lemon
    vinaigrette, pesto, or pico

Instructions

1. Preheat the grill to 350°F.

2. Remove the outer leaves from the cauliflower.

3. Chop down the stem so it sits flat on the cutting board.

4. Use a sharp chef's knife to slice the cauliflower into approximately 1-inch steaks.

5. Put the minced garlic into a bowl with the olive oil and spices.

6. Mix well.

7. Brush both sides of the cauliflower with the olive oil mix.

8. Grill for 5 to 6 minutes (cover closed).

9. Flip and grill for an additional 5 minutes (cover open).

10. When done, they will be golden brown and fork-tender.

Manifestation Fruit Kebab

Energetic Essence: Geometrically, the shortest distance between two points is a straight line. This kabob-style grill represents a direct path toward reaching your goals. You can build the vibrations in this recipe. Start at the bottom with strawberries (your passion). Follow with cantaloupe (good fortune), and finally top it off with pineapple (celebration).

Ingredients

Vegetable oil grill spray

Skewers (metal or wood)

2 cups strawberries (about 1 inch in size)

2 cups cantaloupe squares (1 inch)

2 cups pineapple chunks (1 inch)

Real maple syrup

Greek vanilla yogurt

Substitution

Maple syrup: Honey, molasses, coconut nectar, golden syrup

Instructions

1. Set the grill to high.

2. Spray the grill with vegetable oil to avoid sticking.

3. Soak the skewers (if wooden) for 20 minutes before using.

4. Thread the fruit on the skewers.

5. Lightly brush each skewer of fruit with maple syrup.

6. Place the skewers on the grill for 2 to 3 minutes per side.

7. The fruit should be golden and tender after 10 minutes.

8. Serve with yogurt for dipping.

> ## DIFFERENT GOALS FOR KABOBS
> The symbolism of building energy from the bottom up gives kebabs a lot of uses in the Kitchen Witch's repertoire. Change the ingredients; transform your fate!

Endnotes

1. Pippa Middleton, *Celebrate: A Year of Festivities for Families and Friends*, United Kingdom: Viking, October 20, 2012.

2. Amy Roberts, "11 Facts to Raise your Grilling IQ," CNN, June 14, 2016, https://www.cnn.com/2013/06/21/living/grilling-by-the-numbers/index.html.

3. Matthew Willis, "The Evolution of American Barbecue," *The Smithsonian Magazine*, October 18, 2019, https://www.smithsonianmag.com/arts-culture/the-evolution-of-american-barbecue-13770775/.

4. Jim Shahin, "Smoke Signals: Presidential Grilling," *Washington Post*, February 21, 2012, https://www.washingtonpost.com/blogs/all-we-can-eat/post/smoke-signals-presidential-grilling/2012/02/21/gIQA3OlgRR_blog.html.

5. Four Roses Bourbon, "The History of the Four Roses Legend," January 15, 2021, https://www.fourrosesbourbon.com/blog/history-of-the-four-roses-legend.

6. Brien O'Brien, "The California Cut: Learn How Tri-Tip Steak Is Uniquely Californian," *Active*, August 26, 2009, https://www.activenorcal.com/the-california-cut-learn-how-tri-tip-steak-is-uniquely-californian/.

7. Jessica Roux, *Floriography: An Illustrated Guide to the Victorian Language of Flowers*, Kansas City, MO: Andrews McMeel Publishing, 2020.

8. Lucy Pollok, "The Massachusetts State House: Sacred Cod," Revolutionary Spaces, Accessed September 23, 2023, https://revolutionaryspaces.org/the-massachusetts-state-house-sacred-cod/.

9. Molly Harris, "Here's Why Chefs Season Food From So High Up," *Tasting Table*, March 9, 2022, https://www.tastingtable.com/792845/heres-why-chefs-season-food-from-so-high-up/.

10. Yelang (Son of China), "What Does Peach Symbolize in China?", Son of China, May 18, 2023, https://sonofchina.com/what-does-peach-symbolism-in-china/.

chapter eight
edible petals for spellbinding courses

Flowers are not typically found in everyday meals, so their deliberate inclusion in a dish makes that dish something special, a treat for the receiver. They send a message of freshness and of caring. In some cultures, specific flowers are ritually used to mark festivals and special occasions. In this way, their appearance in a dish elevates it to something beyond the ordinary.
—Constance Kirker[1]

You may wonder, what on earth is a chapter on flowers doing in a cookbook? Guess what? Hundreds of flowers are edible, many of which you are already familiar with, such as roses. Looking through the pages of time, you find the Egyptians, Greeks, Romans, Hindus, and Mayans (well, nearly everybody) all using flowers for their flavors, beauty mixes, and magic.

When you think of a presentation, what is more glorious than a flower on your plate? It brings thoughts of receiving bouquets throughout the year. But there is far more to edible petals than meets the eye, which will please the Kitchen Witch.

There is an unspoken rule of cooking to never put anything inedible on the plate. There is a difference between a garnish and a decoration. The garnish is essential to the plate, enhancing flavor and creating harmony. Anything else is decoration. Flowers fill both designations neatly.

From the perspective of pantry power, flowers are a splendid topping on the proverbial cake. You can swap any spiritual component missing from your recipe with flowers as decoration. Sometimes, you can add their flower right into your fare. Just think about how it may change textures, flavors, and aromas.

Floriography: Conversing through Flowers

Floriography is the language of flowers. Meanings for each blossom come from ancient myths and folklore. There is a charm in petaled presentations, and they blossomed in popularity (something for which the flower industry is very grateful). There were blooms sacred to gods and goddesses and those exchanged by lovers in a quiet corner.

Some petals get their symbolism from color or type of flower or both! From a single bloom to a mindfully assembled showpiece, flowers can convey your feelings and

EDIBLE FLOWER CHART

There is no way for me to convey *all* the edible flowers from which you have to choose. Enjoy this sampling to get those creative juices flowing.

Flower	Parts	Taste	Meaning
Bee balm	Petals, leaf	Oregano, mint	Good health
Borage	Petals, leaf	Cucumber-like	Courage
Carnations	Petals	Clove, nutmeg	Fascination
Chrysanthemum (white)	Petals	Cauliflower-like	Truth
Dandelion	Flower, leaf	Honey-like	Faithfulness, joy
Hibiscus	Fruit, leaf	Cranberry-like	Delicate beauty
Lavender	Flower	Sweet, minty	Serenity, grace
Nasturtiums	Flower, leaf	Watercress-like	Victory
Pansy	Petals	Slightly sweet	Thoughts
Rose (dark pink)	Petals	Fruity notes	Gratitude
Squash flower	Flower	Mild squash	Protection
Sunflower (dwarf)	Bud	Artichoke-like	Adoration
Tulip	Petals	Sweet pea-like	Believe in me
Violet	Petals, leaf	Perfumed, sweet	Watchfulness

As you can imagine, that's just the beginning.

your magical intent without words. You can use a centerpiece for a meal and cook with some flowers from that centerpiece for your dish for a proverbial double whammy.

During the Victorian era, floriography was in its heyday. It was an amusing and suitable hobby for young ladies. However, it was also a way to deliver a secret message to someone who grabbed your attention. Receiving a red rose indicated a crush. A yellow one, in return, said, "No, let's be friends."

Offering a dahlia says, "a committed, lasting bond," which is why they appeared in anniversary gifts. Chrysanthemum was a wish for happiness, and hydrangeas expressed deep gratitude. Poppy is the flower of remembrance and often appears at funerals. Daffodils promise hope and new beginnings, perfect for a house blessing.

It's easy to see the gift nature provides us. It can visually represent your goal. Then, internalize the flower's energetic signature for manifestation.

Precautions

Because many people have never eaten flowers, there is a chance someone may have an allergic reaction. Always tell people about your ingredients. If you intend to forage for items yourself in the forest, one green-leafy thingy can look like another. Be sure of what you use. If you can't be sure, throw it out.

Those who grow their own ingredients know they're organic. If buying from a store, you want to look for organic, too. Treated flowers do not have the same flavor profile or magical aptitude.

〰

My love affair with floral cooking came about in one of the most common ways possible: by accident. I periodically work with rose water in cooking. Since I had an 8-foot strand of roses, I invoked my inner pioneer woman and made some myself, following instructions from a 1920s all-inclusive book.

Once I completed the rose water, it went into a dark jar for storage in a cool place until I needed it, per the instructions. Guess what? I promptly forgot about it. The surprising rediscovery of the bottle was followed by another marvel. I heard a little *"pssst"* upon opening. Quickly closed, the jar awaited someone who could test the results with me (this time, I remembered where I put it).

It appears the flowers were very busy, introducing natural wild yeast, and I now had rose wine. It was kind of fruity yet smelled of roses. Since then, I have made rose wine for couples getting handfasted or married, aging it for a year and a day. Flowers make their way into my summer salads frequently, too.

Here are some petaled recipes for you to try.

ACACIA FAITHFULNESS FLOWER FRITTERS

Energetic Essence: In the language of flowers, acacia *means "secret love." But your devotion need not be a secret. Acacia represents integrity in your interactions and diligence. As an evergreen, its immortal correspondence made it a popular tree for planting near the graves of people's beloveds. You can use acacia in amulets to protect your relationship.*

Ingredients

10 fresh acacia flowers

½ cup flour

½ tsp baking powder

½ cup pilsner beer

1 tbsp light brown sugar

Lemon zest

Substitutions

Brown sugar: Maple syrup

Lemon zest: Orange zest

Pilsner: Pale ale, ginger ale, white wine, white grape juice

Instructions

1. Look over the acacia flowers closely. Give them a gentle shake, encouraging dirt remnants to come off.

2. Combine the flour, baking powder, and beer.

3. Set the deep fryer to 350°F.

4. Dip each acacia flower in the batter (hold them by the stalk end).

5. Let excess batter drip off.

6. Carefully insert the flowers individually into the fryer. Give them space. Crowding deters even cooking.

7. Remove when golden brown.

8. Let the oil drip off onto paper towels.

9. Serve hot with a sprinkle of brown sugar and lemon zest.

   ∽ **NOTE** Squash flowers, zucchini flowers, elder flowers, daylilies, and dandelions all stand up well to deep frying.

Blossoming Spring Salad

Energetic Essence: Spring breezes bring new hope and a sense of renewal. It's a time for starting projects and doing things a little differently. We shift our energy from the enclosure of longer nights to the liberation of longer days filled with sunshine. This salad goes together quickly. Maybe you can enjoy it while doing spring cleaning and home blessings.

Ingredients

1 small, sweet onion
¼ cup raspberry vinaigrette
Organic baby spring greens
   (3 ozs per person)
1 oz edible flower mix
Sliced strawberries (optional)

Substitution
Raspberry vinaigrette: Balsamic
   vinaigrette (this is heavier)
Spring mix: Baby spinach, cabbage

Instructions

1. Peel and slice the onion thinly and evenly.

2. Put the vinaigrette at the bottom of the salad serving bowl.

3. Top with the greens and the onions, toss.

4. Top with flowers.

5. Mix again just before serving. This keeps everything from getting soggy.

Side Dish Suggestions

Cornbread
Cucumber soup
Fried chicken
Whitefish

Potential Additions

Caesar-style croutons
Glazed bacon crumbles
Nuts (chopped)
Sliced egg (another spring symbol)

May Day Fermented Flower Cordial

Energetic Essence: As a child, my mother would take me out looking for wildflowers on May Day. We gathered them and created simple baskets with handles. When all was quiet, we left baskets of flowers on doorknobs as if the fairies had visited. If we were lucky, we would see the delight on the face of someone finding their gift. This fast-fermented floral beverage is perfect for the May Day spirit.

Ingredients

1 pinch of active yeast (~$\frac{1}{16}$ tsp)

2 cups warm water (100–110°F)

1 cup mixed sweet edible flowers
   (rose, pansy, lilac, etc.)

1 cup white sugar

2 tbsps lemon or orange juice

Instructions

1. Begin with a 1-quart glass jar with a secure lid.
2. Wash it with boiling water, then let it cool.
3. Put the yeast in the warm water and wait for 10 minutes.
4. Now, put everything into the jar.
5. Adhere the lid and shake.
6. Keep shaking until you see the sugar dissolve.
7. Remove the lid.
8. Replace it with three layers of cheesecloth.
9. Secure the cloth with a rubber band.
10. Store the jar in a dark, cool area (like a pantry).
11. Once in the morning and once at night, remove the cheesecloth, replace the lid, and shake the jar.
12. After nine days, strain out the flowers.
13. Transfer the mix into a pitcher.
14. Place it in the refrigerator.
15. It has a shelf life of 6 months, but the sweetness declines.

Fruit and Flower Fortification Smoothie

Energetic Essence: Redbud has the spiritual impact of releasing barriers and attracting comfort. It heals guilt, drives away loneliness, and eases heartache. Redbud is a messenger of spring, often blossoming before any other trees.

Ingredients

6 standard-size ice cubes

1 cup pineapple, cut in chunks

1 ripe banana

1 cup firmly packed redbud flowers

½ cup reduced fat milk

1 tbsp raw honey

Instructions

1. Put all the ingredients into a blender.

2. Pulse until the ice starts breaking up.

3. Change to high speed.

4. Taste-test for sweetness and consistency. You can add more ice if it's not thick enough, more milk if it's too thick, and more honey if it's not sweet enough.

5. Serve in tall glasses with some edible petals as garnish.

Fortress Gin Fizz: Refuge from the Storm

Energetic Essence: Under the influence of the fire element and the planet Mars, the black pepper plant is a vining flower from which our table pepper originates. Going back five thousand years or more, it is one of the first spices known to the ancients.[2] The spiritual qualities of pepper include protection from the evil eye or malintent and breaking curses. When you see a storm on the horizon, whip up this feisty brew.

Ingredients

1 tbsp red and pink peppercorns

1 cup orange blossom honey

1 tbsp dried culinary rose petals

1 cup water

2 ozs cherry gin

4 ozs prosecco

½ cup lemon juice, freshly squeezed

Pink peppercorns (garnish)

Organic rose petals (garnish)

Substitution

Cherry gin: Strawberry, orange, or blackberry gin

Instructions

1. Chill two cocktail glasses (coupe style).

2. Mix the peppercorns, honey, rose petals, and water in a small saucepan. Bring to medium heat until it reaches a boil. Let it continue boiling for 10 minutes.

3. Remove from the heat and cool.

4. Strain the blend, discarding the peppercorns and rose petals. It should be syrupy.

5. Put this in a glass container with a lid in the refrigerator until you want to use it.

6. The syrup has a shelf life of three weeks.

7. When ready to consume, pour the gin, prosecco, lemon, and ½ oz of the peppercorn honey into a shaker with ice.

8. Shake well and pour into glasses. If you want a little more fizz, top it with prosecco, any sparkling wine, or club soda.

9. Add garnish and serve cold.

Side Dish Suggestions

Charcuterie

Cucumber sandwiches

Fruit salad

Oysters on the shell

STUFFED SQUASH FLOWER OF FORTUNE

Energetic Essence: Cultivated since ancient times, squash (and its flower) is a versatile plant. Folklore claims the larger the squash you have (and, by extension, squash flower), the greater your abundance and prestige. On top of your fortune, squash flowers promote self-love and positive growth.

Ingredients

1 jar garlic tomato sauce

1 plum tomato, chopped

Pinch red pepper flakes

½ tsp basil

½ tsp sugar

14 squash flowers

1 cup whole milk ricotta

1 egg yolk

⅔ cup parmesan cheese, divided

Pinch salt and pepper

½ cup flour

¾ cup club soda

Substitutions

Club soda: Beer

Stuffing: Lobster, crab, cooked
    shrimp, or mozzarella and bacon

Tomato sauce: Cream or white wine
    sauce

SQUASH BLOSSOMS

Besides stuffing them, you can add delicate squash blossoms to stews, shepherd's pie, and salads, and as a pizza topper. The blossoms have a melt-in-your-mouth goodness with a mild (surprise!) squash flavor.

Instructions

1. Mix the tomato sauce, tomatoes, red pepper flakes, basil, and sugar in a saucepan. Warm over a low flame.

2. Simmer while you prepare the squash flowers for frying.

3. Set the fryer to 375°F.

4. In a small bowl, stir together the ricotta, egg yolk, ⅓ cup parmesan, salt, and pepper.

5. Very carefully put about 2 tsps of the ricotta mix inside the flower.

6. Twist the petals so they cover the filling.

7. Blend the flour, ⅓ cup parmesan, pinch of salt, and club soda in another deeper bowl.

8. Dip each flower in the batter when the fryer is at the proper temperature.

9. Lower the flowers slowly into the fryer. Do not overcrowd.

10. Let the flowers cook for about 2 minutes on each side until they are golden brown.

11. Transfer the flowers to paper towels. Let the excess fat drip off.

12. Serve with tomato sauce on the side for dipping.

Just for the Hal-i-bit

Energetic Essence: Okay, you knew a pun was coming sometime. But, honestly, why not try new things just for the hal-i-bit? You may like it or not. Either way, it's an adventure into creativity. Do a little jig; make some magic.

Ingredients

¼ cup parsley, finely minced

4 tbsps minced nasturtiums, roses,
    garlic chive blossom, wild radish

2 tbsps basil, minced

1 tbsp oregano, minced

¼ tsp each fresh ground sea
    salt and pepper

2 tbsps green onion, minced

4¾ lbs halibut filets

2 tbsps extra virgin olive oil

1 tbsp garlic, minced

1 cup fish stock

1 cup fresh peas

Instructions

1. Combine all the herbs and green onion in a small bowl.

2. Sprinkle the mix on some parchment paper.

3. Pat the fish with a paper towel.

4. Press both sides of the fish into the herb mix.

5. Heat the olive oil in an iron skillet over medium heat.

6. Fry for 4 minutes on one side and 3 on the other.

7. Pour in the fish stock.

8. Add the garlic.

9. Simmer until the halibut is opaque (5 minutes).

10. Add the fresh peas at the 3-minute mark.

11. Serve in soup bowls with broth and peas.

12. Garnish with more fresh flowers.

CHOCOLATE LAVENDER CALMING COOKIES

Energetic Essence: A certain friend of mine has been a source of ongoing inspiration over the years. She works harder than anyone I know, so I wanted to create calming cookies to help her chaotic days (plus, she loves chocolate). Practitioners of aromatherapy use lavender as a means of rebalancing the chakras. It's believed to be a relaxing, healing scent that releases our blockages, opens the spiritual pathways to universal insight, and deters anxiety and depression.

Ingredients

2 tbsps dried lavender buds

1½ cups brown sugar

1 cup white sugar

3 eggs

2 tbsps vanilla extract

4½ cups flour

Pinch salt

1½ tsps baking soda

3 sticks butter

12 ozs chopped chocolate
(white, milk, or dark)

Vanilla ice cream (optional)

Substitutions

Chocolate: Toffee nibs

Lavender: Any edible petal, but rose
goes well with this mixture

∾ **TIP** You can find dried lavender
buds in the produce aisle or you
can pick your own and dry them.

Instructions

1. Grind the lavender into a fine powder.

2. Put the lavender into a mixing bowl, add both sugars, and mix well. Set aside.

3. In a separate bowl, combine the dry ingredients (flour, salt, and baking soda). Set this aside.

4. In a third mixing bowl, whip the eggs and vanilla extract together for 3 minutes (medium speed). They should be frothy.

5. Add the lavender sugar mixture and butter to the whipped eggs. Continue blending on medium until creamy.

6. Once the sugar and butter are creamy, turn the mixer to low and slowly add the dry ingredients. You'll see the flour integrate in 5–6 minutes.

7. Add the chocolate. Beat for 2 minutes.

8. Use a cookie scoop to get an even size. Put each scoop on a cookie tray lined with parchment paper about 2 inches apart. Refrigerate them overnight.

9. Preheat the oven to 350°F.

10. Decorate the middle of each cookie with a flower bud and sea salt if you've opted for it.

11. Bake for 10 minutes, then turn the cookie tray. Bake for another 4 minutes until the edges of the cookies are slightly brown.

12. These taste amazing when warm (try adding a scoop of vanilla ice cream).

13. If you have leftovers you need to store, put them in a food storage bag in the refrigerator.

Potential Additions

Nuts (just reduce the amount chocolate pieces). Walnuts match the energetic essence of this recipe.

PLEASING CANDIED PETALS

Energetic Essence: My grandmother made candied violets. At first, I turned my nose up (hey, I was around ten). Eventually, she worked her magic again when I was more mature. What a pleasant surprise! The vibrational signatures of candied petals come from the plants themselves. Violets inspire devotion, begonias reflect thoughtful communication, pansies equate to all types of love, purple lilacs signify spirituality, borage represents courage...Well, you get the idea.

Ingredients

1 egg white
5 drops of plain vodka
60 flower petals (approximate)
Caster sugar

Substitution
Plain vodka: Flavored vodka (bear in mind this will change the taste)

Instructions

1. Put the egg white into a mixing bowl.

2. Beat it until it's frothy.

STORAGE TIP
Storing delicate dry goods such as flower petals in a dark area where the temperature is relatively constant improves their shelf life. They won't lose as much color or flavor.

3. Add the vodka.

4. Using a small art paintbrush, put a coating of egg white on each petal (both sides).

5. Sprinkle sugar on the petal.

6. Move them to a fine mesh wire rack to dry.

7. After about 36 hours, they should be brittle.

8. Gently transfer the petals to a dark, airtight storage container. They have a shelf life of about 1 year.

Dandelion Rose Restorative Honey

Energetic Essence: While those with tidy lawns may disdain dandelions, you can make them into many things, including wine, salads, and this honey. Blowing on a dandelion head filled with seeds takes your wishes on the winds. The bright yellow of this flower represents hope, health, and growth, all characteristics suited to blending with rose vibrations.

Ingredients

1½ cups freshly picked dandelion flowers (no green stuff)

5 medium-sized Fuji apples

½ cup loose-leaf rose tea

2 quarts milk

¼ lemon, freshly squeezed

4 cups light brown sugar

Instructions

1. Gently and quickly dip the dandelions in water to remove dirt or tiny bugs.

2. Peel, wash, and chop the apples.

3. Put everything into a stock pot except for the brown sugar.

4. Close the lid and let the mixture maintain a low-rolling boil for an hour.

5. Strain out the apples and flowers. Retain the liquid in the pot.

6. Add brown sugar and stir.

7. Return the pot to simmer without a lid for 2 hours or until the liquid reduces by half. Keep an eye on it, but don't stir it too much.

8. Test the consistency of the honey by putting some on a platter and moving it around to coat. It should be reasonably even, and it will get thicker as it cools.

9. At this point, can the honey and let it sit. The longer you let it be, the thicker the honey becomes.

ALL ABOUT APPLES

The use of Fuji apples in this recipe was a nod to their sweetness.[3] You can, however, use other apples so long as you like their flavor. The next four apples in terms of sweetness are:

KIKU APPLE This is actually a mutation of the Fuji apple. It's firm, has a satisfying crunch, and has a high level of natural sugars.

AMBROSIA APPLE If you can find them, it will be during the months of October to March. The Ambrosia apple has a honey-like flavor and plenty of juice.

GALA APPLE You get plenty of sweetness from the Gala, but there's a twist of tartness, too. The flavor notes are akin to pears.

HONEYCRISP APPLE A bold fruit, Honeycrisp apples have a complex flavor because their acids and sugars balance out.

SOLICITUDE PANSY SHORTBREAD

Energetic Essence: Pansies bring a smile to the face. They represent all facets of love, including gentle affection toward another person. The word pansy *comes from the French "pensée." It translates as "thought," giving pansies associations with thoughtfulness and mindfulness toward others.*

Ingredients

½ cup white sugar

2 tbsps fresh orange zest

1 tbsp lemon zest

1 cup soft butter

1½ tbsps vanilla extract

2½ cups baking flour

Fresh pansies

1 large egg white, lightly beaten

Additional white sugar for sprinkling

Substitution

Lemon zest: Lime zest

Instructions

1. Line two baking or cookie sheets with parchment paper (so much easier to clean up).

FANCIFUL PANSY PORTRAITS: THE COLOR SYMBOLISM OF PANSIES

Pansy flowers come complete with colorful options that enhance their meanings. It's their "secret" code.

BLUE Devotion, loyalty, honesty

ORANGE A rare color representing a better attitude, achievement, and hope

PURPLE Authority, dignity

RED All types of love (full spectrum)

WHITE Spirituality

YELLOW Sweet joy and positivity

2. Preheat the oven to 325°F.

3. Put the sugar and zests into a mixing bowl and whisk them gently until well incorporated.

4. Add the butter and vanilla.

5. Beat for about 4 minutes (it should be fluffy).

6. Integrate the flour into the butter slowly.

7. Test to make sure the dough is not sticky. If so, add a little more flour.

8. Divide the blend in half.

9. Shape each half into a ball and cover them completely with plastic wrap.

10. Refrigerate for 30 minutes.

11. Working with the first ball, roll it out on a floured surface. You are looking for about ¼ inch.

12. Using a cookie cutter, make as many as possible but keep the size consistent so they cook at the same rate. Roll up the leftovers, and repeat until all dough is used.

13. Put the cookies 1 inch apart if they are small, 2 inches if they are large.

14. Coat each cookie with a minute coat of beaten egg in the center.

15. Take one pansy flower and press it into the egg white.

16. Top with a sprinkling of sugar.

17. Put the trays on the oven's center rack for 15 minutes (keep an eye on them). If the cookie edges are slightly brown, remove them from the oven.

18. Remove from the oven and let the entire sheet cool for 5 minutes.

19. Now transfer the cookies onto a wire rack until they're cool.

20. Repeat with the second ball of dough.

Potential Additions

1 tbsp fresh, finely minced orange mint leaves

FLOWERING SPRING ROLLS 'N' RICHES

Essential Essence: Spring rolls, also called "chun juan," are a traditional element of Chinese New Year. The golden colors of the finished rolls represent inspiring riches in the coming year. In this case, you'll put edible petals inside as a decorative, celebratory element.

Ingredients

8 small young white radishes

5 green onions

½ seedless cucumber

1 medium green pepper (other colors are fine)

Shredded cabbage

8 8-inch spring roll wrappers

1 clove garlic, finely minced

½ cup whole edible flowers, your choice

Thai chili sauce or dumpling dipping sauce

Substitution

Vegetables: You can change up the vegetable mix here. For example, add fresh bean sprouts, slivered carrots, or mustard greens.

HOMEMADE DIPPING SAUCE

If you want to make dipping sauce for these spring rolls, it's simple. Combine:

1½ tbsps rice wine vinegar

3 tbsps sweet soy sauce

½ tsp ginger powder

½ tsp chili oil

½ tsp sesame oil

1 tbsp green onion, finely minced

1 clove garlic, finely minced

Pinch brown sugar

Place all ingredients in a jar and shake well. Let the mixture age for a week in the refrigerator before using.

Instructions

1. Using a mandoline (see page 89), slice the vegetables into thin strips, slightly shorter than the spring roll wrappers.

2. Prepare a dish with hot water.

3. One at a time, put a sheet of spring roll wrappers in the water for 15 seconds.

4. Transfer it to a damp cutting board.

5. Place edible flower petals in the middle of the sheet.

6. Stack the vegetables on the flowers, leaving 2 inches on the sides.

7. Fold and roll the spring rolls tightly.

8. Repeat with the rest of the wrappers, keeping them under a damp covering until service.

Flower and Wine Pairing

While there were a few beverage recipes in this chapter, I wanted to share with you some flower and wine pairings. Similar to spices and sides, certain blossoms blend well with the flavor of specific wines. You can soak the petals in the wine or float them on top of the glass for a charming touch.

Flower	Wine
Aster	Reds
Carnations	Champagne
Chrysanthemum	Cabernet sauvignon
Daisy	Sauvignon blanc
Gladiolus	Rosé
Jasmine	White dessert wine
Marigold	Zinfandel
Nasturtium	Sauvignon blanc
Peonies	Sparkling rosé
Rose	Pinot noir
Tulips	Riesling
Violet	Merlot
White Orchid	Chardonnay

Endnotes

1. Constance Kirker, *Edible Flowers: A Global History*, London: Reaktion Books, October 15, 2016.

2. International Pepper Community, "History of Pepper," International Pepper Community, September 2013, https://www.ipcnet.org/history-of -pepper.

3. Cassie Marshall, "What Are the Sweetest Apples?", *The Kitchen Community*, June 19, 2021, https://thekitchencommunity.org/what-are -the-sweetest-apples/.

chapter nine

potion notions

And to think, I've been worrying about my potions final.
—RON WEASLEY[1]

Now we get to the water element. When people stop by, we regularly offer a beverage. It's a sign of welcome and hospitality. The history of tea, in particular, has many magical references, including divining by tea leaves (tasseomancy). The recipes in this chapter build off the history of beverages and the meaning of their components.

My interest in potions began with brewing mead. It was fun, and watching the bubbles form as the mead aged was, in my opinion, nature's take on alchemy. The yeast's hard work led to a saying attributed to Trappist monks in Belgium, "Beer should be liquid bread, not colored water,"[2] and they should know. They successfully brewed beer and sold a good quantity of it in the Middle Ages, along with some jams and jellies. When you combine bubbles with intention and ingredients, effervescence happens!

In making beverages of any sort, we should give a nod to water. The only potable drinks were, for a long time, milk and water and some kind of mixture coming from either. The Babylonians had another idea. They started brewing beer about 2700

THE WONDERFUL WORLD OF WATER

The earth has a "closed system" when it comes to water. When you take your next glass of it, ponder how long the molecules in the water have been around—since the planet's beginning. The same rain that fell on the alchemists could be in your next cup of tea.

We hear all about how many cups of water we should drink daily. A simple fact highlights the importance of this. While an average person could have no food for a month before death, it only takes one week without water. Why? Seventy percent of the human body weight is water (trees have a very similar composition, coming in at 80 percent, depending on the tree).

If you're looking for something with high water content for a snack, cucumbers are your friend. They are 95 percent water. In the fruit aisle, grab a watermelon, which is 92 percent water. Watermelon represents love, abundance, and fertility. Cucumber affords health, vitality, and profit.

BCE.[3] From there, we see an abundance of references to cider and mead, along with wine in Greece and Rome. The Greeks brewed up kukeōn, a mix of water, barley, and herbs. Or it might include goat cheese with a splash of honey.[4]

It sounds like a great deal of alcohol until you realize the water quality was sub-par. The brewing processes made unhealthy beverages potable.

Cocktails

No one is certain where the term *cocktail* originated. One theory begins in the tavern. At the end of the day, shopkeepers would gather the dregs (called tailings) from empty barrels and sell them at a lower price. Where did the "cock" come into the picture? It was the term sometimes used in place of the "spigot."[5]

Rum Orange Riches

Energetic Essence: Dreaming of rum portends prosperity. In the baroque era, oranges sym-bolized wealth and wistful thoughts of far-off adventures. Add to oranges' association with overall optimism, and you can consume this beverage when your bottom line needs a little bounce.

Ingredients

1½ ozs dark rum

1 oz Amaro CioCiaro

1 oz sweet vermouth

1 oz Cointreau

1 orange peel, twisted (garnish)

Substitution

Cointreau: Limoncello (use twisted lemon peel). Lemons represent friendship and refreshment.

Instructions

1. Set up 2 old-fashioned glasses with ice.

2. Put everything into a shaker with ice.

3. Shake for 30 seconds.

4. Pour into glasses.

5. Garnish with the orange twist.

SPARKLING TEQUILA SERENITY

Energetic Essence: The Aztecs believed agave was a divine gift to comfort the soul. Agave is the essence of tequila. There is an Aztec goddess, Mayheul, whose dominion was the agave plant.[6] Through her, it obtained a connection with good health, long life, and dancing! Peach offers happiness. Make this beverage while taking some "downtime" to find peace and renew joy. Try sacred dance to reconnect with the Divine.

Ingredients

6 tbsps reposado tequila
  (*reposado* means "rested")

1 lime, juiced

½ tbsp peach-ginger jam

12 ozs Cava

Lime peel, twisted (garnish)

1 fresh peach, sliced (garnish)

Substitution

Peach: Strawberry (abundance, perfection), orange (optimism), mango (happiness, wishes)

TEQUILA VS. MEZCAL

Tequila is limited to one type of agave: blue agave (*Agave tequilana weber*). Mezcal has no such limitation. It can be created out of any kind of agave. Plus, mezcal often has spices, upward of forty, depending on the brand. The tradition of harvesting blue agave by hand continues (hey, quality control). Of the two, tequila has a more refined feel and flavor.

Most mezcals age for between two months and a year or more. Tequila ages from two months to three years. The flavor for both depends heavily on aging. Anejo tequila is smooth with an oak undertone, blanco is similar, and reposado is mellow. By comparison, mezcal retains a smoky aroma with notes of fruits and flowers.

Instructions

1. Put the tequila, lime juice, and jam into a shaker.

2. Muddle the mixture to release the most flavor.

3. Fill the shaker with ice.

4. Shake until the blend is thoroughly cold.

5. Pull out 2 highball glasses.

6. Put a dollop of jam in the bottom of each.

7. Add ice on top.

8. Strain the muddled tequila into the glasses.

9. Top with cava.

10. Garnish with lime twists and peach slices.

Potential Additional Step

Lightly smoke or grill the peaches before putting them in the glasses.

HIBISCUS HAPPINESS

Energetic Essence: The notable component in this cocktail is pink hibiscus. The hue is enough to "tickle you pink." Hibiscus inspires joy and positivity. If you carry a few petals with you, they attract good fortune.

Ingredients

1 cup water

⅓ cup dried hibiscus flowers
(culinary grade)

1 cup white sugar

1 oz vodka

½ oz lemon juice

3 mint leaves

2 ozs sparkling rosé

Instructions

1. Bring to boil 1 cup of water. Steep the hibiscus therein for 10 minutes.

2. Strain the water into a small bowl.

3. Discard the hibiscus petals.

4. Add sugar to the hibiscus water and stir until it dissolves. This make the hibiscus syrup.

5. Combine the vodka, lemon, ½ oz hibiscus syrup, and mint leaves in an ice-filled shaker. Cover and shake.

6. In about 20 seconds, the outside of the shaker should be frosty.

7. Pour this into a champagne glass, topping it with the sparkling rosé.

COFFEE

Coffee comes from the roasted seeds of a tree native to Abyssinia and Arabia. In the early 1500s, Mecca sported the first coffee house.[7] European establishments came around the same time as English ones in the 1600s.[8] No longer beer, the king of breakfast. Welcome, coffee!

GET UP AND GO FROTHY COFFEE

Energetic Essence: Those who adore coffee enjoy the taste and the boost of energy it provides. Coffee represents accomplishment and actualization. There is definitely a coffee culture, individuals who know about every variety of coffee, its flavor profile, and history. Mint symbolizes personal strength. When your "get up and go" got up and went, brew yourself this great cup of sweetened coffee. When paired with ice, it allows you to "keep it cool" and mete out your energy wisely.

Ingredients (1 cup)

8 ozs hot coffee (your choice)

2 tbsps sugar

¼ cup mint creamer

Ice (optional)

Substitution

Mint creamer: Vanilla creamer for soothing and love; hazelnut for fertility and wisdom

Instructions

1. Pour all the ingredients but ice into a blender.

2. Whip until frothy.

3. Put a few ice cubes in a cup.

4. Pour the coffee over the top.

   ∽ **TIP** Freeze some coffee in ice cube trays and use them for this recipe. Your coffee won't get watery.

ICY INSIGHTS

By the way, choosing ice for your iced coffee makes a difference! Large ice is perfect for sipping outside. In the heat, large ice cubes won't melt as fast. Medium-sized ice is the standard of ice cubes, good for any ice coffee recipe. Crushed ice is best for when you're in a hurry because it cools the coffee faster.

South of the Border

Energetic Essence: One of the keynote flavors in this drink is Triple Sec, which is orange. You enjoy it in cosmopolitans and Long Island iced tea. Orange represents prosperity, travel, enthusiasm, warmth, and happiness. Coffee can boost any of those vibrational signatures.

Ingredients

¾ cup hot coffee
Fresh sweet cream, whipped
½ oz tequila
½ oz Kahlua (also coffee flavored)
½ oz Triple Sec
⅛ tsp vanilla extract

Sprinkle of allspice, ginger, or cinnamon (garnish)

Substitution
Triple Sec: Cointreau, Grand Marnier, Orange Curaçao

Instructions

1. Brew a fresh pot of coffee.

2. While you wait, whip up the sweet cream.

3. Mix the coffee with tequila, Kahlua, Triple Sec, and vanilla extract in a coffee mug.

4. Top with a dollop of sweet cream.

5. Sprinkle the chosen spice on top for a finish.

Punch

The word *punch* may have originated in India with the name *paantsch*. It ties to the Hindi term (*pāñĉ*) as well. The word means "five" because the beverage had five components: water, alcohol, lemon juice, sugar, and spices.[9] Punches are lower in alcohol than a typical drink.

Punch appears in English writings during the early 1600s. The ingredients were like wassail, using brandy or wine as a foundation. When rum came on the scene, new rum punch recipes appeared.

TASTE THE RAINBOW MEDLEY

Energetic Essence: Celebrate diversity and hope. The rainbow embraces love and friendship without judgment. Add in the traditional leprechaun at the end of the rainbow, and you have luck for good measure. This beverage has every color of the rainbow.

Ingredients

½ cup fresh strawberries, sliced

½ cup mandarin orange, peeled and divided

½ cup pineapple nibs

½ cup kiwi, peeled and chopped

½ cup blueberries

½ cup champagne grapes

2 cups cold ginger ale

3 cups prosecco

¾ cup pineapple juice

Maraschino cherries (garnish)

Substitution

Prosecco: Cava Brut, English sparkling wine

Instructions

1. Find tall glasses and chill them.

2. Layer a little of each fruit from red to purple up the glass.

3. Make sure to leave room for the liquid.

4. Blend the ginger ale, prosecco, and juice.

5. Pour into each glass and garnish with 1 to 2 cherries.

∽ **NON-ALCOHOLIC TIP** Lemon-lime soda or a fruity sparkling seltzer can replace the alcohol in this recipe.

THE PLEASING PUNCH BOWL

The English were particularly fond of punch. Men's clubs and punch houses served their recipes in a communal bowl. Translate that into metaphysics, and you have a fanciful cauldron.

Early on, punch bowls were silver, which the upper class favored.[10] A punch bowl is versatile. Couple it with fresh flowers and a bottle of champagne, and you have a grand centerpiece. Or it may become a fruit bowl.

We still have one to use on special occasions. When I look at it, I see special memories I treasure.

Hot Cranberry Courage

Energetic Essence: Cranberries ripen during the late harvest festival, explaining their appearance at many tables during this time. Magically, cranberries have pluck and possibilities. Secondary vibrational signatures include taking action (perfect for when you need to be brave), abundance, and gratitude. Heating this beverage puts fervor behind your efforts. This is a set-it-and-forget-it punch.

Ingredients

½ gallon cranberry juice

¾ cup pineapple juice concentrate

2 cups water

8 cinnamon sticks (one per cup)

2 allspice berries

2 whole cloves

Brown sugar or honey to taste

Substitution

Pineapple juice: Apple juice concentrate (self-awareness) or orange juice concentrate (vitality; universal love)

Instructions

1. Put all the ingredients into a slow cooker except for the sweeteners.

2. Cook on high for 20 minutes.

3. Taste-test, adding sugar to taste.

4. Leave it in the slow cooker so folks can help themselves.

Tea

Tea originated in China around 2700 BCE, but it's likely that people used tea far earlier. In this area of the world, tea is a common medicinal. By the third century CE, it moved into favor as a standard daily drink, and the first published instructions for sowing, refining, and drinking tea appeared in 350 CE.[11]

Tea moved to Japan in 800 CE. People began cultivating it here in the thirteenth century. The Japanese elevated tea drinking into a ritual process, the Japanese Tea Ceremony (translated as "the way of tea"). The ceremony begins on a tatami mat floor. It takes several hours intended to express hospitality.

Such tea events had spiritual overtones with strong roots in Zen philosophy. The moment of drinking tea is ephemeral and straightforward. Guests experience a moment of inner harmony before returning to the outside world.

I enjoy tea most late at night. The house is quiet. My one dog snores to his tune. The hush that falls like a cozy blanket room-to-room goes perfectly with warm, comforting tea. While I am by no means a tea snob, my preferred teas are Earl Grey (black tea), Taiwanese oolongs (a category all its own), Japanese Sencha (green tea), and Silver Needle (white tea).

There are, of course, herbal teas with a wide range of aromas and flavors. My choices? Rose-lavender, ginger-lemon, and hibiscus. Periodically I go into a specialty tea store and try something new. It's a great way to get to know your teas. Plus, sometimes you discover a treasure, such as blossoming tea. It comes in a wide range of colors and themes, and as it steams, a tea flower blooms in your cup. Almost too pretty to drink.

GOODWILL RASPBERRY LEMON ICED TEA

Energetic Essence: Raspberry keeps negative spirits at bay while encouraging kindness at the same time. Raspberries are in the same family as roses. While you may only think of them as red, there are yellow, orange, white, and black. Each hue expands their potential spiritual applications through color associations.

Ingredients

2 cups fresh raspberries

1 cup sugar or honey

2¼ cups water, divided

1 drop of lavender extract (optional)

2 black darjeeling tea bags

4 lemons, juiced (¾ cups)

Lemon slices (garnish)

Substitution

Raspberries: Pineapple (hospitality) or add a little juice

Instructions

1. In a non-reactive saucepan, mix the raspberries, sugar, and ¼ cup of water. Add lavender extract if desired.

2. Bring the mix to a boil.

3. Reduce the heat and simmer until the raspberries are soft.

4. Cool.

5. Press the liquid through a strainer into a 4-cup jar you can seal.

6. Set aside.

7. Bring 2 cups of water to a boil, then add the tea bags.

8. Take it off the heat.

9. Steep for 5 minutes.

10. Remove the tea bags.

11. Add the tea to the lemon juice and raspberry blend.

12. Stir thoroughly.

13. Seal the jar.

14. Refrigerate until serving.

15. Use tall glasses with ice and a slice of lemon in each.

THE ORIGIN OF TEA

Japanese mythology explains the origin of the tea plant. A Chinese Buddhist saint Bodhidharma was meditating and fell asleep. This break in his duties bothered him deeply. He removed his eyelids and tossed them to the ground to ensure this shortcoming would never happen again. There they took root and became the first tea plant, providing energy.[12] If you look at a tea leaf, they do indeed resemble eyelids. Talk about fierce dedication.

GINGER CHAI TEA FOR CLEANSING

Energetic Essence: There are several ways to look at this tea. First off, the ginger element is a spice used for offerings to the Buddha. Tibetan Buddhists use it regularly in rituals. This tea certainly has a ceremonial undercurrent.

Other cultures feel ginger promotes peace, prosperity, and love and energizes passion. Overall, ginger brings about positive transformation in your life, starting with spiritual house cleaning. Cardamom marries well with these vibrations by awakening our inner wisdom and uplifting our souls.

Ginger is one of the essential spices in my home. I love the aroma and bright taste.

Ingredients

2 green cardamom

1 cup water

¼ inch ginger root, peeled and grated

⅓ cup milk or cream

Sweetener as desired

1 tsp loose-leaf English breakfast tea

Instructions

1. Remove the seeds from the cardamom.

2. Crush them using a mortar and pestle.

3. Place water in a saucepan over medium flame.

4. Add the cardamom seeds and grated ginger.

5. When the water is hot, add milk and sweetener.

6. Bring everything to a low-rolling boil.

7. Add in the English tea. Simmer for at least 2 minutes (longer if you want a more robust tea flavor).

8. Strain.

9. Serve hot with finger sandwiches.

∾ FACTOID In India, *chai* is not a tea flavor. Instead, *chai* translates as "tea." If you say "chai tea," you're saying "tea tea." While the Western world considers chai a specialized drink, India looks at it as the standard way to prepare tea.

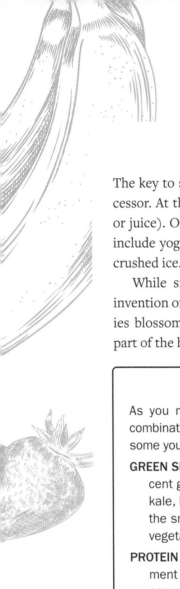

SMOOTHIES

The key to smoothies' "smoothness" is a blender or food processor. At the foundation, a smoothie begins with liquid (milk or juice). Other ingredients that could be put in the smoothie include yogurt, fruit, vegetables, nutritional supplements, and crushed ice.

While smoothies appeared on the West Coast after the invention of blenders in 1930,[13] the true renaissance of smoothies blossomed in the mid-1980s. By 2000, the smoothie was part of the health food culture and everyday life.

TYPES OF SMOOTHIES

As you might imagine, there are as many smoothie combinations as creativity allows. There are, however, some you will see regularly offered at beverage stands:

GREEN SMOOTHIE This drink consists of around 50 percent green leafy vegetables. Examples include spinach, kale, broccoli, collards, and parsley. The remainder of the smoothie is fruit to offset the bitter taste of raw vegetables.

PROTEIN SMOOTHIE In this smoothie, a protein supplement is center stage. It's added to milk or water and sometimes fruits and vegetables.

YOGURT SMOOTHIE As the name implies, this begins with yogurt. Yogurt is incredibly healthy for boosting metabolism and supporting the immune system. Yogurt smoothies might feature seeds, nuts, and fruit.

Smoothies have been a global sensation long before refrigeration. People in Mediterranean regions puréed fresh fruit together, for example. In Persia, you'll find the Sharbat, referenced in twelfth-century writings.[14] Ingredients might include flower petals, fruit, chia seeds, cane juice, and tea.

VERY BERRY BRAIN BOOST

Energetic Essence: This recipe builds on studies linking berries to brain health. Berries have "good for you" stuff including antioxidants, vitamins, and flavonoids. One flavonoid unique to berries supports memory retention, fine motor skills, and keenness. Almonds are friends with our powers of recall, too.

There is absolutely no reason a Kitchen Witch can't find inspiration in the proven health benefits of Mother Nature's garden!

Ingredients (yields 5 cups)

1 ripe banana

1 cup frozen strawberries

1 cup frozen blackberries

1 cup frozen raspberries

½ cup frozen blueberries

1 cup almond milk

¾ cup vanilla Greek yogurt

Honey (to taste if desired)

Instructions

1. Break up the banana and put it in the blender or food processor.

2. Put a portion of each ingredient in the blender and whip them up.

3. Continue adding ingredients for thorough mixing.

4. Serve cold.

Apple of My Eye Smoothie

Energetic Essence: Cinnamon has a vibrational signature perfect for activating your third eye, empowering psychic awareness. Apple brings growth into the picture. Make this when you are focusing on further developing your spiritual arts. Think of it as a tune-up for your soul.

Ingredients

1 apple, peeled

1 cup apple juice

¼ cup dates, chopped

¼ cup raisins (gold is a good choice)

½ tsp cinnamon

¼ tsp ginger

2 tbsps walnuts or pecans, chopped

Substitution

Apple: Pear, which represents a
spiritual work in progress

Instructions

1. Get out a saucepan.

2. Chop and core the apple.

3. Put the chopped apple and apple juice into the pan with all the other ingredients (except the nuts).

4. Bring to a boil over medium-high heat.

5. Remove from the heat.

6. Let the mixture cool for 3 minutes.

7. Carefully pour this mix into the blender. Remember, it's HOT.

8. Add the nuts.

9. Process on high until smooth.

10. Enjoy while still warm.

Milk

While Cleopatra may have bathed in milk to ensure her youthful appearance,[15] we're looking at internalizing milk's natural and spiritual attributes. Did you know just one glass of milk provides 30 percent of your daily calcium intake? Milk is also a source of vitamins A, B12, and D. Accordingly, "health" is undoubtedly one of milk's vibrational signatures.

Two people stand out in the history of milk as we know it today. The first is Louis Pasteur (nineteenth century), who invented the pasteurization technique to inhibit bacterial growth. The following figure is Dr. Hervey Thatcher, the inventor of the milk bottle. This meant milkmen no longer had to ladle milk into a container at a person's home. Afterward, he patented a wooden stopper, securing the bottle. Because of his efforts, Thatcher earned the title "Father of the Milk Bottle."[16]

Spiritually speaking, milk is the essence of the Mother Goddess, filled with fertility and abundance. In Egypt, the goddess Hesat provided humankind with life-supporting milk. Her image, aptly, is a cow. Roman mythology tells us that milk came from Ops (Rhea in Greece).

BANANA CINNAMON COMFORT

Energetic Essence: Banana is a fruit tied to the Sacred Masculine in the universe. It inspires joy while protecting you from negative thoughts and vibrations. Cinnamon has shielding benefits so you can find relief and comfort and focus on self-love.

Ingredients

1 ripe banana, sliced or
    broken into pieces

½ cup of regular milk

¼ cup water

¼ cup crushed ice

1 tbsp maple syrup

1 drop pure vanilla extract

Substitutions

Maple syrup: Molasses, honey,
    corn syrup, coconut nectar

Vanilla extract: Caramel (steadiness),
    cinnamon (luck), coconut
    (versatility), ginger (vitality), mango
    (happiness), pineapple (hospitality)

Instructions

1. Put all the ingredients into the blender or food processor.

2. Mix on high until they are well integrated.

3. Serve cold (it tastes good warm, too).

The Land of Milk and Honey

Energetic Essence: If you want to go to sleep and enjoy sweet dreams, this is the drink for you. The cinnamon and clove provide a warming effect. Cinnamon has healing, soothing properties. Clove supports your immune system, and cardamom soothes anxiety.

Ingredients

2 cups whole milk

1 vanilla bean

1 cinnamon stick

3 whole cloves

1 whole cardamom

1 tbsp honey

Whipped cream (garnish)

Ground cinnamon (garnish)

WHAT'S THE BUZZ?

In a worker bee's lifetime, they make only $1/12$ of a tsp of honey.[17] They travel at speeds up to 15 miles an hour, beating their wings more than 11,000 times a minute (which makes the buzzing sound). To create 1 pound of honey, bees from one hive must visit approximately two million flowers. Honeybees never sleep (talk about focus!).

Honey, as a condiment, has incredible longevity. King Tut's tomb had a pot of honey, still consumable.[18]

Instructions

1. Place the milk and spices into a saucepan over medium heat.

2. Warm the mixture until it's just shy of boiling.

3. Remove from heat.

4. Let the mixture "marry" for 10 minutes.

5. Mix in honey.

6. Strain and serve hot, topped with whipped cream and a dash of cinnamon.

   ~ **TIP** Try different types of honey in this beverage. Ideas include wildflower and orange blossom honey.

HEARTH-MADE HOT CHOCOLATE

Energetic Essence: I cannot think of anything more comforting and cozy than hot cocoa. Making it from scratch allows you to tinker with the depth of flavor and additions to the mix for greater symbolic value. For example, use

- *butterscotch chips instead of chocolate for the blessings of love,*
- *unicorn chips for whimsy,*
- *mint to cool and soothe, and*
- *peanut butter for accurately tuning into signs and omens.*

Ingredients

½ cup sugar (you can adjust for more or less sweetness)

¼ cup cocoa powder, unsweetened

3½ cups whole milk

½ cup baking chips (semi-sweet for traditional)

1 tsp vanilla extract

Whipped cream or mini marshmallows (garnish)

Instructions

1. Get out a saucepan.
2. Place sugar and cocoa powder into it.
3. Add the milk and bring it to a low, rolling boil.
4. Add the baking chips.
5. Whisk continuously until smooth.
6. Turn down the heat.
7. Simmer for 2 minutes.
8. Remove the pot from the heat.
9. Stir in vanilla.
10. Serve hot with whatever toppings suit your fancy.

CHARACTERISTICS OF CHOCOLATE

There are five main types of chocolate. **White chocolate** is easy to recognize because of its color. The aroma white chocolate gives off is tempting vanilla. This is a rich choice with a soft, creamy texture because of sweetened condensed milk and cocoa butter. White represents peacefulness and purity.

Milk chocolate is tried and true, at least in my youth. It's creamy, sweet, and by far the most popular chocolate. It's softer than dark chocolate but not as sugary as white chocolate. Use milk chocolate when working with your inner child.

Dark chocolate is robust, even though it has only two simple ingredients: cocoa and sugar (sometimes vanilla for good measure). The firmness makes it ideal for tempering. In a recipe, there's no mistaking the presence of dark chocolate. This chocolate is energetic, dramatic, and sophisticated.

Next is **bittersweet chocolate**, sometimes called extra-dark chocolate. Bittersweet has a higher cocoa content—often 70 percent or more! For those looking for a chocolate flavor without as much sugar, bittersweet can be a good friend. Chocolate nibs can create a harmonic bridge between sweeter ingredients. This represents cooperation and accord.

Finally, there's **ruby chocolate**. While you might conclude this is just colored white chocolate, it's completely different. Ruby chocolate originates from ruby cocoa beans and is a newcomer to the market (2017). The flavor is like a slightly tart berry. Ruby chocolate attracts wealth and stimulates passion.

Endnotes

1. J. K. Rowling, *Harry Potter and the Sorcerer's Stone*, New York: Scholastic, 1998.

2. Christian Lepage, "Belgian Ardour for Liquid Bread," *Slovak Spectator*, March 17, 2014, https://spectator.sme.sk/c/20050120/belgian-ardour-for -liquid-bread-video-included.html.

3. Tate Paulette, "Brewing Mesopotamian Beer Brings a Sip of this Vibrant Ancient Drinking Culture Back to Life," *The Conversation*, August 24, 2020, https://theconversation.com/brewing-mesopotamian-beer-brings- a-sip-of-this-vibrant-ancient-drinking-culture-back-to-life-142215.

4. The Hellenic Museum, "Kykeon: The Drink of Champions," September 6, 2021, https://www.hellenic.org.au/post/kykeon-the-drink-of-champions.

5. Difford's Guide, "Origin of the Word Cocktail," *Difford's Guide for Dis- cerning Drinkers*, accessed September 26, 2023, https://www.diffordsguide.com/encyclopedia/2292/cocktails/origins-of -the-word-cocktail.

6. Nicoletta Maestri, "Mayahuel, The Aztec Goddess of Maguey," ThoughtCo, April 5, 2023, https://www.thoughtco.com/mayahuel-the -aztec-goddess-of-maguey-171570.

7. Nathans Nyhvrold, "Coffee Origin, Types, Uses, History & Facts," *Ency- clopedia Britannica*, last updated September 11, 2023, https://www.britannica.com/topic/coffee.

8. Mark Pendergast, "The History of Coffee and How It Transformed Our World," Coffee Timeline, September 2013, https://as.vanderbilt.edu /clas-resources/media/Coffee%20Timeline.pdf.

9. Difford's Guide, "The History of Punch," *Difford's Guide for Discerning Drinkers*, accessed September 24, 2023, https://www.diffordsguide .com/g/1129/punch-and-punches/history.

10. University Libraries, "The Punch Bowl Pre-1806," Virginia Tech Univer- sity, January 12, 2023, https://guides.lib.vt.edu/c.php?g=387023&p =3016428.

11. Khado Tsephel, "The History of Tea," *The Science Survey*, July 25, 2022, https://thesciencesurvey.com/spotlight/2022/07/25/the-history-of-tea/.

12. Lisa Dong, "Legends on the Origins of Tea from China, Japan, and Korea," *T Ching*, March 21, 2012, https://tching.com/2012/03/legends -on-the-origins-of-tea-from-china-japan-and-korea.

13. Abdul Alhazred, "Kitchen Blender Where It All Started," History and Headlines, January 2, 2020, https://www.historyandheadlines.com /kitchen-blender-where-it-all-started/.

14. Nazima Kudus, "Of Sorbet, Sherbert, Sarbat and All That Jazz," Uitm Institutional Repository, June 2022, https://ir.uitm.edu.my/id /eprint/63625/1/63625.pdf.

15. Susruthi Rajanala, "Cleopatra and Sour Milk—The Ancient Practice of Chemical Peeling," *Jama Network*, October 2017, https://jamanetwork .com/journals/jamadermatology/article-abstract/2657249.

16. Christina Baker, "Thatcher Glass: A History of Innovation," Corning Museum of Glass, last updated May 10, 2017, https://blog.cmog .org/2017/05/10/thatcher-history/.

17. Maureen Dolan, "Tales from the Hive," Nova Online, last updated October 2000, https://www.pbs.org/wgbh/nova/bees/buzz.html.

18. Jennifer Gaeng, "Discover the Oldest Honey Ever Found (From King Tut's Tomb?), A–Z Animals, February 28, 2023, https://a-z-animals.com/ blog/discover-the-oldest-honey-ever-found-from-king-tuts-tomb/.

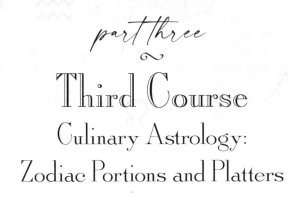

part three

Third Course
Culinary Astrology:
Zodiac Portions and Platters

Astrology is a language. If you understand this language, The Sky Speaks to You.
—MICHAEL R. MEYER, *A HANDBOOK FOR THE HUMANISTIC ASTROLOGER*

The study of astrology looks at personality traits, compatibility, fortunes, and fates for individuals based on the alignment of the stars on their birthdays. Why wouldn't that extend into what foods each sign enjoys? Kitchen Witches are no strangers to using interesting "tools" to achieve wonderful flavors and impressive energies.

Think of astrology as just another layer of mindful energy mixed in for good measure. How does it work? It's easier than you might think. Start with the general characteristics exhibited by each sign. From there, pair various components in your meal with those energy signatures.

It quickly becomes apparent that the zodiac has a far-reaching palate, and such diversity is highly enjoyable. The possibilities go beyond the menu itself. Some people want refined dining atmospheres with an emphasis on finesse. For them, the "experience" is central. Others are content to plop down in a field and enjoy a spur-of-the-moment sandwich. For them, it's the company they are keeping.

Neither end of the spectrum is right or wrong. It's simply a different way of interacting with food. The occasion lets you explain why you chose the setting, serving style, and menu (which makes for pretty cool conversations). No matter what, people will find your thoughtfulness endearing.

The four chapters in Part 3 tackle the idea of mastering food for each sign by elemental correspondence.

chapter ten

cooking for star signs: earth

Persistence overshadows even talent as the most
valuable resource shaping the quality of life.
—ANTHONY ROBBINS[1]

As the name implies, earth signs (Taurus, Virgo, and Capricorn) are...well... down to earth! They never seem to lose their balance. Because they enjoy finer things, they will work hard to accumulate money to meet their needs.

> ⁓ **TIP** When your earthy friend or partner has a bad
> day, assuage them with lovely food and fine wine.

Earth signs prefer small, intimate affairs with good conversation in social settings. The earth signs' motto is "quality over quantity." They are not friend "collectors," nor do they seek minions.

One thing you notice about those born under earth signs is they love routines. They create a rhythm of their life with set patterns. When the structure changes for whatever reason, it makes for an unhappy individual. On a more positive note, if you need someone to create or run a ritual, call on an earth sign.

Building Vibrational Signatures for Earth Element

The work of a Kitchen Witch is never done (well, it is, but you get the drift). There are several elements to making a rock-solid ambiance for earth signs. First, keep in mind that earth signs like to feel secure. A practical approach to your meal always impresses. Your earth element's relationship with food is simple, yet they savor each bite. Let's look at little touches devised with the earth sign's general personality traits in mind.

Color Palette

Integrate earthy colors into your dining room.

> **BROWN** Solidity, reliability, strength, safety, dependability. Promoting appetite. Old-fashioned, established approaches. A warm color.

GREEN New beginnings, abundance, growth, renewal, harmony, safety, wellness. Balance leads to decisiveness—improved efficiency and concentration.

YELLOW Positivity. Enhanced concentration. Stronger analytical thinking. Encourages communication. Enthusiasm, confidence, hope, creativity,

Crystals

Crystals come from the earth, and small ones can make a pretty gift for guests to put near their table setting.

BLACK TOURMALINE Removal of unwanted energies. Protection and grounding. Disperses tension and stress. Cleansing. Improved self-esteem.

GREEN AGATE Compassion, generosity, justice calming, balance. Improved decision-making. Resolving disputes. Emotional flexibility. Reveals natural talents and skills. Truth-telling.

JADE Maintaining the connection between above and below. Relationship with the Sacred Masculine. Strengthening life force (qi). Wisdom and insightful thinking.

JASPER Relieving anxiety. Promoting mental clarity. Grounding. Improved self-confidence, renewed creativity, supporting spiritual growth, nurturing, empathy, stimulates energy.

SMOKY QUARTZ Relieves depression, fear, and negativity. Promotes good thoughts moved into productive action with clarity. Manifesting your goals. Protection from physical danger.

Decorations

Decorations are great mood-setters. Those born with an earth sign favor simplicity. Make sure rooms have breathing space.

In most homes, using a centerpiece is the easiest way to reflect a theme or an energy. First off, a centerpiece can be anything, not just flowers. Look for small vials into which you can place spiritually significant seeds for each guest. They can take home the vial. Another option is to arrange a small bundle of aromatic petals such as primrose, honeysuckle, and magnolia. Mix acorns with pine cones. If you're feeling whimsical, add a gnome figurine.

How about encircling each glass with some green leaves or pine pieces? Bring rustic wood platters into the picture. Create a stick "bouquet."

You can also forgo the centerpiece and other decorations with earth sign guests. They like to see things clearly, especially faces.

Drinks

What do you offer your earth sign to drink?

∾ Apple juice

∾ Black tea

∾ Coffee, no sugar

∾ Gin and tonic

∾ Grape juice

∾ Green smoothie

∾ Malt beer

∾ Martini

∾ Old-fashioned

∾ Pinot noir

∾ Vanilla latte

∾ Zinfandel

Food Presentation

Odd or sloppy-looking foods aren't overly appealing. The way you set the table matters, too. What about rich brown napkins and table runners? Your table doesn't have to be fancy, but the tableware should be well organized to please the earth signs' practical perspective.

Plate your food so it's uncluttered (use white space for this impact). If you decide to use garnishes, they must be edible, such as bright mandarin oranges on an Asian dish, a lime slice for Mexican, or a sprig of mint with a lamb chop.

Flowers

If you like flowers on the table, which ones correspond to the earth element?

∾ Carnations

∾ Chrysanthemum

∾ Dahlia

∾ Fern (for styling)

∾ Hydrangea

∾ Iris

∾ Magnolia

∾ Peony

∾ Tiffany roses

∾ Tulip

Incense

Regarding incense, people born under the earth element prefer lighter scents—ones that don't overwhelm the smell of your cooking. I do not recommend patchouli or frankincense.

∾ Amber

∾ Lemon grass

∾ Narcissus

∾ Rose

∾ Vanilla

Lighting

We've all seen one movie with shadowy lights, candles, and roses. It's your turn to create mood lighting. I do not suggest any harsh illumination. One solution is an adjustable light. Dim it a little. A carved wooden lamp fits the bill, as does a Himalayan salt lamp.

Music

As the saying goes, you can't please all the people all of the time. But when you think about the earth element, the choice is not overly loud but nonetheless joyful. As you might imagine, the earthy songs speak of home, family, tribe, and happiness. Here is a list of songs I think fit the earth element vibe.

ALEXANDER BORODIN In the Steppes of Central Asia

BEACH BOYS Good Vibrations

BEATLES Hey Jude; Here Comes the Sun

BEETHOVEN Symphony 6 in F Major

BOB MARLEY Three Little Birds

CROSBY, STILLS, AND NASH Treat Your Children Well

DAVE AND STEVEN GORDON Earth Drum

ERIC CLAPTON My Father's Eyes

JOAN BAEZ Rejoice in the Sun

JOHN DENVER Earth Songs

KATRINA AND THE WAVES Walkin' on Sunshine

LIBANA The Earth Is Our Mother

LOUIS ARMSTRONG What a Wonderful World

THE JUDDS Love Can Build a Bridge

Tidiness

When you have someone born under the earth element over for an occasion, they prefer clean (don't forget the blinds and windows), organized, and carefully thought-out decor. You might even call them "neat freaks." They will try hard not to notice the dust behind the TV, but all such things catch their eyes.

Now, it is not practicable for you to spend hours making your home into the perfect earth element space. Don't sweat it. If you know you will spend most of your time at the table or entertainment room, focus on those two areas and do your best. Put out something for the specific earth sign you're entertaining. Give the Taurus hand sanitizer, Capricorn a scented soap in a pretty wrapping, and biodegradable napkins for Virgo.

Always remember, it is your sacred space. You are simply being thoughtful. It matters.

Taurus the Bull: April 20–May 20

Bigger Is Better

The Taurus personality combines tenacity and loyalty with being stubborn and headstrong. With Venus ruling this sign, it's not surprising to find Taurus throwing themselves into creative endeavors. They are sensual beings and love the feel of cozy blankets. Add a candle and a well-chosen aroma, and you have a date in the making.

Most Taureans have a taste for the opulent, even if their budget doesn't allow for it. The more luxurious, the better. They are patient, loving, steady, and sure as friends or companions. In work, the Bull focuses on achievement.

Finicky and Fastidious

Where Aries goes with the flow, Taurus brings their personal culinary tools to the party. Of all signs, Taurus can find the subtlest of notes in any recipe. With a person born under this sign, fresher is always better and appreciated, and organic offerings will make them swoon.

DOES THE BULL COOK?

Most Taureans are excellent bakers because they love precision and having high expectations for themselves. When they cook, however, they rarely veer from the ingredients and instructions in front of them. They are not fast and furious in the kitchen. Try not to interrupt them. For the Bull, cooking has a pattern; when it gets disrupted, they become flustered. In the end, the food comes out great. It's just not terribly creative. The presentations rock!

Taurus Taste Buds

People born under the sign of the Bull love to eat. When you're considering an ideal approach to your dinner, dig out luxurious looking but relatively simple concoctions, such as:

- Apple galette
- Butter-poached pears
- Coffee-marinated hanger steak
- Italian fare
- Lobster risotto
- Onion cucumber sweet salad
- Spanakopita

Go with Gourmet

If you skimp on your ingredients, the ever-alert Bull can tell. They may even take you to the best butcher in town and the local farmers' market before your next get-together with a recipe in hand.

Tranquil Settings
Your Taurus will appreciate an ambiance with few distractions. They want to eat slowly, without interruption. Believe it or not, a Victorian-style picnic is ideal, appealing to the Bull's earth energies. Whatever you choose, think about comfort, too.

Keynotes of a Taurus's Diet
Your Taurus will appreciate a meal blending flavors and textures. Now you have wiggle room. Component ideas include:

- Apple
- Asparagus
- Beef
- Berries
- Cauliflower
- Cranberry
- Cucumber
- Dill
- Gravy
- Horseradish
- Peas
- Pomegranate
- Potatoes
- Sprouts
- Swiss chard
- Raisin
- Vanilla bean
- Vine-fresh tomatoes

What to Avoid
- Baked goods
- Heavy carbs
- Lamb
- Liver
- Overly rich food
- Pasta
- Peas
- Processed foods
- Prunes
- Spicy food

SUGGESTIONS
BREAKFAST Ham and egg croissant with cappuccino

LUNCH Cup of Irish stew and buttered bread

DINNER Free-range chicken with honey-sesame glaze

DESSERT Bananas foster

SNACK Aged gouda and cheddar with crackers

Happy Endings Vine-Ripe Roasted Tomatoes

Energetic Essence: This side dish looks beautiful and appeals to the Taurus aesthetic. The color red of the tomato signifies all will be okay, something your Taurus friend will tell you during trying times.

Ingredients

Cherry tomatoes (5–7 per person)

Extra virgin olive oil

Balsamic

Black pepper, freshly ground

Sea salt

Fleur de Sel

Basil leaves, chiffonade (garnish)

WHAT IS CHIFFONADE?

Chiffonade is a French cooking technique. The word means "little ribbons," and when you see the outcome of a chiffonade cut, the reason for the name becomes apparent. Typically, culinarians use this slicing method for leafy green vegetables and herbs such as spinach, Swiss chard, basil, sage, and mint. The little strands then top soups and pasta.

Pick a few herb leaves and stack them one atop the other. Roll up the herb like a jelly roll as tightly as possible. Rest your knife against the flat part of your knuckles and begin slicing from one end to the other in small increments. Ensure your blade stays in contact with your cutting board and keep cutting until complete.

Instructions

1. Set the oven to 350°F.

2. Line an oven tray with parchment paper.

3. Spread the tomatoes evenly over the surface.

4. Drizzle with olive oil and balsamic.

5. Sprinkle the pepper and sea salt on top generously.

6. Roast for 12 minutes (until the tomatoes just begin bursting).

7. Lay them on a serving tray.

8. Use the Fleur de Sel as a finishing touch along with the basil garnish.

Potential Additions

For a hardier side dish, you can add more vegetables to your cooking tray. Use sliced bell peppers (tenacity), corn (faith to succeed), green beans (positive developments), pearl onions (healing), and thin zucchini slices (growth).

Virgo: August 23–September 22

Mom's Soup and Strategy

When you need someone to bring you back down to earth, seek a Virgo. They approach life with systematic strategies. Virgos always want to perfect themselves. As a result, they will practice arts or hobbies again and again.

Being ruled by Mercury, Virgo gathers information, processes it, and meticulously organizes it. Clarity is the name of the game. More importantly, Virgos are helpers. They engage in any opportunity where their knowledge and skills might help uncover a reasonable solution. This is why you see many Virgos involved in healing arts in some manner.

Meticulous Management

Regarding food, Virgo is hyperaware—all sense and sensibility. They like a mindful framework for their meal plan. These folks will plan out menus weeks in advance and put them on the calendar. Don't do "fast food" with your Virgo. They prefer eating slowly.

The Tasteful Table

Your Virgo loves structure. For them, a well-appointed table is pleasing. If you have special wine glasses, use them. If there's a story attached to anything, share it! Stick with classic and uncluttered.

> ## DOES VIRGO COOK?
> Virgos make excellent bakers because they pay attention to technicalities. Even if it seems something has gone wrong, they're quick thinkers who can fix it. On the cooking side, Virgos make every recipe precisely as directed, just like Taurus. Yet somehow, their food tastes terrific (better than the original).
>
> Beware: Because Virgo is such a perfectionist, they never really feel their effort met an impossible goal they had in mind. They may talk about too much salt, for example. Let those mentions pass and keep complimenting the food (in detail).

Healthy Fare

Virgos often lean into what they see as healthy lifestyles, such as vegetarianism. No matter what, they like fresh and wholesome food at the top of their list. Virgos don't mind leftovers one bit. Eating leftovers is frugal and wastes nothing. Think in terms of:

- Barley or lentil soup
- Leftover casserole wonders
- Mixed greens salad with pine nuts
- Pan-seared salmon with apples
- Turkey bacon egg cups

Appreciate the Moment

An attentive Virgo knows only some meals can have a pristine presentation or fancy location. They are grateful for your efforts and will always focus on communication while eating (you may have to warm portions up as chatting ensues).

Keynotes of a Virgo's Diet

Virgos are not people who go to "all you can eat" places. They prefer small portions. Some components you can select in cooking for your Virgo include

- Apricots
- Bay
- Brown rice
- Caraway
- Cauliflower
- Cheese
- Chickpeas
- Dill
- Eggs
- Fruit juice
- Grains
- Green tea
- Greens
- Lean meat
- Lemon
- Oats
- Oranges
- Peas
- Potatoes
- Sprouts
- Sunflower seeds
- Tomato
- Tuna
- Wheat bread
- Yogurt

What to Avoid

- Chocolate
- Coffee
- Cold drinks
- Fried food
- Gravy
- Hot spices
- Oily food
- Processed food
- Red meat
- Sauces
- Sugary foods

SUGGESTIONS

BREAKFAST Popovers with homemade jelly and butter

LUNCH Grilled corn salad

DINNER Meatloaf with sauce

DESSERT Chocolate orange truffles

SNACK Stuffed figs

SUNWISE GREEK ROULADE

Energetic Essence: This recipe is ideal for those walking through a doorway. The feta cheese offers a "fresh slice" of life. Spinach represents manifestation, and sun-dried tomatoes have condensed energy for stepping into a new phase of life.

Ingredients

1½ lbs flank steak

2 cups tomato-basil feta
  cheese crumbles

½ cup sun-dried tomatoes, chopped

½ cup red onion, chopped fine

3 cups baby spinach (not frozen)

Flour (for sprinkling)

½ tsp sea salt

½ tsp large grind black pepper

2 tbsps olive oil

1 cup beef bone broth

1½ tbsps Worcestershire sauce

⅓ cup red wine

Egg noodles (optional)

Instructions

1. Place plastic wrap on top of the meat.

2. Pound it with a meat mallet until it reaches ½-inch thick (this also serves to tenderize the meat).

3. Layer the cheese, tomatoes, onions, and spinach equally on the meat, leaving 1 inch at the border.

HOMEMADE SUN-DRIED TOMATOES

Dehydration is the key to sun-dried tomatoes. Without their natural moisture, their flavor increases. They are tangy, chewy, and sweet. Sun-dried tomatoes are great additions to pasta and salad, and you can easily make your own!

If you want sun-dried tomatoes quickly, begin with tiny cherry tomatoes. You'll want lots of them. Twenty pounds of tomatoes make 2 cups of sun-dried tomatoes. That's a whole lot of tomatoes!

Next, rinse the tomatoes, pat dry, and slice them in half. Remove the seeds and juice. Line a cookie tray with parchment paper. Add flavor by placing them in a bowl with just a hint of olive oil, sea salt, basil, and oregano (you can just use salt if you wish).

Set the oven to 250°F. Cook the tomatoes for 2.5 hours, flip them, then cook for another 2 hours. If you feel they're not dry enough, leave them longer, flipping again for even cooking. Cool completely before transferring into a jar with garlic cloves and other desired herbs, cover with olive oil, and secure the lid.

SUNWISE GREEK ROULADE

∽ CONTINUED ∽

4. Start rolling the meat from the long side near you (like a jelly roll).

5. Tie the roll with butcher's string every 2 inches.

6. Sprinkle all sides with flour, salt, and pepper.

7. Fire up a large skillet with oil (medium heat).

8. Place the roulade inside, browning on all sides.

9. Transfer into a slow cooker.

10. Mix the broth, Worcestershire, and wine, placing them in with the meat.

11. Cook on low for 7 hours (meat will be tender).

12. Remove the roulade to sit for 10 minutes.

13. In the meanwhile, put the juices in a saucepan and bring them to a boil. You can add cornstarch if you want the au jus thickened.

14. If you want egg noodles, prepare them now.

15. Cut slices of the roulade to about 2 inches each, laying them on the plate with a douse of the gravy.

Capricorn: December 22–January 19

The inherent beauty of Capricorns is they keep everything velveteen rabbit real. You never have to second-guess them. They are reliable truth-tellers. Caution: When you ask for an opinion, you will get it without a buffer. When Capricorn takes on a project, it always reflects their standards and values. After all, Saturn rules Capricorn, the planet of responsibility and hard work.

The sensual aspect of the Sea Goat engages the Kitchen Witch. You can make them a fantastic meal, and they will appreciate every bite. Their sensuality pours over into a sophisticated wardrobe, always appointed correctly.

Mission: Tradition

If Capricorn had a motto, it would be, "Work hard, play hard." They feel this is a reasonable approach to life. Sea Goats have honed-in focus, so they often get what they want. There's no lack of motivation here.

People born under this sign strive to be self-reliant in every way, often creating a means of being their own boss. If impossible, they will use their wits to find a strong circle of people supporting the Sea Goat's long-term goals, which isn't as difficult as it might seem. Capricorn has a propensity for being able to size up a person at first sight.

Capricorns will sometimes seem risky, but they have calculated the potential outcomes long beforehand. Overall, if you want to enjoy the company of someone who is "drama-free," honest, and sensitive, the Sea Goat is perfect. If you have grand ideas, Capricorn will help you review them, adjust them, and then move things forward.

> ## DOES THE SEA GOAT COOK?
> Capricorns don't just cook; they like to teach people how to cook. Their kitchen feels like an earlier era and focuses on one-culture items. The meal plans are those they learned at the stove with family. The Sea Goat strives for perfection in their healthy, mouthwatering fare.
>
> Cooking is a coping mechanism when a Capricorn becomes stressed out. People need to eat. Food is practical. It's an ideal relaxing activity.

Don't Be Late for Your Date!

Capricorns work best with a consistent structure. Following schedules to the minute is imperative. Schedules and punctuality are part of respect, and Capricorn always arrives 10 minutes early. Being late means something went terribly wrong. Besides, tardiness for a meal is an insult to the host.

Once ensconced in the occasion, the Sea Goat moves slowly, taking in every bit of ambiance and enjoying flavors to the fullest.

Meat and Potatoes, Please

Food-wise, Capricorns love the edibles with which they grew up. It provides comfort. While cooking simpler recipes might disappoint a "foodie," Capricorn appreciates your efforts. Look for hearty and healthy ingredients. Treat them to:

- Apple pie
- Butter-basted carrots and cabbage
- Cottage cheese with mandarin oranges
- Spinach salad with strawberries
- Traditionally cooked salmon with garlic and lemon

Keynotes of a Capricorn's Diet

Capricorns are not frilly people. Nonetheless, they will not turn down a luscious lobster occasionally. Some components of Capricorn fare include

- Apple
- Cinnamon
- Coriander
- Corn
- Cumin
- Dragon fruit
- Eggs
- Fennel
- Ginger
- Lemon
- Lentil
- Marjoram
- Molasses
- Oysters
- Potatoes
- Sage
- Salmon
- Tofu
- White pepper
- Whole wheat

What to Avoid

- Bread
- Chocolate
- Heavy food
- High salt
- Legumes
- Spicy food

SUGGESTIONS

BREAKFAST Sweet potato pancakes (use real maple syrup)

LUNCH Stuffed pita with Gouda, sprouts, cucumber slices, and ranch dressing

DINNER Chickpea ham soup with buttered kaiser rolls

DESSERT Crème brûlée

SNACK Tempura pickles or stuffed figs

TIPS ON TEMPURA

Tempura batter is light and crispy. You can use it for deep-frying shrimp, sweet potatoes, chicken fingers, fish, broccoli, mushrooms, and eggplant, just to name a few. It's simple to make, and you can have a little fun with it.

Begin by heating your fryer to 350°F. You want it ready when you finish the batter. Use 1⅔ cups of flour, 1½ cups of cornstarch, and 2 cups of ice-cold club soda. Whisk the ingredients and dip your items in it. Let excess drip off. Slowly lower the battered item into the oil. You can fry more than one at a time but don't overcrowd them. Fry until it's light brown. Cool on a wire rack.

The fun part? Use beer instead of club soda.

~ **FACTOID** The word *brûlée* comes from the French, meaning "burned."[2] In sweet dishes, *brûlée* begins by adding a thin layer of superfine sugar (turbinado sugar) or brown sugar on top. Next, the sugar meets a flame, such as a kitchen torch. It melts, then cools, and it cracks when you take your first bite.

Whimsical Vanilla Butter Snowballs

Energetic Essence: To fulfill the Capricorn love of customs, butter cream has been around since the early 1900s.[3] I discovered when you shape it and either refrigerate or freeze it, you end up with a decadent treat, tasting like rich vanilla ice cream. Vanilla in this recipe represents the warmth and caring between us (with just enough shenanigans to keep things interesting).

Ingredients

1 cup unsalted butter, softened
3 cups confectioner's sugar, sifted

2 tsps vanilla extract
¼ tsp almond extract
1 tbsp heavy cream
Shredded coconut

CONFECTIONER'S SUGAR VS. POWDERED SUGAR

Confectioner's sugar appeared in the 17th century. Because refined sugar varied in texture, bakers separated small crystals from the large ones. Confectioner's sugar deftly includes cornstarch to keep it from sticking together. In an interesting twist, the cornstarch helps the sugar adhere to baked goods.[4]

Powdered sugar has no cornstarch. Instead, it's processed several times until it becomes a fine powder. There are different levels of refinement for powdered sugar. If you look at a number on sugar product labels, it tells you the extent of milling. The most common powdered sugar receives six turns through the process. There are finer powdered sugars (like 10x),[5] but they are difficult to find.

Instructions

1. In a large mixing bowl, beat the butter with half of the confectioner's sugar until thoroughly mixed.
2. Slowly add the remaining confectioner's sugar.
3. Continue beating.
4. Add the vanilla and almond extracts.
5. Begin adding the heavy cream.
6. Add a little more sugar for a thicker frosting.
7. Continue beating for 2 minutes.
8. Chill in the refrigerator until you can easily shape it with your hands.
9. Make 12 balls, rolling them in coconut.
10. Transfer to a cookie pan lined with parchment paper.
11. Place in the freezer.
12. Once set, you can store them in a food storage bag so you can take out what you want, when you want.

Endnotes

1. Anthony Robbins, "Empowering Quotes from Tony Robbins," accessed September 12, 2023, https://www.tonyrobbins.com/tony-robbins-quotes.

2. Vicki Hayman, "Impressive Crème Brûlée," University of Wyoming Extension, accessed September 12, 2023, https://uwyoextension.org /uwnutrition/newsletters/impressive-creme-brulee/.

3. True Treats, "The History of the Illustrious Butter Cream," True Treats Historic Candy, accessed September 22, 1923, https://truetreatscandy .com/the-history-of-the-illustrious-buttercreams/.

4. The Sugar Association, "Types of Sugar: A Crash Course on the Many Types of Sugar," accessed September 12, 2023, https://www.sugar.org /sugar/types/.

5. Lynn Oliver, "Confectioner's Sugar," Food Timeline, accessed September 12, 2023, https://www.foodtimeline.org/foodcandy.html#powdered.

chapter eleven
cooking for star signs: air

The three air signs are Gemini, Libra, and Aquarius, and they're the thinkers, communicators, and doers of the zodiac. They analyze, synthesize, and probe. They breeze through life, never stopping to catch their breath. They have a "live and let live" mentality, and their intelligence helps them make decisions easily.
—LISA STARDUST[1]

Go outside when the breeze is gently flowing or just after a rainstorm. Take a deep breath. It's sublimely refreshing. Air is indeed the breath of life.

Individuals born under air signs (Gemini, Libra, Aquarius) are an independent lot. Don't try to tie them down. If they wish to be "settled," it will definitely be on their terms. Keynotes in the air personality include adventure, curiosity, keen-mindedness, and liberation.

To some, they seem flighty, but the air is elusive and intangible. People born under this sign innately know they can do much without being seen.

Sometimes air-born people are challenging to understand. They dig deep into mounds of research while their mind wanders into incredible places unsuitable for a layperson. Their projects are ever evolving. Whatever process they begin will keep breezing along until they reveal the results, which can border on genius.

Now, that doesn't mean air signs are boring and never leave their desk. Anything but. They have a cutting wit and can talk to nearly anyone. If you want a long, detailed conversation, find an air sign. Prepare. They think and talk quickly. If you have a question, gently interrupt them for more detail. These traits make air signs perfect lawyers, public speakers, comedians, doctors, and writers. In their spare time, you'll find air signs tinkering with customizing toys, restoring old cars, whittling, candle making, leather working, and building models.

The one thing air signs must watch for is getting too caught up in thought. You start at ten a.m., and suddenly it's five p.m. You don't recall if anyone passed by or said anything to you. During this time, you'll likely overthink something pretty straightforward. Surround yourself with people who can spot this habit and bring you back to the present.

If there is one word summing up the air signs' needs, it's *stimulation*. They love a challenge at work and having a partner who can keep up with all their motivation.

Air signs can be exhausting, particularly as children. There are never enough puzzles, and they are always on the move.

Building Vibrational Signatures for the Air Element

Color Palette

The color palette for air signs is typically light to the point of being ambiguous.

WHITE White embodies much of the air element's personality. It celebrates all the colors of the spectrum. White is virtuous, fair-minded, hopeful, and optimistic, and it emits sound judgment. It is a blank slate for someone to write about their future. In New Age philosophy, white light describes protective and even divine energy. White amplifies the energies with which a person is working.

WISPY PASTEL Pastels are bright but less saturated, naturally creating a soothing vibe. Each color—pale pink, light blue, creamy green, soft yellow, muted lilac, and peach (just to name a few)—has its own vibrational imprint based on the primary hue. If you had a dimmer switch, pastels would take things down a notch. For example, instead of intensely energetic yellow, pastel yellow becomes happy and slower paced.

YELLOW Yellow is the sun in splendor. It's joyful and incredibly spirited. It's an excellent color, in moderation, for people with depression. Yellow helps release creative blockage, supports a clear perception, and improves one's studying focus. Like these signs, this hue wants to shine on every dark corner and bring things into the light.

Crystals

Air crystals spark ingenuity, particularly in presenting your side of things. These stones help people in transition to remain focused on the positives, allaying fear.

BLUE LACE AGATE This crystal is serene and improves a person's ability to speak truthfully. Blue lace agate is a fantastic ally for those looking inward for more authenticity and clarity.

CITRINE Citrine boosts self-confidence and motivation. It empowers your spirit, stimulates creativity, and promotes manifestation. Intent becomes a reality.

CLEAR QUARTZ The transparent nature of clear quartz symbolizes spiritual manifestation. Energetically, it's an amplifier for intent and facilitation. Clear quartz is an ideal stone for meditation and healing.

FLUORITE Fluorite is exceptional for air signs as it helps organize a chatty mind. For students, it supports enhanced mental growth. It often bears the name "genius stone" for this reason.

TANZANITE This high-vibration crystal transforms old, unhealthy patterns so you can move forward with a strong sense of purpose. Tanzanite opens the crown chakra, allowing for enhanced psychic abilities.

YELLOW JASPER Yellow Jasper is a warm stone known for its nurturing nature. When times are difficult, it comforts and helps allay stress. It improves the head-heart balance for a sense of calm.

Decorations

Options include images of birds, dragons, the sky, or clouds in the dining area. A ceiling fan certainly represents the air element. At the doorway into your home, place some pleasant chimes. In other areas of the house, you can use incense (or any aromatic compound), bells, attractive hand fans (perhaps antique), and streamers to represent air.

Drinks

- Banana almond milk
- Beer (hops)
- Berry smoothies
- Dandelion juice
- Dark and stormy
- Frozen daiquiri
- Grapefruit tonic
- Lavender gin fizz
- Nutty irishman
- Pinot grigio
- Rose water
- Shiraz

Food Presentation

Anything feeling fresh and calm. Not overcluttered, with hints of romance and nostalgia, perhaps some flower petals on the table. Air people enjoy interactive meals, such as "make your own," where you provide components, and they can assemble what they wish.

Flowers

Ahhh, there's nothing like petal power!

- Acacia
- Air plants
- Anemone
- Chamomile
- Cottonwood
- Dandelion
- Ferns (intermixed)
- Lavender

Incense

The air element embodies scents with aromatic appeal. They travel on the winds with a hint of magic.

- ∿ Bergamot
- ∿ Lavender
- ∿ Lemongrass
- ∿ Peppermint
- ∿ Sage
- ∿ Sandalwood
- ∿ Spruce

Lighting

If you were to go to several people born under air element signs, you might well find at least one unique lighting piece hanging from the ceiling (in the air!). They like the sparkle too. Other features include wall sconces, adjustable lighting fixtures, and a disco ball if you feel retro.

Music

Music for the air element includes instruments in the "air" portion of an orchestra. Think about flute, saxophone, tuba, and other woodwinds. There is a reflective, thoughtful element to air music and a sense of liberation, too.

ABBA Chiquita

ALEXANDER BORODIN Symphony No. 2 in B Minor—Allegro

BACKSTREET BOYS I Want It that Way

BETTE MIDLER Wind Beneath My Wings

BOLLYWOOD Any dance music

BOB SEGER Against the Wind

DUA LIPA Physical

ELTON JOHN Candle in the Wind; Your Song

CHRISTOPHER CROSS Ride Like the Wind

GEORGES ENESCU Romanian Rhapsody No. 1

FLUTE MEDITATION MUSIC The Secret of Peace

HOLST "The Planets" Suite, Op. 32—Venus

KANSAS Dust in the Wind

MOGLI Wanderer

PETER, PAUL, AND MARY Blowing in the Wind

SAM COOKE They Call the Wind Maria

SANTANA Song of the Wind

SEALS AND CROFT Summer Breeze

Tidiness

The wind is erratic. It can make quite a mess with anything light lying on the ground. Similarly, those born under an air element sign won't fixate on a few things askew in a room.

Gemini: May 21–June 20

Of Two Minds

Gemini is a mutable sign, and with two minds in one body, it makes perfect sense. A Gemini is constantly changing and may contradict itself within minutes. If you've discussed a menu, clarify it beforehand. Even then, they may switch. Hmm...maybe surprise them?

Their love of banter makes them adept table companions, no matter the occasion. Being ruled by Mercury, the planet of communication, this trait is very prominent. Geminis know how to make people around them feel comfortable, often through light-hearted wit.

To use an old saying, Gemini "can charm the pants off anyone." In ancient times, they may well have been alchemists, searching for gold through transmutation. Today, Geminis do well in jobs that involve sales and entertainment and spearheading transformational projects. If they can improve something, they will.

Tweaking comes with cooking too. Don't be surprised if your Twins sneak into the kitchen wanting to fuss with your recipe. How much "hands-on" time you offer is up to you. Their enthusiasm might be contagious, but it could also ruin a dish.

At the table, Gemini talks better than they listen, not to be rude but because their minds move at 100 mph, zigging and zagging between topics. You may have to redirect them to the discussion's keynote. And by all means, do NOT let a Gemini bring their cell phone to dinner. They will constantly check it and write reminder notes. Gemini loves communicating with their hands, and typing (even on a cell phone) falls under that umbrella.

Gemini Light Grazing

Trying to feed your Gemini is an endeavor requiring a deft hand. You are dealing with two personalities. Hot vs. cold, sweet vs. savory. If there is one sign appreciative of umami, it's Gemini.

One thing you know for sure is they love to nibble. Respond by leaving some handy snacks available to them. You can make a variety of one item and wrap the options individually. For example, create a mayo, garlic, onion, and celery base. Take pieces of bread and cut off the edges. Now, mix a little flaked ham with some of the dressing and some hard-boiled eggs with the rest. Ham and egg salad finger sandwiches on the go!

The Gemini Palate

Think diversity when feeding your Gemini. Ask them about family meals they loved. The trick is your Gemini isn't a real sit-down eater. Keep things tidy. Ever the student, Geminis also appreciate historical fare such as:

- Goulash (ninth century)[2]
- Couscous (thirteenth century)[3]
- Wassail (fifteenth century)[4]
- Italian Wedding Soup (fifteenth–sixteenth century)[5]

FOCUS: FINGER SANDWICHES

Finger sandwiches bear another name, tea sandwiches, because they were part of many afternoon teas. It kept hungry people from pestering the cook before dinner. The best finger sandwiches should be a three-bite culinary perfection. The shape is usually rectangular or triangular, made from white bread with the edges removed. Some people lightly toast the bread with butter, so the ingredients don't make for a mushy mouthful. Besides white bread, sourdough, rye, and pumpernickel are all favorites. As for fillings? Cream cheese with sliced cucumber, olive tapenade, watercress, or smoked salmon all fill the bill.

DO THE TWINS COOK?

Your Gemini loves it when they can cook for you, friends, or their family. Recipes are like a coloring book for this sign, and they never stay inside the lines. How much onion powder, you ask? They don't have any idea, but the food tastes terrific.

Twin Tenor

You'll find those born under this sign appreciate low-key places. They want to converse, not shout. With all the talking, you may think your Gemini isn't paying attention to the food. Don't worry; one of them will remember all the details and rave about it later.

Keynotes of a Gemini's Diet

The Twins eat for two, loving hearty portions of beef, lobster, and eggs. Here are some other components to consider in your menu planning:

- Apricot
- Broccoli
- Celery seed
- Cola
- Ginger
- Grape juice
- Green beans
- Hazelnuts
- Oats
- Oranges
- Parsley
- Pomegranate
- Sesame
- Spinach
- Tomatoes

What to Avoid

- Alcohol
- Beets
- Carrots
- Coffee
- Flavorless food
- High-carb foods
- Junk food
- Potatoes

SUGGESTIONS

BREAKFAST A fresh, in-season fruit salad

LUNCH Shrimp taco bowl

DINNER Garlic linguine with chicken meatballs and spinach

DESSERT Chocolate-cherry muffins, fruity pie, citrus sorbet

SNACK Relish tray with crispy pickles, olives, cheese cubes, carrot sticks, cherry tomatoes, etc.

Oat-Hazelnut Creativity Cookies

Energetic Essence: The hazelnut tree is one of inspiration and wisdom, especially among the Celts.[6] Oats appear in Chinese medicine to calm qi *("life force"),[7] helping Gemini's ever-restless soul.*

Ingredients

1 cup unsalted butter, room temperature

1 cup brown sugar, packed firmly

¼ cup white sugar

2 large eggs

2 tbsps vanilla extract

1 tbsp orange blossom honey

1½ cups flour

1 tsp baking soda

3 cups rolled oats

½ tsp table salt

1 cup chopped praline hazelnuts

Substitution

Vanilla: Hazelnut extract

Potential Additions

Butterscotch or chocolate chips

Instructions

1. Place the softened butter in a mixing bowl and cream it with both sugars until well integrated.

2. Add 1 egg and blend. Follow with the second egg, and blend.

3. Scrape the sides of the bowl, adding in the vanilla and honey.

4. In a separate bowl, stir the flour, baking soda, oats, and salt.

5. Using a mixer on low, slowly add the dry ingredients to the butter mixture. Make sure all the ingredients distribute evenly.

6. Hand-fold the nuts into the batter.

7. Refrigerate for 30 minutes.

8. Meanwhile, set the oven to 350°F.

9. Line a cookie sheet with parchment paper.

10. Form the cookies out of 2 tbsps batter each.

11. Space them 2 inches apart.

12. Bake for 12 minutes (the edges will be toasty brown). Don't worry, the center is supposed to be a bit shiny.

13. Cool on the sheet before removing them to a tray.

Libra: September 23–October 22

A Table for Two, Please

Those born under the sign of Libra dislike having meals alone and will often skip eating for that reason. Regarding food, Libra sees it as a glorious gesture. Bring on the pampering and leave quarrels for afterward! Touches of beauty soothe the Libra soul and always bring a smile. Even a pretty wine glass will do the trick. Alternatively, pack a luscious picnic basket and head to a pre-prepared location where nature surrounds. If you have an ornate garden, it's perfect.

It's better to tell your Libra what you're preparing rather than ask. Their natural impulse is to overthink what *everyone* will enjoy instead of sharing their preferences. While designing and serving your meal, let your Libra participate in some manner. They genuinely thrive on making people happy and creating a harmonious experience.

At the table, Libra likes to share. Be ready to take a bite off their plate, or vice versa.

CHARCUTERIE VS. ANTIPASTO

Charcuterie and antipasto have some similarities. Charcuterie comes from France and can be hot or cold, whereas antipasto comes from Italy and is only served at room temperature. Both presentations include cured meats.

Items commonly featured on a charcuterie board include crackers, cheese, fruits, nuts, olives, and crusty bread. As for antipasto, expect artichoke hearts, capers, roasted red peppers, cheese, mushrooms, bruschetta, pepperoni, and salami.

Bite-Sized Bliss

A tasting table is ideal for Libras. They enjoy the diversity and will ask you about each element you prepare, for example:

- ⁓ Charcuterie
- ⁓ Fresh antipasto plate
- ⁓ Fruit or vegetables with herbs
- ⁓ Wine and cheese pairing

Take them to a potluck and watch their eyes light up.

Symmetry Seals the Deal

Those born under the sign of the scales appreciate balance. If there's a candle on one table, another must be at the opposite end. They find mishmash decorations distracting. This goes for your food presentation, too. For example, if serving a soup with a crouton garnish, each bowl must have the same number of croutons. Yes, it's a little more trouble, but you want to focus on each other, and this is one way to keep the ambiance alive.

Keynotes of a Libra's Diet

Don't worry about HUGE flavors with Libra. They like flavors that gently mix, balance, and mingle.

∽ Asparagus	∽ Honey
∽ Brown rice	∽ Parsnip
∽ Carrots	∽ Peas
∽ Eggs	∽ Raisins
∽ Fennel	∽ Shellfish
∽ Ginger	∽ Vegetable juice

What to Avoid

∽ Alcohol	∽ Pork and beef (moderate)
∽ Carbonated beverages	∽ Refined sugar
∽ Heavily spiced foods	∽ Starchy foods
∽ High-fat foods	

SUGGESTIONS

BREAKFAST Bagel with a "shmear"

LUNCH Cranberry spinach salad

DINNER Lemon-basil shrimp over wild rice

DESSERT Honeyed figs, berries in cream, banana split

SNACK Trail mix

DOES LIBRA COOK?

If Libra cooks for you, prepare for a complete flop or the meal of a lifetime. This sign cooks through their emotions, which end up in the food. If they are upset about something, you will know from bite one. They adore any embellishments making the meal appear lovely, even if the recipe turns out lackluster.

Asian Sesame Salad with Swag

Energetic Essence: Normally made with pasta, this recipe uses cabbage instead (better for the Libra diet). Feng shui says cabbage is an emblem of wealth, while sesame brings good fortune. This dish provides gainful vibrations from hard work without sidestepping a little fun.

Ingredients: Salad

1½ cups white cabbage

1½ cups red cabbage

1½ cups napa cabbage

1 medium carrot

1 cup sugar snapped peas or raw peas

3 large green onions

⅓ cup celery

⅓ cup cucumber

½ cup toasted peanuts

1 tbsp toasted sesame seeds

Instructions: Salad

1. Thinly slice all of the cabbage and place it in a large salad bowl.

2. Julienne the carrots.

3. Chop the snap peas at an angle.

4. Dice the onions, celery, and cucumber.

5. Add the vegetables along with the nuts and seeds into the bowl.

6. Toss everything thoroughly and make the dressing.

Ingredients: Salad Dressing

4 tbsps toasted sesame oil

4 tbsps rice wine vinegar

2 tbsps wildflower honey

2 tbsps lemon juice

2 tsps freshly grated ginger

2 tsps garlic, minced

½ tbsp brown sugar

½ tsp white ground pepper

Instructions: Salad Dressing

1. Place all the ingredients in a saucepan.

2. Warm them gently, just enough to integrate the flavors.

3. Cool before serving. (Do not refrigerate. The honey will become too thick to pour.)

4. Pour over the salad, mixing as you go.

Aquarius: January 20–February 18

Food for Thought

Aquarians have a lot of mental energy. They examine every detail if they're pondering something, even food. If you make interesting dishes, they'll love discussing the components and process with you. Listen closely. They may inspire innovation in the recipe. Trendsetter, thy name is Aquarius. Of course, this can cause distraction. Keep paying attention to yourself and the recipe, too. You can always talk about the fine print and footnotes later. Hey, why not make a recipe card for your guest?

Water Bearers appreciate health-conscious appetizer choices, but the occasional "food fad" appeals to their sense of whimsy. Your food, to them, is an extension of your friendship. While they love flavors, they don't get uppity about the occasional lack of salt.

Ordinary or Extraordinary?

Homemade food makes your Aquarian delirious. It shows thoughtfulness. They appreciate the tried-and-true endeavors. A recipe from your childhood with a story makes an excellent experience for the Water Bearer who wants to know the details. The history is intriguing and makes the food taste special.

But if you're making something wholly new or odd, ask if they'd like to help. International fare from "across the pond" appeals, for example:

- ∾ Beef Wellington
- ∾ Cornish pasty
- ∾ Fish and chips
- ∾ Full breakfast fry-up
- ∾ Shepherd's pie

Aquarian Ambiance

The idea of formal affairs makes most Water Bearers cringe. They like to be comfortable when they eat. Think boho! Toss a tie-dye tablecloth out, mix and match the patterns of your napkins, and use different styles of plates and glasses. It's all FUN.

DOES AQUARIUS COOK?

Absolutely. The Water Bearer always looks for novel recipes, garden-to-table ideas, and fusion food to let their imaginations run wild. They are always three steps ahead of culinary trends and have no issue saying, "I told you so," with a whimsical wink. However, no matter what they create, there will always be some type of personal signature, such as a secret spice. The Water Bearers' motto in the kitchen is "Make it memorable." By the way, don't be afraid to offer a hand. Aquarians enjoy cooking with other people.

Keynotes of an Aquarian's Diet

When an Aquarian is deep in thought, they may reach for convenience foods with empty calories. Make efforts to have healthier options available. When reminded to eat better, they will listen because their health matters greatly to them. Food textures are enticing.

- Almonds
- Carrots
- Figs
- Five-spice blend
- Garlic
- Ginger
- Mustard seed
- Ocean fish
- Oranges
- Pears
- Protein smoothies
- Radishes
- Rice
- Sage
- Tofu (fried)
- Turnip
- Walnuts
- Yogurt

What to Avoid
- Bagels
- Carbonated beverages
- Coffee
- Fast food
- High-fat foods
- Refined sugar

SUGGESTIONS

BREAKFAST Honey nut granola

LUNCH Quinoa salad with lemon

DINNER Tuna steak wild rice and pine nuts

DESSERT Nut tarts, croquembouche, brown butter cookies

SNACK Vegetable tray with dips

TRANQUIL TEATIME

Energetic Essence: Since caffeine isn't a great option for the Aquarian, try having a relaxing teatime using decaffeinated tea. Tea has a culture filled with soothing energy, perfect for conversing (leave the cell phone elsewhere).

Ingredients

Water (8 oz per person)

Decaffeinated Earl Grey tea bags

Milk or cream (optional)

Sweetener (optional; sugar, honey, agave, maple syrup, artificial sweeteners)

Lemon wedges (optional)

Instructions

1. Boil the water to 200°F.

2. As the water comes up to temperature, set out creamers, sweeteners, and snacks such as scones, finger sandwiches, and biscuits with honey butter.

3. Place one tea bag in each cup.

4. Fill the cup, leaving some space at the top to avoid spilling.

5. Give the tea a good stir and wait 4 minutes (longer if you like strong tea).

6. Remove the tea bag. (DO NOT SQUEEZE IT. Your cup will be bitter.)

7. Your guests can then add what they wish to their cups.

TEATIME ETIQUETTE AND TIPS

For a traditional British-style teatime, the host or hostess should always pour the first cup. You raise the saucer with one hand and pour with the other. No pinky finger lifting allowed, and no adding sugar cubes with your fingers.[8]

If using loose-leaf tea, you'll need about ½ tbsp per cup. Make sure your water is not scalding hot. It can burn the tea. Remove the slice of lemon before drinking.

Stick to Your Roots Soup

Energetic Essence: The three root vegetables in this blend are sweet potatoes, parsnip, and carrots. In some areas of the world, sweet potato represents true peace of mind and a state of prayerful living. Carrots offer clarity. Parsnips support a healthy brain and symbolize grace.

Ingredients

¼ cup extra virgin olive oil

2 cups white onion, chopped

Freshly ground black pepper

Kosher salt

4 cloves garlic, chopped fine

1 tsp curry powder

1 tsp chipotle powder

2 large sweet potatoes (or yams)

2 large carrots

1 parsnip

8 cups vegetable stock

Green onion and croutons (garnish)

GROUNDING AN AIR SIGN

Sometimes those born under the air sign need to come to earth and put foundations under their concepts and contrivances. The best approach is using root vegetables (you can't get much more grounded!).

Instructions

1. Pull out a stockpot and heat the olive oil.

2. Add the onions and season with pepper and salt to your taste.

3. Stir in garlic, curry, and chipotle when the onions are translucent. Mix for 1 minute.

4. Peel and chop the sweet potatoes, carrots, and parsnip.

5. Pour in the stock and add the vegetables. Cook for 25 minutes (you want the vegetables fork-tender).

6. Take one-half of the mixture and purée it with an immersion blender, and then mix it back into the pot.

7. Serve hot topped with green onion and croutons.

HOMEMADE CROUTONS

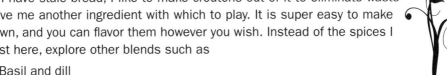

When I have stale bread, I like to make croutons out of it to eliminate waste and give me another ingredient with which to play. It is super easy to make your own, and you can flavor them however you wish. Instead of the spices I suggest here, explore other blends such as

- ～ Basil and dill
- ～ Paprika, chipotle, and onion
- ～ Parmesan, garlic, and parsley
- ～ Parsley, sage, and rosemary

If you don't feel like mixing spices, try using powdered soup or salad dressing mixes.

Preheat your oven to 375°F. Prepare a cookie sheet with parchment paper.

This recipe begins with one loaf of stale bread. Use white, wheat, sourdough, pumpernickel...whatever you enjoy. Cut the bread into ¾-inch cubes (smaller if you like a tidy bite). Squares represent the four corners of creation and earthiness, perfect for this soup's intended goal.

Mix ¼ cup olive oil or melted butter with 2 tbsps Italian seasoning, 2 tsps garlic powder, 1 tsp onion powder, ¾ tsp salt, and ½ tsp pepper. Slowly pour this over the cubes while stirring so they coat evenly.

Spread the croutons over the parchment paper evenly and put them in the oven. After about 10 minutes, turn them for even browning. They're ready in about 10 more minutes. Cool completely. Use a food storage bag or container to house them until you can use them. Because they are dry, you can freeze them for about two months.

Croutons have many uses, including as a substitute for bread in French onion soup, as a thickener for chowder, broken up fine for meatloaf, as stuffing, as a casserole binder, and as a crumbled topper for scrambled eggs, and that only scratches the surface.

Endnotes

1. Lisa Stardust, "All About Air Signs, the Zodiac's Social Smarties," *Cosmopolitan*, January 23, 2023, https://www.cosmopolitan.com/lifestyle/a33314375/air-signs-astrology/.

2. Britannica, the editors, "Goulash," *Encyclopedia Britannica*, September, 15, 2022, https://www.britannica.com/topic/goulash.

3. Charles Perry, "Couscous and Its Cousins," *Oxford Symposium on Food and Cookery 1989*, Prospect Books, accessed September 22, 2023, https://www.google.com/books/edition/Oxford_Symposium_on_Food_Cookery_1989/I15eJt6U3gMC.

4. Beth McKibben, "The Centuries-Old History of Wassail," Tales of the Cocktail Foundation, November 30, 2015, https://talesofthecocktail.org/history/history-wassail-punch/.

5. Ian Macallen, "The Marriage of Meat and Leafy Greens: the History of Italian Wedding Soup," America.Domani, December 29, 2022, https://americadomani.com/the-marriage-of-meat-and-leafy-greens-the-history-of-italian-wedding-soup/.

6. Paul Kendall, "Hazel Mystery and Folklore," Trees for Life, accessed September 22, 2023, https://treesforlife.org.uk/into-the-forest/trees-plants-animals/trees/hazel/hazel-mythology-and-folklore/.

7. Dr. SK Mao, "Oats," Foods Natural Health Dictionary, accessed September 23, 2023, https://askdrmao.com/natural-health-dictionary/oats/index.html.

8. Erika Robertson, "25 Fascinating Tea Etiquette Rules You Need to Know," *Teabloom*, August 27, 2022, https://www.teabloom.com/blog/25-fascinating-tea-etiquette-rules-you-need-to-know/.

chapter twelve
cooking for star signs: fire

Adventure is worthwhile in itself.
—AMELIA EARHART [1]

Moving on to hot-hot-hot fire signs (Aries, Leo, Sagittarius), we see expansive passion and thirst for spirituality. Fire signs see where they are going and focus on what they want. Exploration is life's blood for these signs. They will be the eternal students in life's classroom.

People born under a fire sign want to know the internal workings of just about anything. This makes it fun to cook for them. If you have a new kitchen gadget, spice, or culinary approach, share it! Watch the excitement grow.

Fire signs are typically not loners. They like having companions who lift them up and who they can likewise encourage. Fiery folk do, however, like to wander, following where their curiosity leads them. Sometimes it's hard to develop long-term relationships. If you want to pack up a camping kitchen and go with them, you will make your fire sign ecstatic, indeed. The more the merrier in a fire sign's book. They are always inspiring others to get involved in some unexpected shenanigans.

Fire signs are brash yet charming, unreliable but filled with endless enthusiasm, and chaotic but often brilliant. These are tell-it-like-it-is folk. If you want an honest opinion about a new recipe, ask a fire sign. Just prepare. They don't gild the lily.

In the proverbial game of life, fire signs are doers. Sitting on the sidelines drives them crazy. As a result, these individuals are often trendsetters, blazing a trail for highly original and ingenious thoughts and actions. If there's a leap of faith to be made, you can count on a fire sign to be first in line to volunteer. Fire-born people always feel ready for anything.

Of course, a fire sign can get unruly and hot under the collar. In such cases, try to redirect the energy toward something else. If you have something with which they can help at a gathering, express how much it would mean for them to handle it. The project gives a fire sign time to cool off and reconsider the intensity of their reaction. And if not, try ice cream.

Building Vibrational Signatures for the Fire Element

Color Palette

If you look into a fire, you'll quickly see the color palette for the fire element emerging.

GOLD The color of good fortune, generosity, and power. Gold celebrates the illuminating nature of fire and how light manifests in positive ways, including wealth and status.

ORANGE Orange is an attention-grabbing hue perfect for the fire sign on the go. Orange radiates optimism, determination, encouragement, stimulation, positivity, and the excitement fire-born people naturally exude. Use touches of orange in your decor when you're preparing a healthy meal.

RED Red is where the passion and sexuality of the fire signs come out prominently. It's a color indicative of the courage a fire-born person has burning within.

WHITE The color of honesty, a trait common to fire signs. It represents the clarity and perfection these individuals try to achieve throughout their lives. White evokes fresh ideas.

YELLOW Yellow is warm, welcoming, and filled with hospitality. It's both optimistic and energetic. Like fire signs, yellow is confident and curious. Using yellow at the dining table makes for cheerfulness.

Crystals

Fire crystals make excellent amulets, burning away any negativity in your presence. If you're dragging your feet, carry one for improved energy.

AMBER Amber is a protective stone, especially in matters of love and passion. It attracts good fortune, improves personal confidence, and keeps your mind clear.

BOTSWANA AGATE When you think of cozy warmth, that's Botswana agate. It diminishes a person's dark thoughts and anxiety over difficulties.

CARNELIAN Carnelian is vibrant, manifesting courage, leadership, and motivation. Ancient warriors might well wear one for the power to overcome their foes. On the days when a fire sign might not feel quite so sparky, carnelian stimulates confidence, eloquence, and inventiveness. Carnelian is a lucky stone, too.

FIRE AGATE True to its name, the fire agate looks like it burns from within with the light of a thousand stars. The flashes of green and gold create a spiritual vibration, bringing joy to the gods of fire. When pleased, the Divine offers guidance on an important forthcoming action.

GARNET Garnet is an emotional stone. It symbolizes the feelings we have just beneath the surface. Carrying garnet helps keep your mood in check before it bubbles out of control. Garnets act as healers for any period of transformation in which someone purges a harmful behavior. It's useful for grounding while meditating and accessing the energies of endurance and strength. And, true to the fire element, garnet intensifies passion.

LAVA STONE These literally come from volcanic activity, making them unique in the world of sacred stones. All that energy sparks an unquenchable fire in a person's soul. When facing challenges, you could not ask for a better crystal ally. If lava stone had a mantra, it would be "seek to find." You can discern the truth using this gemstone, as long as you put forth effort.

RUBY Wake up in the morning and face sunward. It is a new day and a new opportunity to reach goals. This is the power of a ruby. It boosts virtue by calming anger and negativity. Ruby makes some serious sparks in the bedroom.

SUNSTONE The fire of the sun burns in this crystal, making it vibrant, warm, and resilient. It is an excellent choice for people reclaiming their power and place. It is nearly impossible to be sad while carrying or wearing sunstone. Your mind strengthens as well as your body, and inspiration renews itself. Sunstones bring luck as a talisman for success. It will help you remain connected to the wisdom you've gained in all your lifetimes.

Decorations

Candles are an obvious choice for fire decorations, as are incense burners. You can look for tablecloths or napkins with zigzag patterns representing fire. If you're cooking outdoors, the open fire pit or grill becomes the fire element at center stage.

Drinks

- Bloody Mary
- Cinnamon cider
- Flaming margarita
- Ginger beer
- Jalapeño mule mocktail
- Nevada Reaper soda
- Spiced honey punch
- Sweet heat beer
- Syrah
- Turmeric milk
- Whiskey sour

Food Presentation

A small fondue with hot cheese makes a fantastic appetizer and interactive dish. Any type of fondue recipe does the trick.

Flowers

Many of these selections visually look like fire.

- Angelica
- Blaze orange Asiatic lily
- Bloodflowers
- Calendula
- Carnation
- Dutch Carnival dahlia
- Eucalyptus leaves (in the centerpiece)
- Fire lily
- Fire poppy
- Larkspur
- Marigold
- Orange cosmos
- Red hibiscus
- Red tulips
- Sunflower

Incense

- Almond
- Amber
- Cedar
- Cinnamon
- Frankincense
- Geranium
- Ginger
- Neroli
- Sandalwood

Lighting

Try lava lamps placed around the room. If you are outdoors, get paper lanterns in a variety of colors. Depending on the mood, the fire element's lighting can blaze bright or low and mellow.

Music

Fire music expresses deep emotions and sensual rhythms. It can sometimes be whimsical and often features brass instruments.

ABBA Lay All Your Love On Me

ADELE Set Fire to the Rain

ALICIA KEYS Fallin'

ANDREWS SISTERS Boogie Woogie Bugle Boy

BRUCE SPRINGSTEEN I'm on Fire

DESTINY'S CHILD Say My Name

EDWARD ELGAR Variations on an Original Theme (Enigma) Op 36

FLEETWOOD MAC Dreams

JERRY LEE LEWIS Great Balls of Fire

PINK Just Like Fire

RALPH VAUGHAN WILLIAMS Fantasia on Greensleeves

SCHUBERT Symphony No. 8 in B Minor, D. 759 Unvollendete

SHANIA TWAIN That Don't Impress Me Much

THE DOORS Light My Fire

YANNI From the Vault

Tidiness

Always shine for your fire sign at the start of dinner service. They do value tidiness, but the actual deep-down cleanup can wait until morning.

Aries the Ram: March 21–April 19

No Fuss, No Muss

Aries is the leader of the pack—the first sign of the zodiac and its story. In some ways, Aries-born people are a bit like the Fool card of the tarot. They're optimistic and trust easily. They set their sights on a new adventure all the time. Anything that appears as a good choice for upward mobility catches the Ram's eye quickly. It is in the Ram's nature to work constantly toward the best version of themselves, not just at their jobs but in relationships, too.

Aries are born leaders who truly believe fortune favors the bold. When they attend your dinner or event, they'll often fall into a managerial role, fixing tableware and making strong suggestions on your ingredients. You don't have to accept the idea, but please acknowledge it. This sign has an excellent track record for initiating something amazing.

People born under this sign can sometimes act impulsively and rarely change their minds once in action. Within, the fire of *joie de vivre* burns intensely. Trying to match the Aries' enthusiasm is a tough challenge.

Sitting down for dinner? Good luck. The Ram is on the go and needs edibles matching its fidgety nature. When you invite them, this is a perfect moment for tasting stations. Have one pairing wine with cheese and another area with types of hummuses to try, for example. This way, your Aries can revel in the food but also keep moving. You do not have to be frilly with Aries. They have a strong appetite and are more concerned with flavor and fellowship.

> ∼ **TIP** Make sure your food is ready on time. Aries
> have a habit of being very impatient.

Spices Win the Day

Speaking of flavors, spicy, multidimensional food wins. Running out of hot sauce never happens in the Ram's home. Seriously, they'll stop everything and go get some.

∼ Asian: hot and sour

∼ Chiles rellenos

∼ Noodles with Malaysian Sambal sauce

∼ Ragin' Cajun

∼ Smoky hot sauce barbecue

∼ Thai green curry

While you may be accustomed to your Aries talking non-stop, food changes the dynamic. Their focus is on the flavor profiles presented.

> ### DOES THE RAM COOK?
> Rams can learn to cook, but baking isn't the best option. They are results-oriented, so rushing a recipe is a common shortcoming. When making a meal, a Ram nibbles on everything to the point of filling themselves up before dinner.

Make Meals Fun

Those born under the sign of the Ram *love* to play with their food. Give them some fortune cookies and watch their smile grow.

Keynotes of an Aries' Diet

In order to make a meal, first you have to have a handle on the best components for your hearthside magic. Options include (but are not limited to)

∼ Asparagus

∼ Black beans

∼ Cappuccino

∼ Curry

∼ Flounder

∼ Garlic

∼ Ginger

∼ Horseradish

∼ Leeks

∼ Lime

∼ Mustard seed

∼ Onions

∼ Radishes

∼ Red wine

∼ Spinach

∼ Tarragon

∼ Veal

∼ Walnuts

What to Avoid
- Alcohol
- Coffee
- Junk food
- Salt

SUGGESTIONS

BREAKFAST American style with spicy sausage and eggs

LUNCH Buffalo chicken wrap

DINNER Sriracha chicken with walnut-strawberry salad

DESSERT Chocolate-dipped fruit, very lemony tarts, tiramisu

SNACK Garlic-ginger edamame or fresh sweet potato chips

BUFFALO-STYLE CHICKEN

The idea of "buffalo" chicken, born in western New York, is firmly rooted in the chicken wing. In 1964, the owner of the Anchor Bar, Teressa Bellissimo, invented buffalo wings somewhat by whimsy. From a butcher's standpoint, chicken wings seemed useless. But one night her son's friends were hungry. She fried up the wings and tossed them in sauce, and a legend was born.[2]

The most traditional buffalo sauce is Frank's Hot Sauce with butter. Other common components include Worcestershire sauce, vinegar, cayenne, and garlic powder.

SIMPLICITY SHRIMP

Energetic Essence: Shrimp's energy signature meshes perfectly with the Aries' unfussy approach to food. The spicy elements in this dish (sriracha, ginger, chili) help fuel the Ram's ongoing energy levels, keeping the proverbial tank full.

Ingredients

1 tbsp sesame oil (plus ¼ tbsp)

1 small red onion

2 cloves garlic, minced

2 tsps fresh ginger root, minced fine

½ each red and yellow sweet peppers, sliced thin

1 cup pineapple, cubed (fresh if possible)

8 large shrimp

1 tbsp hoisin sauce

1 tbsp rice vinegar

½ tsp sriracha

Pinch brown sugar

½ cup cooked rice

¼ Fresno chili, sliced thin (garnish)

2 scallions, sliced thin (garnish)

½ fresh lemon, cut in wedges (garnish)

Substitutions

Fresno chili: Jalapeño

Hoisin: Tamari or soy sauce

Rice vinegar: White vinegar

Instructions

1. Using a small wok or skillet, heat the sesame oil over medium flame.

2. Sauté the onion to crunchy-tender and move into a stovetop pan.

3. Sauté the garlic and ginger until fragrant. Transfer to the pan with the onions.

4. Sauté the peppers until they get a slight brown edge. Transfer into the pan as well.

5. Caramelize the pineapple, adding it to the rest of the mixture (about 5 minutes).

6. Cook the shrimp until opaque. Set aside with the rest of the fried ingredients.

7. In a saucepan, simmer the hoisin, vinegar, sriracha, and sugar for 2 minutes (make sure the sugar dissolves). Turn off the heat.

8. Turn up the temperature on the wok to medium-high. Add ¼ tbsp oil. Quickly stir fry the rice.

9. Mix the rice with all the fried ingredients, then toss with the sauce.

10. Garnish with chilis, scallions, and lemon wedges.

Potential Additions

Broccoli florets (health), water chestnuts (luck), chopped celery (victory)

Pork and Green Bean Spiritual Rebirth Stir Fry

Energetic Essence: Green beans are no stranger to the world of symbolism because they are one of the first crops of the harvest. This provides green beans with energies for spiritual renewal and reawakening (making them ideal for spring celebrations and the Aries-born enthusiasm). Green beans often bear a second crop, as if to say, "Keep going." This recipe gives a nod to traditional pork and beans; I give it a 5-star rating.

Ingredients

1 lb ground pork

3 tbsps dark soy sauce

¼ tsp white pepper

¼ cup chicken stock

3½ tbsps hoisin sauce

¼–½ tsp red pepper flakes

1 tbsp rice vinegar

½ tsp cornstarch

1¾ cups toasted sesame oil

12 ozs green beans, trimmed

3 tbsps garlic, minced

¼ inch fresh ginger, peeled and grated

Substitution

Hoisin sauce: Teriyaki, oyster
    sauce, tamari sauce

Instructions

1. Put the ground pork into a small mixing bowl.

2. Add 2 tbsps of soy sauce and white pepper.

3. Mix and set aside.

4. In another bowl, mix the stock, hoisin, red pepper, rice vinegar, cornstarch, and 1 tbsp soy sauce.

5. Heat the wok until hot. Coat with sesame (or peanut) oil. Add the green beans.

6. Stir until the beans look wrinkled (about 4 minutes).

7. Remove the beans and let them drain on a paper towel.

8. Add the garlic and ginger to the wok. Once fragrant, add the pork.

9. Stir fry the pork until it's no longer pink.

10. Add the stock mixture into the wok, stirring.

11. Bring everything to a boil, watching for it to thicken.

12. Return the green beans to the wok and drizzle with a little sesame oil (and add sesame seeds if you wish).

13. When everything warms through, serve hot.

Side Dish Suggestions

Dim sum

Green salad with ginger dressing

Sesame noodles

Spring rolls

Leo: July 23–August 22

Luxurious and Lucious

If you had to sum up the Leo personality, it would be boisterous, dramatic, fierce, and expressive. When Leo enters a room, their aura arrives 10 minutes earlier. It *seems* like Leo is arrogant (and they can be), but some of this presentation is a facade for insecurity and intense sensitivity.

It is a rare occasion when you find an unmotivated Leo. Exhilaration runs in their DNA. The sun rules this astrological sign. The brightness coming from the Lion certainly illustrates the connection.

Leos are loyal and very protective of those in their inner circle. For the Lion, there is time for play and time for swift action. Are people arguing at the table? Leo leaps into the fray, trying to redirect the issue.

Having a Leo friend or partner is a blessing. They are generous to a fault and have a heart as big as, well, a Lion. Even though they enjoy the spotlight, they revel in bringing lightheartedness to any event. If you're looking for someone to put in the role of maître d' for a special dinner, ask a Leo. They're a perfect choice.

Most Leos enjoy the idea of having a family, but at home, they are the rulers of the roost (or so they think). Jealousy and possessiveness are two traits Leo must work to avoid. When Leo finds a good partner, the family dynamics sing harmoniously.

Extravagant Delights

The average Leo is very persnickety about food. They know what they want (with footnotes) and when they want it. Leo is not a "drive-through" person. Luxury is the name of the game. If there is entertainment and astonishing cocktails, all the better. The setting is just as important as the edible options.

Make It Marvelous

Your Leo is a curious Lion. They will want to try the odd, exotic fare. Think in terms of making a grand meal, going around the world, in four courses:

- Alligator
- Blood sausage
- Cactus fries
- Chicken feet
- Fried silkworm
- Frog legs
- Geoduck
- Molokhia soup
- Pigeon

Now, you may not find the taste of your completed recipe to your liking, but Leo rejoices in your efforts. PS: Have your sub sandwich joint's delivery number handy.

Puttin' on the Ritz

From tea and appetizers to a meal with several courses, think about all the decorations you put out. The table should always look lavish and classy. Make sure the forks are in the right place! It's not just the ambiance, however. If you can present your meal elegantly and sensually, your Leo's eyes will light up.

Keynotes of a Leo's Diet

As a rule of thumb, Leo is a one-meal person, and that meal has to be voluptuous. Ingredient ideas include

∾ Avocado toast

∾ Basil

∾ Bread

∾ Cinnamon

∾ Eggs

∾ Garlic

∾ Ginger

∾ Goat cheese

∾ Lemon

∾ Peach

∾ Rosemary

∾ Spinach

∾ Tarragon

∾ Tomahawk steak

∾ Watermelon

∾ Whole baked fish

∾ Whole roast chicken

What to Avoid

∾ Dairy

∾ Fatty food

∾ Gluten (excess)

∾ Processed food

∾ Sugary drinks

SUGGESTIONS

BREAKFAST Eggs benedict and/or a TALL stack of fresh pancakes

LUNCH Poutine

DINNER Crown roast with spring rolls

DESSERT Coffee cake, Earl Gray pudding, jam-filled cookies

SNACK Brownie toffee bars

DOES A LEO COOK?

Leo doesn't offer to cook very often. But when they do, prepare for a flame in your future. The Lion sees culinary efforts as an artistic outlet. Stay out of the Lion's way and prepare for a memorable meal.

Fulfillment Fajitas

Energetic Essence: When you have a goal requiring personal modifications, this recipe fits the bill. Chili powder provides a little luck, sweet pepper supports change for the better, and corn suits rituals focused on growth and transformation.

Ingredients

1 tbsp dark brown sugar

1 tbsp chipotle powder

½ tsp kosher salt

1 lb flank steak

12 miniature sweet peppers (red, yellow, orange), sliced

1 medium sweet yellow onion, sliced

12 cherry tomatoes

2 ears fresh corn

4 cups romaine lettuce

2 tbsps fresh cilantro, chopped

Lime vinaigrette

1 package fajita wraps
(10-count small; 8-count large)

Substitution

Lime vinaigrette: Chipotle vinaigrette or creamy Southwest dressing

Instructions

1. Mix the brown sugar, chipotle, and salt together.

2. Apply the mix on both sides of the flank steak.

3. In a grill pan, grill the peppers and onions together over medium heat until they have slightly browned edges and are tender and crisp (about 10 minutes).

4. At the 8-minute mark, add the tomatoes.

5. Remove and set aside.

6. Put the steak and corn on the grill for 10 minutes, turning after 5, and close the lid.

7. For a medium-rare steak, the internal temperature should read 135°F. Give the meat 10 minutes to rest before slicing.

8. While the steak is resting, cut the corn off the cob.

9. Mix the lettuce with the cilantro in a large mixing bowl. Top with vinaigrette and toss.

10. Top a fajita wrap with even amounts of lettuce, corn, tomato, onion, peppers, and strips of steak.

11. Roll the wrap and enjoy!

Sagittarius: November 22–December 21

Multicultural Cuisine

Sagittarians have some things in common with air signs. The Archer wants freedom. Once they're in motion, you might as well stand back and watch.

Your Sagittarian is a philosopher in the making. They're always trying to decipher life in a deeper sense. And they crave people who truly understand their spiritual leanings.

Self-confidence and assurance emanate from the Archer. In part, this is thanks to Jupiter's rulership, bringing blessings and good fortune. Throughout life, your Sagittarian has seen things simply "work out."

Archers surround themselves with people who challenge them in various ways. Traveling to other countries and immersing themselves in the local culture delights the Archer's soul. The Sagittarian mind is always hungry for input. Often, you'll see hints of their experiences displayed in their home, each with a story to tell.

> ### DOES A SAGITTARIUS COOK?
> Personality-wise, Sagittarians prefer to direct a show rather than get into the fray. They can create wonderful menu plans, complete with every element you desire. The Archer will help by giving people suitable tasks. Your Sagittarius may even bring some kitchen curios collected in their travels if they think it will prove useful.

You know the age-old question, what came first, the chicken or the egg? It was probably first pondered by a Sagittarian. They love quandaries and puzzles. If you present a truly unique meal with diversified elements for them, the conversation will be replete with questions.

If you are feeding an Archer regularly, remember to change things. They quickly become bored with repeated dishes, even if they liked them originally.

One word of caution. If you ask a Sagittarian for their opinion, it will be as sharp as your chef's knife. If they see issues, they illustrate them. However, if they like what they see, you will have someone jumping for joy.

Bounteous Plates

Toss out any ideas of petite foods. They are not the Archer's style. No matter where they eat, they always pile their plates high. Sagittarians have a hardy appetite. Offer food storage options for "doggie bags." The Archer is someone on the move. Sometimes they grab their treasure and head out to whatever issue caused a distraction. Don't feel shorted. Your Archer will come over later and tell you all about the food in meticulous detail. Have them bring the wine.

Keynotes of a Sagittarius' Diet

Anything you can cook outdoors works well for the Archer, who finds comfort in nature. Grilled dishes or picnic baskets are welcome. Ingredients aligned with Sagittarians include

- Bacon
- Banana
- Carrot
- Cheese
- Cinnamon
- Curry
- Endive
- Fig
- Garlic
- Ginger
- Ham
- Nuts and seeds
- Onions
- Pears
- Plums
- Radishes
- Saffron
- Squash
- Turbot
- Whole grains

What to Avoid

- Butter
- Chocolate
- Cream
- Fats
- Gravy
- Honey
- Oatmeal

SUGGESTIONS

BREAKFAST Fresh doughnuts or Belgian waffles

LUNCH Grilled cheese with tomato sandwich

DINNER Braised pork with fruity pico

DESSERT Confetti cake, sundaes, grapefruit granita

SNACK Carrot cake or muffins

MASHED POTATO PIZZA

Energetic Essence: Potatoes symbolize financial blessings, providence, and continuance. The Archer is hitting an important mark in obtaining their goals.

Somehow, I always manage to make more mashed potatoes than we can eat. One day I tried something different. I used mashed potatoes as the foundation for a pizza. It was yummy, and I didn't share (sorry...it was a craving). This recipe is for two people unless you're really hungry.

Ingredients: Crust

2½ tbsps butter

1 cup seasoned breadcrumbs

2 cups leftover mashed
  potatoes (separated)

1 tbsp parsley flakes

Salt and pepper

Instructions: Crust

1. Cut a circle of parchment paper to fit within the diameter of an air fryer and put it in the bottom.

2. Melt 2 tbsps butter in a small pan.

3. Pour in the breadcrumbs and stir until they are lightly browned.

4. Sprinkle the crumbs evenly over the surface of the parchment paper.

5. Spread out 1 cup of the mashed potatoes over the breadcrumbs (I find using fingers works best for keeping the crust intact).

6. Put down the remaining butter in small pats on the potatoes.

7. Sprinkle top with parsley, salt, and pepper.

SEASONING THE POTATOES

You can season your potatoes in any way you wish, specifically to match your intended toppings. For example, use garlic, onion powder, lemon zest, and parsley in the potatoes for a baby shrimp "pizza." For a taste of the islands, use ginger as part of a Hawaiian pizza. Greek pizza can benefit from a base of crumbled bacon and fresh spinach leaves. You want to build flavors.

MASHED POTATO PIZZA
∿ CONTINUED ∿

Instructions: Toppings

What next? Well, you can use pizza sauce with traditional sauce, pepperoni, and mozzarella cheese. Sauce, however, is not a necessary component to your magical medley. Toss on some green onions and banana peppers and cook it up. Or try leek with shallots and broccoli. If you want meat, try Polish sausage with fried onions.

1. Air fry for 7 minutes.

2. Check the pizza.

3. For a good crust, turn the fryer to the broil setting for 3 minutes. If it's not as crunchy as you want, continue to broil for 1 to 2 minutes more.

4. Remove the parchment paper with the "pizza" from the air fryer. Careful—it will be hot.

5. Create a second pizza with remaining potatoes.

Endnotes

1. Amelia Earhart, "Amelia Earhart Quotes," accessed September 12, 2023, https://www.ameliaearhart.com/.

2. Anchor Bar, "History-Anchor Bar," Anchor Bar, accessed September 23, 2023, https://anchorbar.com/history/.

chapter thirteen
cooking for star signs: water

Be happy. Be yourself, the day is about a lot more.
—ANNE HATHAWAY[1]

The three signs come under the elemental rulership of water: Cancer, Scorpio, and Pisces. Water signs have strong empathic capabilities. Because of this, they sometimes have to step away from emotional overload, making them somewhat mysterious. Feeling *too* much distracts water signs from mundane and spiritual goals. Water signs also sometimes push down their feelings, not wanting to make others uncomfortable.

Water signs are dreamers and visionaries with eerily accurate intuition. They are aware of patterns in the world, the signs and omens, and the ebb and flow of things. If a water sign tells you something is coming, prepare.

Having a casual dinner date with a water sign is rarely *really* casual. They see potential partners idealistically. Water-born people move into relationships quickly, wanting love, connection, and security. Expect personal questions. For the water-born, this tendency leads to many missteps and broken hearts.

Excitement precedes reality, clouding warning signs. Finding out a person is not as they seem or that they purposefully manipulated a water-born individual's sentiment is akin to an unforgivable sin. Unless circumstances are very unusual, once you've broken trust with a water sign, you'll never get it back.

But, back to food. Water people always try to find something good to say. They are courteous guests and appreciative of your efforts.

Building Vibrational Signatures for the Water Element

Color Palette

When you think of the colors of water, look at the richness of the oceans. From shallow crystal blue to the deepest depths of almost black, there's a lot in between.

AQUAMARINE Green and blue balance symmetrically in this color. It's soothing and refreshing. Spiritually, aquamarine embodies tranquility, reliability, and trust.

BLACK If you think of the Mariana Trench, water-black is rich with the unknown. The depths here are an enigma, revealing their secrets slowly. Black represents a sense of luxury, initially appearing dramatic and bold. But it's a ruse. There's more to discover.

DARK BLUE A more mysterious color, suggesting something just beneath the surface. It represents using authority, power, and knowledge responsibly.

PURPLE True confession time: this is my favorite color. It symbolizes dignity, pride, creativity, wisdom, devotion, honor, and peace. Egyptians see purple as an emblem of faith and virtue. As the hue associated with the crown chakra, it also represents universal consciousness.

SEA GREEN Sea green exudes mindfulness, health, and harmony. It helps stabilize emotions run amok, offering security and a safe spiritual haven in your soul. This is a fortunate color, suggesting growth and prosperity are on their way.

SILVER If you look at a wave as it crests, it looks silverish, particularly by moonlight. Silver has healing and lunar overtones, and connections with wealth.

Crystals

Water crystals feel like the waves of the ocean, gently rolling through your aura.

AMETHYST This is a highly intuitive stone. Many partiers trusted it as an amulet, protecting the bearer from temptations like drunkenness. Think of it as a sober crystal, clearing your mind for effective decision-making. Da Vinci felt amethyst could banish evil. Amethyst makes an excellent meditation stone when you're having trouble quieting your mind.

AQUAMARINE Water appears in the name of this sacred stone. Aquamarine helps people deal with inner struggles and find long-sought-after solutions. It inspires a sense of trust in yourself. When your inner voice speaks, listen. For those who struggle with communication, wear an aquamarine as a necklace.

BLUE FLUORITE Blue fluorite represents the cleansing nature of water. Get rid of old clutter and let the qi flow. Purging disarray goes for your mind, too. Put together your thoughts before speaking, especially when teaching. This sacred stone encourages you to remain true to yourself and strive for the greatest good. When you work with blue fluorite, it may manifest a couple of spiritual "ah ha!" moments.

BLUE LACE AGATE When you are down in the dumps, blue lace agate inspires emotional well-being and serenity while calming confusion. It strengthens the connection between emotion and body. This sacred stone connects with your heart chakra, improving your ability to give and receive love.

BLUE TOPAZ Blue topaz bears the label "clarity stone." Its energy accentuates your inner wisdom, from which solutions flow. Roman warriors carried this sacred stone for protection. Some claimed if you held this crystal near a poisoned item, it would warn you by changing color. This could apply to toxic people, too. The Egyptians felt the Sun god, Ra, empowered topaz with special supernatural powers.

CORAL Living in the ocean gives coral a unique relationship with the water element. Coral symbolizes the joy and wisdom developed through modesty. It allays fear, apprehension, and depression. Those seeking a mate would do well to wear coral as an amulet. Better still, when you meet someone, coral helps you leave your past behind and move forward confidently.

FOSSILIZED SEA URCHIN Another gift from the ocean, bearing all the power and wonder of the sea. When you carry one, the ebb and flow of life become clearer. You can achieve balance by overcoming barriers. The sea urchin attracts good fortune.

LARIMAR At the top of my list of favorite gems, Larimar is unpretentious yet simply captivating. It is a stone of enlightenment and healing and, in my opinion, it is essential for any water Witch's kit. Larimar facilitates moving an idea from the mind and bringing it into reality. For people suffering from stress-related conditions, Larimar is your go-to sacred stone. It calms phobias, panic attacks, and unfounded fears. Larimar puts you back in touch with your inner child for joyful release.

OPAL Opal amplifies energy. It raises hope and directs you toward an intimate divine connection. Opal embodies deep spirituality and the quest for inner peace. The colors dance in the sun, attracting harmony and luck in your life. As a sacred stone, opal brings all colors into your aura, filling your emotional body with light and helping you with karmic issues. Creativity and insight soar.

PEARL Pearl has a graceful feel to it. The synergy with water is unmistakable. Pearl has additional associations with the lunar sphere, looking much like a full moon. It invigorates magic and inner wisdom. Pearl is an excellent gem for meditation when you want to strengthen your relationship with the Sacred Feminine. Pearl truly offers you "pearls" of wisdom.

SELENITE The name of this gem reveals its relationship to the moon and, thereby, water. Selenite has powerful feminine energies that nurture new beginnings. Use this sacred stone when looking within yourself to find treasures you've overlooked. Selenite activates the crown chakra, encouraging a greater connection with the universe.

Decorations

When decorating with the water element in mind, avoid harsh corners (water is smooth). Some trinkets include shells, sea stars, sand in a bottle, nautical maps, seafaring ropes, water-smoothed stones, fish tanks, and miniature waterfalls.

Drinks

Beverages for those born as water signs include

- Blue curaçao mojito
- Blue Moon beer
- Blue Hawaiian
- Blue raspberry soda
- Brut
- Cloudberry liqueur
- Green tea
- Heineken
- Melon ball
- Orange pineapple juice
- Purple cosmopolitan
- Purple haze wine
- Sparkling water
- Zinfandel

Food Presentation

Food presentation for water signs follows the same concept as decoration. Focus on soft shapes on the plate. Classic silhouettes also inspire appreciation. Make swirl motifs in the mashed potatoes. Have wine charms for each guest.

Flowers

Water element flowers include those growing in water and those appreciative of a wet environment.

- Apple blossom
- Aster
- Cherry blossom
- Gourd
- Iris
- Larkspur
- Lilac
- Lotus
- Passionflower
- Periwinkle
- Pickerelweed
- Rose
- Water hyacinth
- Water iris
- Water lily
- Water poppy
- Willow
- Wisteria

Incense

- African violet
- Chamomile
- Gardenia
- Geranium
- Ginger
- Honeysuckle
- Night jasmine
- Orange blossom
- Peony
- Sage
- Tea rose
- Tea tree
- Ylang-ylang

Lighting

Use gentle light, such as amber bulbs. Even better is ambient, natural light.

Music

Emotive, sentimental music moves water-born people's souls.

ADELE Water Under the Bridge

BEATLES All You Need Is Love; Hey Jude

BON JOVI Livin' on a Prayer

BRUCE SPRINGSTEEN Glory Days

CALVIN HARRIS Feels

CARLY RAE JEPSEN Shooting Star

DEEP PURPLE Smoke on the Water

DURAN DURAN All Along the Water

EARTH, WIND, AND FIRE I'll Write a Song for You

GUS DAPPERTON My Favorite Fish

THE INCREDIBLE STRING BAND The Water Song

MAC DEMARCO My House by the Water

NEIL YOUNG Down by the River

PACHELBEL'S CANON Played on hydraulophone[2]

PASSENGER Coins in a Fountain

PORCHES Underwater

QUEEN The Show Must Go On

THE ROLLING STONES As Tears Go By

SIMON AND GARFUNKEL Bridge Over Troubled Waters

Tidiness

It's not orderliness that appeals to water signs. They want comfort and focus on the moment. Cleanups can wait until the next day off. Think of the feel of a book nook.

Cancer: June 21–July 22

Sweet Snacker

Cancers are sentimental and love foods with memories attached, so by all means, tell the story. They look for ease in their menu. One thing the crab *always* wants is sweets. If you're making homemade candy, they'll swoon. And put out small bowls of snacks around the space.

Cancer is the first of the water signs. These people thrive on security. They seek out people who show compassion and sensitivity. Cancers can be class clowns, wanting to make everyone happy, even at dinner. They will take extra time to adjust flavors, hoping everyone comes away satisfied.

If you swing by a Cancerian's house, they welcome you with warm tea and good company. No topic is off the table save for ones that are sad, vexed, and filled with conflict. This water sign loves to show off their home. They are what you might call determined nesters. There's something in each room reflecting Cancer's family and good memories.

> ### DOES A CANCER COOK?
> The answer is a vehement YES. People born under this sign not only love to cook but do it exceptionally well. They lean toward fresh ingredients and tried-and-true methods. Make them happy by asking for the recipe!

Distraction Tactics

When your Cancer is, well, crabby, you can easily distract them with a good meal. It helps redirect their minds away from the worries of the day, especially their career. Some ideas include:

- ~ Coconut rum with pineapple juice for sipping
- ~ Moon cakes (Cancer is ruled by the moon)
- ~ Smoked crab (yes, there is an irony here) or any seafood
- ~ A special recipe complete with anecdotes
- ~ Sushi (mixed platter)

Keynotes of a Cancer's Diet

Your Cancer appreciates traditional meals you want to eat again and again. Deep-fried chicken, anyone? Here are some components you might include in your culinary magic:

- ∾ Banana
- ∾ Beans
- ∾ Cauliflower
- ∾ Cheese
- ∾ Coconut
- ∾ Cucumbers
- ∾ Lemon
- ∾ Melon
- ∾ Milk
- ∾ Parsley
- ∾ Sage
- ∾ Thyme
- ∾ Vanilla
- ∾ Whole grains

What to Avoid

- ∾ Horseradish
- ∾ Hot pepper sauce
- ∾ Oily foods
- ∾ Salt
- ∾ Starches
- ∾ Wasabi

SUGGESTIONS

BREAKFAST Chocolate chip crepes

LUNCH Watercress on rye

DINNER Four-cheese mac 'n' cheese with toasted breadcrumbs

DESSERT Dark chocolate snack bites, crème brûlée, apple crostata

SNACK Vegetable smoothie

INNER CIRCLE CHICKEN POT PIE

Energetic Essence: Cancerians have nurturing natures. What better way to express it than with comfort food? The peas in this dish offer peace and happiness. Chicken represents service to others, and carrot supports a healthy diet (something for which Cancer strives).

Ingredients

½ cup butter

1 white onion, chopped

½ cup celery, chopped

2 carrots, diced

3 tsps garlic, minced

¾ cup flour

3 cups chicken bone broth

¼ cup heavy cream

3 cups cooked chicken, shredded

1 cup petite peas

1 tbsp parsley

Fresh ground salt and pepper

8- or 9-inch premade pie dough

1 egg

∾ **TIP** If you don't want to make your own cream sauce, buy chicken gravy or cream of chicken soup instead (eliminating the broth and flour for the roux).

Instructions

1. Preheat the oven to 375°F.

2. Put the butter, onions, celery, and carrots in a pot and stir over medium heat until they soften some (10 minutes).

3. Add garlic.

4. Stir in the flour, and keep stirring as the flour becomes golden and the butter thickens.

5. SLOWLY whisk the chicken broth into the pan.

6. Once thickened, add the heavy cream, chicken, peas, parsley, salt, and pepper. Now's the time to test the filling and adjust the spices.

7. Butter the pie pan, and place one of the premade crusts inside.

8. Pour in the filling, making sure it's even.

9. Add the second pie crust over the top. Secure it to the bottom crust by pinching the two together.

10. Put some slits in the top to allow for venting.

INNER CIRCLE CHICKEN POT PIE
~ CONTINUED ~

11. Beat the egg and then brush it on top of the crust.

12. Bake for about 45 minutes until the crust is golden brown.

13. Cool for 15 minutes before cutting into it.

FOUR AND TWENTY BLACKBIRDS?

The custom of making pot pies began in the Roman Empire. Did you know the rhyme about four and twenty blackbirds was based on a real thing?[3] The idea was to tuck the birds inside so they would fly out with the first slice. During the Elizabethan era, chefs made extravagant pot pies topped with all manner of decorations and filled with meats like venison and lamb.

Across the pond, the first published recipe for pot pie appeared in 1796, "American Cookery." And it wasn't just one pie! The book included stew and sea pie, too. By the 1950s, pot pie became a staple in American households. Supermarkets offered frozen meals created by well-known names like Morton and Stouffer's.

Pot pie is a way to use up leftovers. You can tinker with the recipe using crumble crust or phyllo dough. Classic ingredients include potatoes, peas, carrots, celery, onions, and meat.

Scorpio: October 23–November 21

It's All in the Details

For being a water sign, Scorpio comes under the rulership of Mars, which is all fire. This creates a vast store of energy and the desire to act. You might think Scorpios are elusive or sneaky. Nope! They are simply private people. They don't randomly open up about personal matters to others reading their Facebook page.

It's easy to find yourself drawn to a Scorpio. You like the mystique, fierceness, and cleverness. As a partner, your Scorpio never disappoints in the bedroom. Do not, however, try to change Scorpio's beliefs. They are firm as a rock.

One trap Scorpios must try to avoid is getting too caught up in trying to uncover deep truths about self, others, life-death, and the universe. If they go too far, they lose track of what's right in front of them. In this case, it's dinner!

Scorpio's intensity and passion emerge when trying new food adventures. They love exploring unique food and dabbling to create a perfect "new" recipe. This means your Scorpio might want a snake or spider as a gnash. Caviar? Ooooh, yes, please!

Think of weird and wonderful ideas like

- ∾ Alligator
- ∾ Antelope
- ∾ Caviar limes
- ∾ Durian fruit
- ∾ Frog legs
- ∾ Ground elk
- ∾ Octopus
- ∾ Quail

I personally recommend trying small portions of such exotic food. Not all of it will be to everyone's liking, even your Scorpio.

> ## DOES A SCORPIO COOK?
> Yes, Scorpios are refined cooks who love spices and pungent odors, such as feta cheese. They like presenting a dramatic flair. For example, they might surprise you with freshly pickled vegetables or a flambé. Your Scorpio may mix and match cultures, too. Just don't get in your Scorpio's way in the kitchen. They are protective of the space.

Talking at the Table

If you're looking for a quiet meal, don't bring a Scorpio. They have the gift of gab in abundance. Posing questions about the meal is normal (read the fine print). Offer to send them the details by email later.

Keynotes of a Scorpio's Diet

Scorpios are on the move. They get hungry quickly. Have snacks to go! Here are some components for the recipes you create for your Scorpio.

- ∾ Almonds
- ∾ Artichokes
- ∾ Beets
- ∾ Black cherry
- ∾ Cauliflower
- ∾ Cloves
- ∾ Cottage cheese
- ∾ Cucumbers
- ∾ Curry
- ∾ Garlic
- ∾ Lemon
- ∾ Lentils
- ∾ Mushrooms
- ∾ Onion
- ∾ Oysters
- ∾ Root vegetables
- ∾ Vanilla
- ∾ Watercress

What to Avoid

- ∾ Alcohol
- ∾ Oils (heavy)
- ∾ Red meat
- ∾ Yeast breads

SUGGESTIONS

BREAKFAST Peanut butter and banana toast

LUNCH Bento box

DINNER Lobster mac 'n' cheese

DESSERT Baklava, chocolate wine, rum-raisin truffle

SNACK Chicken wings

DESTINY CHICKPEA BOWL

Energetic Essence: In Jewish tradition, chickpeas represent passion, compassion, earnestness, and devotion, all traits Scorpios have in spades. Also known as garbanzo beans, chickpeas supports your efforts to discover your true purpose.

Ingredients

2 halfway roasted sweet potatoes

4 tbsps extra virgin olive oil

1 medium-sized onion
   (you will only need ¼ of it)

1 cup broccoli crowns

1¾ cups chickpeas

½ tsp chipotle chili powder

Salt and pepper to taste

1½ cups baby kale

1 clove minced garlic

Instructions

1. Prepare a cooking sheet with parchment paper.

2. Slice the potatoes lengthwise and place them on the sheet.

3. Pour 1 tbsp olive oil over them. Bake at 350°F for 5 minutes.

4. Cut the onion into quarters. Pull apart the petals from one quarter and add it to the sheet.

5. Mix in the broccoli crowns.

6. Add 1 tbsp olive oil.

7. Cook for 10 minutes.

8. In the interim, drain the chickpeas and put them in a small mixing bowl.

9. Mix them with 1 tbsp olive oil, chili powder, salt, and pepper. (Don't resist the urge to add onion and garlic powder.)

10. Heat the last tbsp of olive oil in a sauté pan.

11. Crisp the chickpeas in the pan until light brown (about 15 minutes) then drain on paper towels.

12. Put the kale and garlic on the baking sheet and bake for 5 minutes.

13. Assemble!

CHECKING UP ON CHICKPEAS

Garbanzo beans have the honor of ranking second most widely grown crop in the world, the soybean landing in first place. Historians believe people began domesticating crops around 11,000 years ago. It didn't take long to gain popularity. By the Bronze Age, you could find chickpeas in both Greece and Rome.

Around 800 CE, chickpeas appeared in literature. Charlemagne describes the growth of the plant on a manor's lands.[4] The name *garbanzo bean* originated in Spanish, translating as "dry seed."

Pisces: February 19–March 20

Concoction Connections

Pisceans land at the end of the celestial story. And like many happy endings, people born under this sign are empathic, artistic, eternal romantics, and very sensitive. It's not uncommon for a Piscean to use their art as a way of keeping ahead of emotion, which can sometimes overwhelm them. This is true with food. You will know what your Fish feels while cooking every—single—time. As a person born under this sign, I try to avoid cooking until my head and heart settle.

If a spirited conversation naturally grows at dinner, the Piscean will be the voice of reason. They will encourage people to listen and weigh all sides. Mind you, Fishes know when they're swimming upstream. Talk about politics? Nope. That causes indigestion.

At the end of the day, you'll appreciate the Piscean's helpfulness. Want the table cleared or the trash taken out? No problem! Pisces understands and enjoys helping out.

LOVE LANGUAGES

According to experts, there are five love languages people use as a way of giving and receiving love.[5]

ACTS OF SERVICE Actions matter to service-oriented people. They don't simply talk the talk but walk the walk. In effect, actions speak louder than dissertations.

AFFIRMATION Those with the affirmation love language use written and verbal means of illustrating their feelings. Letting people know you appreciate them and showing gratitude are both part of the equation.

GIVING AND RECEIVING GIFTS Mindful choices are the foundation of this language of love. This isn't about materialistic gestures; just little things letting people know you're thinking about them (or they, about you).

PHYSICALITY Even a hand on a shoulder is appreciated by those whose language of love is physical touch. Hold hands and snuggle more.

QUALITY TIME Work and home life balance is a struggle many face. When a person's love language is quality time, moments of uninterrupted intimacy and engagement are a must for their mental and emotional well-being.

Pisces Preferences

Truth be told, Pisces will overlook problematic portions of the meal because it's more about the time you spend together. Pisceans do, however, eat with their eyes, so try and create a pretty presentation.

- ∾ Cucumber canapés or finger sandwiches
- ∾ Fruit and mozzarella skewers drizzled with warm honey
- ∾ Grilled shrimp tacos with pesto
- ∾ Pork served in a pineapple half decorated with hibiscus
- ∾ Tuna stuffed tomatoes with crackers and chive garnish

DOES A PISCES COOK?

Oh, absolutely. Those born under this sign may not be the most organized culinarians, but boy, do they understand flavor combinations. When it seems like there's nothing to eat, watch with wonder as your Pisces grabs this, that, and the other thingy. The results? Surprisingly pleasing.

Keynotes of a Pisces' Diet

While it seems a little contrary, one of the best and most satisfying foods for your Pisces is fish. This includes fish-related items such as seaweed. Here are some more components for consideration for your Piscean menu.

- ∾ Basil
- ∾ Beans
- ∾ Beets
- ∾ Cranberries
- ∾ Eggs
- ∾ Flavor extracts
- ∾ Grapes
- ∾ Honey mustard
- ∾ Lamb
- ∾ Lemon
- ∾ Lentils
- ∾ Olives
- ∾ Oranges
- ∾ Oysters
- ∾ Peaches
- ∾ Peppercorn
- ∾ Plums
- ∾ Raw sugar
- ∾ Sage
- ∾ Smoked paprika
- ∾ Spinach
- ∾ Vinegar
- ∾ Whole grains
- ∾ Wine

What to Avoid

- ∿ Alcohol (moderation)
- ∿ Artificial ingredients
- ∿ Breads
- ∿ Coffee (moderation)
- ∿ Dairy
- ∿ Grapefruit
- ∿ Jalapeño
- ∿ Oily foods
- ∿ Salt (moderation)
- ∿ Sugar (moderation)

SUGGESTIONS

BREAKFAST Large cinnamon roll

LUNCH Sushi with fried rice

DINNER Coconut shrimp with risotto

DESSERT Vanilla bean ice cream, toffee cake, rose-strawberry custard

SNACKS Rice marshmallow treats (use colored marshmallows)

Strawberry-Lavender Chicken Wings

Energetic Essence: This is one of my family's favorite barbecued chicken recipes, especially Firne. If I ask what to make when he visits, this is at the top of the list. The request makes me smile and supports our bond in ways I can't really describe.

This unique recipe has a lovely flavor and distinctive lavender aroma that teases from your grill. Strawberries symbolize Venus, the Roman goddess of love (Aphrodite in Greece), thanks to their red color and heart shape. Adding to the magic of affection, lavender represents devotion and serenity. Wings bring the element of air into the picture, supporting healthy conversations and inspiration.

Ingredients: Marinade

2 tbsps balsamic vinegar

1 cup strawberry wine

¾ cup strawberry daiquiri
condensed juice (frozen)

¼ slice of fresh ginger, peeled

1 tsp onion powder

1 tsp garlic powder

½ tsp culinary lavender

Chicken wings (1½ lbs–2 lbs per person)

Instructions: Marinade

1. Mix all the ingredients in a large, sealable container or food storage bag.

2. Put the chicken in the marinade.

3. Set aside in the refrigerator the night before you make the chicken.

Ingredients: Chicken Sauce (4 servings)

½ tsp olive oil

¼ cup onion, finely minced

2 tbsps balsamic vinegar

2 tbsps honey

½ tbsp garlic, minced

½ tsp salt

1 tsp ginger powder

1 cup strawberries, finely minced

½ cup (4 ozs) strawberry
daiquiri condensed juice

½ cup pink Moscato

1–2 drops of lavender extract

STRAWBERRY-LAVENDER CHICKEN WINGS
∽ CONTINUED ∽

Instructions: Chicken

1. Let the chicken come to room temperature.
2. Preheat the grill to medium-high (375–400°F).
3. While the grill heats, put together the chicken sauce ingredients in a saucepan.
4. Heat to mix and reduce by ¼ cup or until thickened.
5. Remove the chicken from the marinade and pat dry (this will improve crispness).
6. Place the wings on the grill.
7. Get a good sear on both sides (about 2.5 minutes each).
8. Close the lid and cook for 3 minutes.
9. Turn the wings; wait 3 more minutes.
10. Put sauce on the upward side and flip it.
11. Put sauce on the other side.
12. Grill for 5 more minutes and check for doneness.
13. The wings should be 165°F when finished.

Finishing Touch

Sprinkle the wings with honey powder as they come off the grill.

BAVARIAN STRAW-BERRY CUSTOM

In Bavaria, come spring, people hang small baskets filled with wild strawberries on their cattle's horns.[6] The berries are an offering to elves. If the elves are pleased, the cattle will have an abundance of milk and birth healthy calves.

Side Dish Suggestions

Cheesy garlic knots

German potato salad

Greek-style macaroni salad

Grilled cauliflower steaks

Mini peppers stuffed with cream cheese and bacon

Pizza

Potential Condiments

Ranch or blue cheese dressing for dipping

A dash of hot sauce in the glazing mix

Endnotes

1. IMDb, "Anne Hathaway Biography," accessed September 12, 2023, https://www.imdb.com/name/nm0004266/bio/.

2. Ryan Jazen, "Hydraulophones: Acoustic Musical Instruments and Expressive User Interfaces," TSpace Library, 2008, https://tspace.library .utoronto.ca/bitstream/1807/25712/1/Janzen_Ryan_E_200811_MASc _thesis.pdf.

3. Jim Hurley, "Live 'Blackbird Pie' Thankfully No Longer in Fashion," *Irish Independent*, February 10, 2017, https://www.independent.ie /regionals/kerry/lifestyle/live-blackbird-pie-thankfully-no-longer-in -fashion/35432920.html#.

4. Tori Avey, "The Fascinating World of Chickpeas: History, Science, and Culinary Delights," Tori Avey, 2022, https://toriavey.com/the-history -science-and-uses-of-chickpeas/.

5. Heidi Borst, "The 5 Love Languages—And How To Use Them To Strengthen Your Relationship," *Forbes Health*, acessed January 23, 2023, https://www.forbes.com/health/mind/what-are-the-five-love-languages/.

6. University of Illinois Extension, "Strawberries and More," College of ACES, accessed September 1, 2023, https://web.extension.illinois.edu /strawberries/history.cfm.

appendix one
kitchen hacks

There are many things about being a Kitchen Witch that are, well, mundane. The sensibility in tips and tricks gives you more time to focus on the magic you're building. These tested ideas help preserve goods, enhance flavors, and honor the concept of no-waste cooking.

Baked Goods
Put a piece of plain white bread in the storage container. It helps keep the items soft.

Baking Rack Fat Reducer
If you put things in the oven (such as meatballs) with high-fat contents, place them on a baking rack. Below it, put another tray with aluminum or parchment paper to collect the drippings.

Cake and Cupcake Moisture
Adding instant pudding to the recipe improves initial moisture and moisture retention.

Food Separators
If you have a picky eater or prefer to keep small edibles separate from each other, use cupcake liners. You'll be able to set them out decoratively, too.

Fresh Herbs Single Serve
If you buy too many fresh herbs, mince them and freeze them in ice cube trays with olive oil. Once frozen, pop them into a labeled food storage bag and pull out only what you need for a recipe. This method works for sauces, too.

Ice Cream: Keeping It Cold
You can use bubble wrap to keep your ice cream cold longer. Just cover the outside completely except for the top.

Oatmeal
Use the bag from an instant oatmeal packet to measure the water necessary for heating.

Over Salting

If you have stock with too high salt levels, put two slices of apples or potatoes in the pot. Simmer for 10 minutes. Discard or compost. Sometimes adding an acid such as vinegar helps, too.

Paper Towel Power

Paper towels serve many functions in your kitchen besides cleaning up. You can put one under a bowl on a countertop to keep it from sliding, for example. Here are several more:

- ∾ Sprout garden seeds inside a folded, damp paper towel. Spritz periodically and then transfer into pots.
- ∾ Make one into an "in a pinch" coffee filter.
- ∾ Extend the crispness of your vegetables by wrapping them in dry paper towels. These absorb the dampness leading to wilting.
- ∾ Getting a grip on slippery items. One example is using a paper towel to release the silver skin from the back of beef and pork ribs.

Plastic Bag Piping

You may have seen this already, but if you haven't and want pretty presentations, you'll love this. Let's say you're making deviled eggs for a party. Once you've mixed the stuffing, fill a plastic bag and just cut a corner off rather than needing a fancy piping kit. Squeeze gently to fill the egg halves.

Recipe Ingredient Organization

Use a countertop lazy Susan and place all the components of your recipe into it. You can spin it and grab it as you go.

Ripening Fruit

If you need under-ripe fruit to move along quickly, store it in a paper bag. It will speed up the process.

Rolling, Rolling, Rolling

Not every kitchen has a rolling pin. Substitutes include a wine bottle, a dowel, a straight-sided drinking glass, and a soda can (full).

Scoop It!

Use an ice cream scoop to clean the seeds out of squash and pumpkins. For smaller fruits, use a watermelon baller.

Separate Eggs

Crack an egg into a bowl. Using a clean plastic bottle, push the sides in a bit. Now, place the bottle opening over the yolk. Release the squeeze, and up the bottle goes the yolk.

Steak Fries

Cut one end of the potato, then push it through an apple slicer for even pieces.

Table Top Chiller

Fill a large food storage bag with ice. Put it into a bowl or a square pan. Cover with lettuce for a pretty presentation, and lay your food on top.

appendix two

metric conversion table

Volume	
¼ tsp	1.2 mL
½ tsp	2.5 mL
1 tsp	5 mL
1 tbsp	15 mL
¼ cup	60 mL
⅓ cup	80 mL
½ cup	120 mL
⅔ cup	160 mL
¾ cup	175 mL
1 cup	240 mL

Mass	
1 oz	28 grams
4 ozs	110 grams
8 ozs	224 grams
12 ozs	340 grams
16 ozs	455 grams

Temperature	
350°F	180°C
375°F	190°C
400°F	200°C
425°F	220°C

appendix three

meat doneness

Protein	Doneness	Temperature
Fish	Safe cooking	145°F (62.5°C)
Ground meat	Safe cooking	160°F (71°C)
Ham (fresh)	Safe cooking	145°F (62.5°C)
Ham (cooked)	Safe cooking	140°F (61°C)
Lamb	Rare	135°F (57°C)
Lamb	Medium rare	145°F (62.5°C)
Lamb	Medium	160°F (71°C)
Lamb	Well done	165°F (74°C)
Pork	Safe cooking	145°F (62.5°C)
Poultry	Safe cooking	165°F (74°C)
Sausage	Safe cooking	160°F (71°C)
Steak/Beef	Rare	120°F (50°C)
Steak/Beef	Medium rare	130°F (55°C)
Steak/Beef	Medium	140°F (61°C)
Steak/Beef	Medium well	150°F (67°C)
Steak/Beef	Well done	160°F (71°C)

online recommended resources

The internet is replete with information. After a while it can become frustrating to find trustworthy information. Over time, I discovered several websites that I really enjoy from individuals who know their craft. Here are some I've assembled for you. Please note that some require a paid subscription to access.

Barbecue

Cuso Cuts
https://cusocuts.com/
Chef Jack Mancuso's creative smoking and grilling recipes, cutlery, and spices

Great British Chefs: Barbecue
https://www.greatbritishchefs.com/features/barbecue
Everyday recipes, including dietary information, how to cook, food trends, educational articles

Harvard Gazette: Barbecue's Beginnings
https://news.harvard.edu/gazette/story/2012/04/barbecues-beginnings/
A look back on barbecue history

MSU: Smoking As a Food Cooking Method
https://www.canr.msu.edu/news/smoking_as_a_food_cooking_method
General introduction to smoking meat

USDA: Barbecue Food Safety
https://www.sccmo.org/DocumentCenter/View/1655/Barbecuing-and-Food-Safety-PDF
Keeping your food safe during the barbecue process

Beverages

Delishably
https://delishably.com/food-industry/what-is-fusion-cooking
Fusion cooking overview, world cuisine, food and beverage recipes

Drink Business
https://www.thedrinksbusiness.com/2013/01/top-10-wine-gods-and-goddesses/
Beverages of the gods

Harvard: A History of Coffee
https://sites.duke.edu/rethinkingglobalcities/files/2014/09/64Kafadar16
    -coffeehistory.pdf
The history of coffee

The Nibble: Great Food Finds. The Smoothie
https://blog.thenibble.com/2022/10/03/history-of
    -smoothies-smoothie-recipes-for-global-smoothie-day/
A peek at the development of smoothies

UCSC: Coffee 1400–1800
https://humwp.ucsc.edu/cwh/brooks/coffee-site/index.html
The history of coffee

University Libraries: Cocktail History in America
https://guides.lib.vt.edu/specialcollections/cocktailhistory
Cocktails in American history

Yale Global Online Tea: Still Hot after 5000 Years
https://archive-yaleglobal.yale.edu/tea-still-hot-after-5000
    -years
History of tea

Culture & Regional Cooking

A Few Good Things
https://vak1969.com/
A blog compiling "good things"—perspectives on travel, food, spirituality, and daily living

CN Traveler
https://www.cntraveler.com/story/a-guide-to-barbecue-around-the-world
Destinations, food, and culture

Delishably
https://delishably.com/food-industry/what-is-fusion-cooking
Fusion cooking overview, world cuisine, food and beverage recipes

Eat Right: Cultural Cuisines and Traditions
https://www.eatright.org/food/cultural-cuisines-and-traditions
Recipes from around the world, including holiday ideas

Food Timeline
https://www.foodtimeline.org/
A concise review of foods as they came into use among various cultures

House and Garden
https://www.houseandgarden.co.uk/gallery/table-setting
Recipes, interior design, table setting (history and cultural significance)

Spruce Eats
https://www.thespruceeats.com/
Step-by-step photos, regional recipes

Wander Lush: UNESCO Food Culture
https://wander-lush.org/food-culture-unesco/
Exploring food culture, beliefs, and practices

Yummly
https://www.yummly.com/
Meal planning, regional foods, guided recipes

Entertaining

Delish
https://www.delish.com/
The online version of *Delish* magazine, new daily recipes, party ideas, tips and tricks

Epicurious
https://www.epicurious.com/
Recipes, menu ideas for all occasions, informative articles, shopping strategies

Food
https://Food.com
Seasonal, healthy cooking, holidays, food trends

Martha Stewart
https://www.marthastewart.com/
Food, entertaining, holidays

Southern Living: Entertaining
https://www.southernliving.com/food/entertaining
The ultimate insiders' guide to Southern culture, recipes, travel, and events

Flower Cookery

*The Guardian: Blooming Delicious! How to cook with flowers–
from delicate crushed roses to tangy camomile salt*
https://www.theguardian.com/food/2022/mar/02/blooming-tasty-a-beginners-guide
    -to-cooking-with-flowers

An introduction to flower cookery

Michigan State University: Edible Flowers
https://www.canr.msu.edu/news/edible_flowers_adding_color_flavor_and_fun_to
    _your_dinner_plate
Edible flowers: Adding color, flavor, and fun to your dinner plate

University of MN Extension: Edible Flowers
https://extension.umn.edu/flowers/edible-flowers
Using edible flowers

Food History, Trivia

Food Timeline
https://www.foodtimeline.org/
A concise review of foods as they came into use among various cultures

Harvard: A History of Coffee
https://sites.duke.edu/rethinkingglobalcities/files/2014/09/64Kafadar16
    -coffeehistory.pdf
The history of coffee

Harvard Gazette: Barbecue's Beginnings
https://news.harvard.edu/gazette/story/2012/04/barbecues-beginnings/
A look back on barbecue history

Just Fun Facts
https://justfunfacts.com/category/food/
Interesting, quirky trivia and facts about food

Scholarship: An Appetite for Metaphor
https://thescholarship.ecu.edu/handle/10342/3535
Food metaphors in literature

Smithsonian Magazine
https://www.smithsonianmag.com/innovation/brief-history-crock-pot-180973643/
A brief history of the Crock-Pot

University Libraries: Cocktail History in America
https://guides.lib.vt.edu/specialcollections/cocktailhistory
Cocktails in American history

Food Safety

Food Safety Agency: Avoiding Cross Contamination
https://www.food.gov.uk/safety-hygiene/avoiding-cross-contamination#:~:text
    =Cross%2Dcontamination%20is%20what%20happens,cause%20of%20most
    %20foodborne%20infections.
Safe preparation and storage

USDA: Barbecue Food Safety

https://www.sccmo.org/DocumentCenter/View/1655/Barbecuing-and-Food-Safety
-PDF-
Keeping your food safe during the barbecue process

USDA Safe Food Handling and Preparation

https://www.fsis.usda.gov/food-safety/safe-food-handling-and-preparation
Essential review of safe food handling practices

USDA Safe Minimal Temperature Chart

https://www.fsis.usda.gov/food-safety/safe-food-handling-and-preparation/food
-safety-basics/safe-temperature-chart
Internal food temperatures for safety

Fusion Cooking

Delishably

https://delishably.com/food-industry/what-is-fusion-cooking
Fusion cooking overview, world cuisine, food and beverage recipes

Escoffier: What Is Fusion Cusine?

https://www.escoffier.edu/blog/world-food-drink/whats-the-status-of-fusion
-cuisine/
School of Culinary Arts—fusion cuisine

Science Direct: International Journal of Gastronomy and Food Science

https://www.sciencedirect.com/science/article/abs/pii/S1878450X18300787
Contemporary fusion foods: How are they to be defined, and when do they succeed/
fail?

Wolfgang Puck

https://www.foodnetwork.com/shows/wolfgang-puck/recipes
Episodes, recipes

How To

All Recipes

https://www.allrecipes.com/recipes/
A–Z recipes; how to

Brit + Co

https://www.brit.co/food

Food news, healthy eating, DIY recipes, kitchen tools, videos, recipes, and more

Epicurious

https://www.epicurious.com/

Recipes, menu ideas for all occasions, informative articles, shopping strategies

Gordon Ramsay

https://www.gordonramsay.com/gr/recipes/

Classes and recipes

Great British Chefs: Barbecue

https://www.greatbritishchefs.com/features/barbecue

Everyday recipes, including dietary information, how to cook, food trends, educational articles

House and Garden

https://www.houseandgarden.co.uk/gallery/table-setting

Recipes, interior design, table settings (history and cultural significance)

Martha Stewart

https://www.marthastewart.com/

Food, entertaining, holidays

Spruce Eats

https://www.thespruceeats.com/

Step-by-step photos, regional recipes

Western Virginia University Extension: Cooking

https://extension.wvu.edu/food-health/cooking

Cooking for one, slow cooking, family nutrition, home preservation

Nutrition

America's Test Kitchen

https://www.americastestkitchen.com

Thousands of tested recipes, nutrition information

Brit + Co

https://www.brit.co/food

Food news, healthy eating, DIY recipes, kitchen tools, videos, recipes, and more

Edamam

https://www.edamam.com/

Nutritional values, more than two million recipes

Food

https://Food.com

Seasonal, healthy cooking, holidays, food trends

Jamie Oliver

https://www.jamieoliver.com/

Budget-friendly fare, healthy meals, nutrition

MyNetDiary

https://www.mynetdiary.com/library.html

Food search engine, a resource for various dietary needs

Western Virginia University Extension: Cooking

https://extension.wvu.edu/food-health/cooking

Cooking for one, slow cooking, family nutrition, home canning and preserving

Recipes (general)

A Couple Cooks

https://www.acouplecooks.com/

Simple, tasty cooking

All Recipes
https://www.allrecipes.com/recipes/
A–Z recipes; how to

America's Test Kitchen
https://www.americastestkitchen.com
Thousands of tested recipes, nutrition information

Brit + Co
https://www.brit.co/food
Food news, healthy eating, DIY recipes, kitchen tools, videos, recipes, and more

Cuso Cuts
https://cusocuts.com/
Chef Jack Mancuso's creative smoking and grilling recipes, cutlery, and spices

Delish
https://www.delish.com/
The online version of *Delish* magazine, new daily recipes, party ideas, tips and tricks

Eat Right: Cultural Cuisines and Traditions
https://www.eatright.org/food/cultural-cuisines-and-traditions
Recipes from around the world, including holiday ideas

Edamam
https://www.edamam.com/
Nutritional values, more than two million recipes

Epicurious
https://www.epicurious.com/
Recipes, menu ideas for all occasions, informative articles, shopping strategies

Gordon Ramsay
https://www.gordonramsay.com/gr/recipes/
Classes and recipes

Jamie Oliver
https://www.jamieoliver.com/
Budget-friendly fare, healthy meals, nutrition

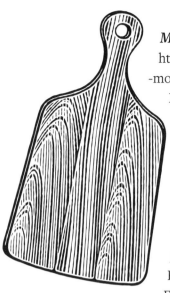

Masaharu Morimoto
https://www.foodnetwork.com/profiles/talent/masaharu
-morimoto/recipes
Many Asian-themed recipes

PBS: Food Recipes
https://www.pbs.org/food/recipes/
Great search function for their available recipes

Pioneer Woman: Best Crock-Pot Recipe Resource
https://www.thepioneerwoman.com/food-cooking
/meals-menus/g32264194/best-crock-pot-recipes/Online
Resource/
Food and recipes; home and life, slow cookers

Rachael Ray
https://rachaelray.com/
30-minute meal recipes

Spoonacular
https://spoonacular.com/
Meal planner, recipe organizer

Tasty
https://tasty.co/
Tips, tricks, easy meals, work lunches, family dinners

Wolfgang Puck
https://www.foodnetwork.com/shows/wolfgang-puck/recipes
Episodes, recipes

Spirituality

A Few Good Things
https://vak1969.com/
A blog compiling "good things"—perspectives on travel, food, spirituality, and daily living

Astrosage
https://horoscope.astrosage.com/food-astrology-remedies/
Food astrology, palmistry, numerology, tarot

Science Direct: International Journal of Hospitality Management
https://www.sciencedirect.com/science/article/abs/pii/S0278431920300463
Exploring the relationship between food and spirituality: a literature review

Spirituality & Health: Your Sacred Relationship with Food
https://www.spiritualityhealth.com/articles/2018/10/16/your-sacred-relationship
    -with-food
Ayurvedic insights

UCDavis: Astrological Zodiac Traits/ Sun Sign Personalities
http://nuclear.ucdavis.edu/~rpicha/personal/astrology/
A one-stop brief overview of astrological traits and personalities

Tips, Tricks, Tools, and Techniques

Brit + Co
https://www.brit.co/food
Food news, healthy eating, DIY recipes, kitchen tools, videos, recipes, and more

Cuso Cuts
https://cusocuts.com/
Chef Jack Mancuso's creative smoking and grilling recipes, cutlery, and spices

Decore Tips
https://decortips.com/homes/design-harmony-how-to-create-harmony-in-a-space/
Fundamentals of spatial harmony

Delishably
https://delishably.com/food-industry/what-is-fusion-cooking
Fusion cooking overview, world cuisine, food and beverage recipes

Epicurious
https://www.epicurious.com/
Recipes, menu ideas for all occasions, informative articles, shopping strategies

Escoffier: The Art of Food Presentation
https://www.escoffier.edu/blog/culinary-arts/the-art-of-food-presentation/
School of Culinary Arts—food presentation

Iowa State Extension: Design: Exploring the Elements & Principles
https://www.extension.iastate.edu/4hfiles/statefair/EEHandbook/EEHJPDesign4H
    634.pdf
Home Design: shapes, colors, rhythm, space, texture, balance, inspiration

Kitchen Essentials: Kitchen Essentials List
https://www.mealime.com/kitchen-essentials-list
71 of the best kitchen cookware, utensils, tools and more

Tasty
https://tasty.co/
Tips, tricks, easy meals, work lunches, family dinners

bibliography

Alhazred, Abdul. "Kitchen Blender Where It All Started." History and Headlines. January 2, 2020. https://www.historyandheadlines.com/kitchen-blender-where -it-all-started/.

Anchor Bar. "History-Anchor Bar." Anchor Bar. Accessed September 23, 2023. https://anchorbar.com/history/.

Avey, Tori. "The Fascinating World of Chickpeas: History, Science, and Culinary Delights." 2022. https://toriavey.com/the-history-science-and-uses-of-chickpeas/.

Baker, Christina. "Thatcher Glass: A History of Innovation." Corning Museum of Glass. May 10, 2017. https://blog.cmog.org/2017/05/10/thatcher-history/.

Beitler, Mandy Lim. "Why We Eat Pineapple Tarts During CNY and the Meanings Behind Other Goodies." AsiaOne. January 23, 2017. https://www.asiaone.com/food /why-we-eat-pineapple-tarts-during-cny-and-meanings-behind-other-goodies.

Borst, Heidi. "The 5 Love Languages—And How To Use Them To Strengthen Your Relationship." *Forbes Health*. January 23, 2023. https://www.forbes.com/health /mind/what-are-the-five-love-languages/.

Cheung, Victor. "A Simple Guide to the Feng Shui Five Elements Theory (Wu Xing)." Feng Shui Nexus. January 16, 2020. https://fengshuinexus.com/feng-shui -rules/feng-shui-five-elements-guide/.

Child, Julia. *People Who Love to Eat Are Always the Best People: And Other Wisdom*. New York: Alfred A. Knopf, 2020.

China Highlights by Cindy. "10 Amazing Chinese New Year's Desserts to Ring in 2023." Last updated July 20, 2023. https://www.chinahighlights.com/travelguide /chinese-food/chinese-new-year-desserts.htm.

Choi, Elizabeth. "Moon Rabbits, Leaping Hares, and Emblems of Rebirth in Art." Sothebys. September 13, 2019. https://www.sothebys.com/en/articles/moon -rabbits-leaping-hares-and-emblems-of-rebirth-in-art.

Claiborne, Craig. *Craig Claiborne's Kitchen Primer (Basic Cookbook)*. New York: Vintage, January 1, 1972.

Cloake, Felicity. "Deconstructing Cassoulet, the Classic French Stew." *National Geographic*. March 15, 2023. https://www.nationalgeographic.com/travel/article /deconstructing-cassoulet-classic-french-stew.

Collins Dictionary. "Janus Definition in American English." *Collins Dictionary*. Accessed October 18, 2023. https://www.collinsdictionary.com/us/dictionary /english/janus.

Colwin, Laurie, in Whitney Hopler. "Famous Quotes on Cooking and Wellbeing." *University News*. Accessed September 28, 2023. https://wellbeing.gmu.edu /famous-quotes-on-cooking-and-well-being/.

Difford's Guide. "The History of Punch." *Difford's Guide for Discerning Drinkers*. Accessed September 24, 2023. https://www.diffordsguide.com/g/1129/punch -and-punches/history.

———. "Origin of the Word Cocktail." *Difford's Guide for Discerning Drinkers*. Accessed September 26, 2023. https://www.diffordsguide.com/encyclopedia/2292 /cocktails/origins-of-the-word-cocktail.

Dolan, Maureen. "Tales from the Hive." Nova Online. October 2000. https://www.pbs.org/wgbh/nova/bees/buzz.html.

Dong, Lisa. "Legends on the Origins of Tea from China, Japan, and Korea." *T Ching*. March 21, 2012. https://tching.com/2012/03/legends-on-the-origins-of-tea-from -china-japan-and-korea/.

Druckman, Charlotte. "Judith Jones In Her Own Words." *Eater*. September 23, 2015. https://www.eater.com/2015/9/23/9355183/judith-jones.

Earhart, Amelia. "Amelia Earhart Quotes." CMG Worldwide. Accessed September 12, 2023. https://www.ameliaearhart.com/.

Flora, Martin. "Potluck Meal Innovation Due to Depression: Guests Chip in With Part of Dinner." *Chicago Tribune*. January 27, 1933. http://archives.chicagotribune .com/1933/01/27/page/14/article/potluck-meal-innovation-due-to-depression.

Forbes, Jack D. "Indigenous Americans: Spirituality and Ecos." Daedalus: American Academy of Arts and Science. Fall 2001. https://www.amacad.org/publication /indigenous-americans-spirituality-and-ecos.

Four Roses Bourbon. "The History of the Four Roses Legend." January 15, 2021. https://www.fourrosesbourbon.com/blog/history-of-the-four-roses-legend.

Frayer, Lauren. "In Spain New Year's Is All About the Grapes." *Morning Edition*, NPR. December 27, 2016. https://www.npr.org/sections/thesalt/2016/12/27 /506484561/in-spain-new-year-s-eve-is-all-about-the-grapes-save-the-bubbly-for -later.

Gaeng, Jennifer. "Discover the Oldest Honey Ever Found (From King Tut's Tomb?)." A–Z Animals. February 28, 2023. https://a-z-animals.com/blog/dis-cover-the-oldest-honey-ever-found-from-king-tuts-tomb/.

Garfinkel, Perry. "Puck Goes Back to His (Ginger) Roots." *Huffington Post*, February 3, 2012. https://www.huffpost.com/entry/wolfgang-puck-spago_b_1253197.

———. "Wolfgang Puck Fusion Veteran." *Wall Street Journal*, February 1, 2012. https://www.wsj.com/articles/BL-SJB-8547.

Gelling, Natasha. "Sorry, Wolfgang, Fusion Foods Have Been with Us for Centuries." *Smithsonian Magazine*. July 24, 2013. https://www.smithsonianmag.com/arts -culture/sorry-wolfgang-fusion-foods-have-been-with-us-for-centuries -17238814/.

Harris, Molly. "Here's Why Chefs Season Food From So High Up." *Tasting Table*. March 9, 2022. https://www.tastingtable.com/792845/heres-why-chefs-season-food-from-so-high-up/.

Hayman, Vicki. "Impressive Crème Brûlée." University of Wyoming Extension. Accessed September 12, 2023. https://uwyoextension.org/uwnutrition /newsletters/impressive-creme-brulee/.

Hellenic Museum, The. "Kykeon: The Drink of Champions." September 6, 2021. https://www.hellenic.org.au/post/kykeon-the-drink-of-champions.

Heller, Susie, and Thomas Keller. *The French Laundry Cookbook*. Yountville, CA: Artisan Books, 2016.

Higham, Nick. "Did the English Invent Bubbly Before Dom Perignon?" *BBC News*. May 20, 2017. https://www.bbc.com/news/uk-england-gloucestershire-39963098.

History.com, the editors. "Julian Calendar Takes Effect for the First Time on New Year's Day." *History*. July 21, 2010. https://www.history.com/this-day-in-history /new-years-day.

Hurley, Jim. "Live 'Blackbird Pie' Thankfully No Longer in Fashion." *Irish Indepen-dent*. February 10, 2017. https://www.independent.ie/regionals/kerry/lifestyle /live-blackbird-pie-thankfully-no-longer-in-fashion/35432920.html#.

IFSG. "The Feng Shui Bagua." International Feng Shui Guild. Accessed October 18, 2023. https://www.ifsguild.org/the-feng-shui-bagua/.

IMDb. "Anne Hathaway Biography." Accessed September 12, 2023. https://www.imdb.com/name/nm0004266/bio/.

———. "Quotes Will.i.am." Accessed September 12, 2023. https://www.imdb.com/name/nm1443238/bio/.

Ingall, Marjorie. "Meet the Jewish Inventor of the Slow Cooker." *Tablet Magazine*. August 5, 2017. https://www.tabletmag.com/sections/food/articles/jewish-inventor-of-slow-cooker-irving-naxon.

International Pepper Community. "History of Pepper." International Pepper Community. September 2013. https://www.ipcnet.org/history-of-pepper.

Jazen, Ryan. "Hydraulophones: Acoustic Musical Instruments and Expressive User Interfaces." TSpace Library. 2008. https://tspace.library.utoronto.ca/bitstream/1807/25712/1/Janzen_Ryan_E_200811_MASc_thesis.pdf.

Jolley, Annalise. "Basque Cider Houses." *National Geographic Travel*. Accessed September 9, 2023. https://www.nationalgeographic.com/travel/article/basque-cider-houses-keep-cultural-and-culinary-history-alive.

Kelly II, M. J. "Discovering the True Meaning of Blessing: A Closer Look at the Hebrew and Greek Words." *Medium*. March 20, 2023. https://medium.com/@mjkelleyII/discovering-the-true-meaning-of-blessing-a-closer-look-at-the-hebrew-and-greek-words-e8ff1de56024.

Kendall, Paul. "Hazel Mystery and Folklore." Trees for Life. Accessed September 22, 2023. https://treesforlife.org.uk/into-the-forest/trees-plants-animals/trees/hazel/hazel-mythology-and-folklore/.

Kirker, Constance. *Edible Flowers: A Global History*. London: Reaktion Books, October 15, 2016.

Kudus, Nazima. "Of Sorbet, Sherbert, Sarbat and All That Jazz." Uitm Institutional Repository. June 2022. https://ir.uitm.edu.my/id/eprint/63625/1/63625.pdf.

Lepage, Christian. "Belgian Ardour for Liquid Bread." *Slovak Spectator*. March 17, 2014. https://spectator.sme.sk/c/20050120/belgian-ardour-for-liquid-bread-video-included.html.

Lid & Ladle. "How Much Is a Pinch?" *Sur la table*. April 4, 2023. https://learn.surlatable.com/how-much-is-a-pinch/.

Macallen, Ian. "The Marriage of Meat and Leafy Greens: The History of Italian Wedding Soup." America.Domani. December 29, 2022. https://americadomani.com/the-marriage-of-meat-and-leafy-greens-the-history-of-italian-wedding-soup/.

Maestri, Nicoletta. "Mayahuel, The Aztec Goddess of Maguey." ThoughtCo. April 5, 2023. https://www.thoughtco.com/mayahuel-the-aztec-goddess-of-maguey-171570.

Mao, Dr. SK. "Oats." Foods Natural Health Dictionary. Accessed September 23, 2023. https://askdrmao.com/natural-health-dictionary/oats/index.html.

Mark, Joshua. "The Hymn to Ninkasi, Goddess of Beer." *World History Encyclopedia*. November 11, 2022. https://www.worldhistory.org/article/222/the-hymn-to -ninkasi-goddess-of-beer/.

Marshall, Cassie. "What Are the Sweetest Apples?" The Kitchen Community. June 19, 2021. https://thekitchencommunity.org/what-are-the-sweetest-apples/.

McKeever, Amy. "Every Season Actually Begins Twice—Here's Why." *National Geographic*. May 31, 2003. https://www.nationalgeographic.com/environment/article /history-science-of-meteorological-astronomical-seasons.

McKibben, Beth. "The Centuries-Old History of Wassail." Tales of the Cocktail Foundation. November 30, 2015. https://talesofthecocktail.org/history/history -wassail-punch/.

Meyer, Michael R. *A Handbook for the Humanistic Astrologer*. Berkeley, CA: Khaldea, 2000.

Middleton, Pippa. *Celebrate: A Year of Festivities for Families and Friends*. United Kingdom: Viking, 2012.

Milano Style. "Wear Something Red on New Year's Eve." *Milano Style*. December 21, 2010. https://www.history.com/this-day-in-history/new-years-day.

Mooney, Michael. "Guy Fieri Shares What Feeds His Appetite for Life." *Success*. May 19, 2016. https://www.success.com/guy-fieri-shares-what-feeds-his-appetite-for -life/.

Nash, Thomas. *Strange Newes, of the Intercepting Certaine Letters and a Convoy of Verses*. United Kingdom, 1870. https://www.google.com/books/edition /Strange_Newes_of_the_Intercepting_Certai/L55TAAAAcAAJ.

Nations Online. "Food Symbolism During Chinese New Year Celebrations." Nations Online. Accessed September 22, 2023. https://www.nationsonline.org/oneworld /Chinese_Customs/food_symbolism.htm.

New Mexico State University, Onion Breeding Program. "History." Accessed September 12, 2023. https://onion.nmsu.edu/history.html.

Nyhvrold, Nathans. "Coffee Origin, Types, Uses, History & Facts." *Encyclopedia Britannica*. Last updated September 11, 2023. https://www.britannica.com/topic /coffee.

O'Brien, Brien. "The California Cut: Learn How Tri-Tip Steak Is Uniquely Californian." *Active*. August 26, 2009. https://www.activenorcal.com/the-california-cut -learn-how-tri-tip-steak-is-uniquely-californian/.

Oliver, Lynn. "Confectioner's Sugar." Food Timeline. Accessed September 12, 2023. https://www.foodtimeline.org/foodcandy.html.

Panza, Carlotta. "How Italians Eat: Explore the History of a Meal." Italy Segreta. September 2021. https://italysegreta.com/exploring-the-history-of-a-meal/.

Paulette, Tate. "Brewing Mesopotamian beer brings a sip of this vibrant ancient drinking culture back to life." *The Conversation*. August 24, 2020. https://theconversation.com/brewing-mesopotamian-beer-brings-a-sip-of -this-vibrant-ancient-drinking-culture-back-to-life-142215.

Pendergast, Mark. "The History of Coffee and How It Transformed Our World." Coffee Time-line. September 2013. https://as.vanderbilt.edu/clas-resources/ media/Coffee%20Timeline.pdf.

Perry, Charles. "Couscous and Its Cousins." *Oxford Symposium on Food and Cookery*. United Kingdom: Prospect Books, 1989. Accessed September 22, 2923. https://www.google.com/books/edition/Oxford_Symposium_on_Food _Cookery_1989/I15eJt6U3gMC.

Pollok, Lucy. "The Massachusetts State House: Sacred Cod." Revolutionary Spaces. Accessed September 23, 2023. https://revolutionaryspaces.org/the -massachusetts-state-house-sacred-cod.

Rama Rau, Santha. *Cooking of India*. Foods of the World. Chicago, IL: Time Life Education, 1969.

Robbins, Anthony. "Empowering Quotes from Tony Robbins." Accessed September 12, 2023. https://www.tonyrobbins.com/tony-robbins-quotes.

Roberts, Amy. "11 Facts to Raise your Grilling IQ." CNN. June 14, 2016. https://www.cnn.com/2013/06/21/living/grilling-by-the-numbers/index.html.

Robertson, Erika. "25 Fascinating Tea Etiquette Rules You Need to Know." *Teabloom*. August 27, 2022. https://www.teabloom.com/blog/25-fascinating-tea-etiquette -rules-you-need-to-know/.

Ross, Adrianne. "What's in a Name? Months of the Year." The British Museum. December 29, 2017. https://www.britishmuseum.org/blog/whats-name-months -year.

Roux, Jessica. *Floriography: An Illustrated Guide to the Victorian Language of Flowers*. Kansas City, MO: Andrews McMeel Publishing, 2020.

Rowling, J. K. *Harry Potter and the Sorcerer's Stone*. New York: Scholastic, 1998.

Shahin, Jim. "Smoke Signals: Presidential Grilling." *Washington Post*. February 21, 2012. https://www.washingtonpost.com/blogs/all-we-can-eat/post/smoke-signals -presidential-grilling/2012/02/21/gIQA3OlgRR_blog.html.

Sibal, Vatika. "Food Identity of Culture and Religion." ResearchGate. September 2018. https://www.wathi.org/food-identity-of-culture-and-religion-researchgate/.

Sifton, Sam. "Crema." *New York Times Food*. Accessed September 26, 2023. https://cooking.nytimes.com/recipes/1018885-crema.

Simpson, Jacqueline. *A Dictionary of English Folklore*. Oxford: Oxford University Press, 2003. https://www.oxfordreference.com/display/10.1093/oi /authority.20110803100117959.

Smith, Jenny. "Wheat Berries: A True Whole Grain." University of Illinois Extension. January 10, 2018. https://extension.illinois.edu/blogs/simply-nutritious -quick-and-delicious/2018-01-10-wheat-berries-true-whole-grain.

Sorgi, Gregorio. "Leicestershire Monks Brew UK's first Trappist Beer." *BBC News*. June 25, 2018. https://www.bbc.com/news/uk-england-leicestershire-44581210.

Stardust, Lisa. "All About Air Signs, the Zodiac's Social Smarties." *Cosmopolitan*. January 23, 2023. https://www.cosmopolitan.com/lifestyle/a33314375/air-signs -astrology/.

Sugar Association. "Types of Sugar: A Crash Course on the Many Types of Sugar." Accessed September 12, 2023. https://www.sugar.org/sugar/types/.

Susruthi Rajanala. "Cleopatra and Sour Milk—The Ancient Practice of Chemical Peeling." *Jama Network*. October 2017. https://jamanetwork.com/journals /jamadermatology/article-abstract/2657249.

Tablet. "Meet the Jewish Inventor of the Slow Cooker." *Tablet Magazine*. August 5, 2017. https://www.tabletmag.com/sections/food/articles/jewish-inventor-of-slow -cooker-irving-naxon.

Thorsson, Edred. *Futhark: A Handbook of Rune Magic*. Newburyport, CT: Samuel Weiser Inc., 1992.

TIME staff. "A Brief History of Salt." *TIME Magazine*. February 8, 2021. https://time .com/3957460/a-brief-history-of-salt/.

Traverso, V. M. "The Catholic Monasteries that Invented Our Favorite Cheeses." Aleteia.Org. April 6, 2022. https://aleteia.org/2022/04/06/the-catholic -monasteries-that-invented-our-favorite-cheeses/.

True Treats. "The History of the Illustrious Butter Cream." True Treats Historic Candy. Accessed September 22, 1923. https://truetreatscandy.com/the-history-of -the-illustrious-buttercreams/.

Tsephel, Khado. "The History of Tea." *The Science Survey*. July 25, 2022. https://thesciencesurvey.com/spotlight/2022/07/25/the-history-of-tea/.

University Libraries. "The Punch Bowl Pre-1806." Virginia Tech University. January 12, 2023. https://guides.lib.vt.edu/c.php?g=387023&p=3016428.

University of Illinois Extension. "Strawberries and More." College of ACES. Accessed September 1, 2023. https://web.extension.illinois.edu/strawberries/history.cfm.

Walker, Jake, and Robert S. Cox. *A History of Chowder*. Charleston, SC: The New History Press, 2011.

Walsh, Karla. "How to Use a Mandoline Slicer." *Better Homes and Gardens*. September 5, 2022. https://www.bhg.com/recipes/how-to/foodstorage-safetyx/a-mandoline-saves-time/.

Waxman, Olivia. "Spam Is Turning 80. Here's How the Canned Meat Took Over the World" July 5, 2017. *TIME*: History Food and Drink. https://time.com/4827451/spam-history-80th-anniversary/.

Willis, Matthew. "The Evolution of American Barbecue." *The Smithsonian Magazine*. October 18, 2019. https://www.smithsonianmag.com/arts-culture/the-evolution-of-american-barbecue-13770775/.

Wilmes, Brittany. "Pear Symbolism for the New Year." USA Pears. December 12, 2010. *https://usapears.org/blog/pear-symbolism-year/*.

World Archeology. "Crete: Olives." *World Archaeology* issue 48. July 7, 2011. https://www.world-archaeology.com/features/crete-olives/.

Wright, Janeen. "The Herb Society of America Essential Guide to Dill." The Herb Society of America. Accessed September 26, 2023. https://www.herbsociety.org/file_download/inline/0191822e-0527-4cac-afb6-99d2caab6b78.

Yelang (Son of China). "What Does Peach Symbolize in China." Son of China. May 18, 2023. https://sonofchina.com/what-does-peach-symbolism-in-china/.

index